25-
op

# The
# METROPOLITAN
# CLUB
*of*
# NEW YORK

Paul Porzelt

The
METROPOLITAN
CLUB
of
NEW YORK

RIZZOLI
NEW YORK

Published in the United States of America in 1982 by
RIZZOLI INTERNATIONAL PUBLICATIONS, INC.,
712 Fifth Avenue, New York NY 10019

Copyright © Paul Porzelt, 1982

ISBN: 0-8478-0423-2
LC:    81-52827


Color photographs by Joseph Farber
Artwork by Jan Fairservis


Designed by John Bradford
Composition by Adroit Graphic Composition Inc., New York
Printed and bound by Arti Grafiche Amilcare Pizzi, S.p.A., Milan, Italy

# Table of Contents

# Foreword
by Nicholas King

The Metropolitan Club is a monument, a monument of New York and a monument in New York. The reasons for its eminence are easily discovered. First of all, it is one of the city's most magnificent buildings, a masterpiece by Stanford White, conceived and executed at the height of the American Renaissance. Then it provides a historical focus of striking importance in the annals of the city, created and nurtured as it was by the titans of American finance and industry at a time when their power was supreme in the land. Finally, it has endured as a bastion of social and civic influence, its splendor intact and its life and spirit strong when many other proud institutions have foundered and disappeared in a modern world they could not survive.

Most New Yorkers know the club as the great greyish-white building on the corner of Fifth Avenue and Sixtieth Street that overlooks the southern confines of Central Park and the Fifty-Ninth Street Plaza. The structure is as imposing as a Roman palace, and the interior, with its huge central hall rising forty-five feet to a coffered ceiling, is probably the grandest private space in the whole of New York City. New Yorkers may know, too, that the Club continues its tradition of distinguished membership while it is becoming a center of community life, making it far more than a private club of the old school.

But many have forgotten the role of the private club itself, and its influence in the life of the city during the last hundred years. The Metropolitan Club and its sister institutions were, in fact, gathering places for the nation's elite, indoor forums where the generals of industry, finance, and of taste, too, met in an atmosphere of cordiality and trust. The clubs were ostensibly established for the pleasure and entertainment of the members. They were comfortable and often sumptuous havens where the rich and powerful hobnobbed with their peers as they took the temperature of the world, of society and of affairs. It was natural that the clubs should also be places of private meetings and deliberations, where unwritten, gentlemanly contracts were made, and advice given and received by those who held the reins of political and economic power.

The clubs provided intimate and even personal settings for these magnates, and so they also reflected the artistic expression and domestic manners of the time. Membership in a good club was the pinnacle of many a social ambition and many a business or professional career.

New York club life, which had its beginnings before the Civil War, flowered during the years of the nation's industrial and commercial expansion that followed it. But towards the end of the century, the existing New York clubs and their buildings failed to match the growth of the wealth and power of the country and the need for a progressive new club with a more imperial building became increasingly obvious. What crystallized this dissatisfaction was the famous incident of the blackballing by the old and old-fashioned Union Club of one of J. Pierpont Morgan's friends and business associates. Furious—according to legend—he summoned Stanford White to his presence and said: "Build a club fit for gentlemen. Damn the expense."

But whatever Morgan may have said to Stanford White, clubmen were clearly longing for the spacious, indeed the grandiose, on a European scale. Many of the London clubs had built superb palaces, and the Metropolitan drew its cue from them. White did magnificently by the Club. The Building itself cost nearly two million dollars, a sum soon pledged by the 700 members originally enrolled. It was finished in 1894, opened to the Members and, for a day, to an astonished press which could only gape in awe at the splendor of the marbles, the richness of the gilding, the sparkle of the chandeliers and the glow of the panelling that decorated the vast interior. From the bowling alleys in the basement to the thirty-four bedrooms on the top floor, the club was pronounced a marvel and a cynosure.

All this and a great deal more is recounted by Paul Porzelt in the following pages with care, wit and a lively eye—and scruple—for historical detail. Mr. Porzelt is himself a long-time Member of the Club, and has been for some years in the forefront it its leadership. His book is a labor of love, but it is also an achievement in historical and social perspective which deserves a wide audience.

His account of the Club Building, examining in fascinating detail as it does the palatial scale and wealth of its ornament, is in itself an outstanding piece of research. His survey of New York life, as seen both through its clubs and in the lives and works of prominent New Yorkers, constitutes a series of historical and social insights of enduring value.

This is particularly so in view of the current cultural interest in the period of the Club's genesis and original growth. The seal of Stanford White's genius is deeply stamped on American architecture and on the Metropolitan Club. White's houses have become in their way temples, grand or modest, of kinship with the national past. Their perspectives, both interior and exterior, have the power to frame spiritual outlooks, and often do so. I live in a Stanford White house, and worthy or not, such an idea has from time to time occurred to me.

This book will be read with much appreciation by the Metropolitan's Members, and also by all those who are interested in or influenced by the history of New York, of which the great Building on Fifth Avenue is such a visible and dynamic part.

# Preface

At a dinner party ninety years ago—on Friday evening, February 20, 1891—the idea of the formation of the Metropolitan Club was presented to the Founding Members. No book has ever been written about the Club's rich history, although the Governors were aware of the need for one. In 1936, they appointed a Member to undertake the task. A letter exists, dated December 14, 1936, written by the Chairman of the Library Committee, Ernest H. Wands, to William M. Kendall who had been Stanford White's staff architect, asking for data to be used for a proposed Club history. Lamentably, nothing came of the attempt; half-a-dozen Charter Members were still alive then and they would have been a rich source of information. On July 24, 1962, the Board asked Charles J. McCarty to compile a complete history of the Club; once again, nothing happened.

My involvement in the writing of this book was unpremeditated. About two years ago, President Hamilton asked my wife Klara, then Chairman of the Women's Committee, to oversee the publication of the Club's Monthly Bulletin. Knowing of my interest in events of the past, she asked me to contribute a short article each month on the history of the Club. I agreed, not anticipating what I had let myself in for. I had visions that past Bulletins would be a rich and easy source of information, but this was not the case. Their comments on the history of the Club were sketchy at best and full of mistakes to boot. The Club's files contained nothing helpful except for the Minutes of the

Board of Governors or Executive Committee meetings. The most interesting Minutes book, the first one covering the early years, has been lost. Minute books give names of new Members, deaths, resolutions and statements of profit and loss (mostly the latter), but tell nothing of the life in the Clubhouse. To make matters worse, the Club has always avoided any publicity and its "no reporters, no photographers" dictum was an obsession with early Members. The only exception is the records of the Metropolitan Club Bridge Dinner Club, a satellite organization which I ran across accidentally and which is a rich source of information about life among the Members compiled by the Members themselves seventy-five years ago. Nevertheless, my "Historical Notes" were received with such great interest that the idea of a book slowly took form.

Soon I was spending my days in research libraries reading books about architecture and the social life at the turn of the century. I decided soon that I would not write a conventional history; I had read too many of those and had found them boring. Furthermore, the necessary facts and information were lacking. I had become entranced with the age, the gilded age, of the early years of the Club's existence and with the men who made up the Membership then, an aristocracy of achievement. Despite the books of Gustavus Myers and the belittling remarks of Henry Adams or Albert Jay Nock, I found these Clubmen interesting, strong men, builders of a continent. They lived like kings of old: they endowed colleges, gave magnificently to hospitals and museums, donated state parks and churches. We would not have museums full of priceless art treasures if Morgan and Frick, Huntington and Havemeyer, Kress and Widener had not spent fortunes ransacking Europe for them. These men employed great architects, artists and craftsmen to build mansions and museums and they have given us something comparable to the ancient castles and palaces of Europe, adding a lustre to our cities which they would otherwise lack.

My book, therefore, is selective; it provides Historical Notes and Vignettes and leaves much of the more recent history of the Club to the research and pen of a better-qualified future historian. The Building, this masterpiece of Stanford White, fascinated me above all else: its exterior classic, severe and aloof, reflecting the character of the Founders; its interior exuberant, opulent and elegant, like their mode of living.

All mentions of the Metropolitan Club, the Building and the Rooms in it have a capital letter; for example, West Lounging Room, Main Hall.
Dates in parenthesis after a Member's name indicate the year he joined the Club.

To my unforgettable Klara

*They are not long, the weeping and the laughter,*
  *Love and desire and hate:*
*I think they have no portion in us after*
  *We pass the gate.*

*They are not long, the days of wine and roses:*
  *Out of a misty dream*
*Our path emerges for a while, then closes*
  *Within a dream.*

                              Ernest Dowson

# Chapter 1

# MEN'S CLUBS
# IN LONDON AND NEW YORK

Men have congregated in associations, whether military, religious, literary or political, since the beginning of civilization. The ancient Greeks had their *hetaireia,* the Romans their *sodalitates.* But modern men's clubs, such as the Metropolitan Club, are direct descendents of the British clubs of the eighteenth and nineteenth centuries.

English clubs first appeared in Elizabethan times and they were literary in character. Later their interests changed and they became more social in nature. "We now use the word 'clubbe' for a sodality in a tavern," wrote John Aubrey in 1659. During the reign of Charles II, clubs became increasingly political, but changed their character again in the late 1600s.

In 1693, an Italian known as Francis White, whose real name probably was Francesco Bianco, founded White's Chocolate House. Started as a restaurant, it became the greatest gambling center in London. Then, as the eccentricities of the eighteenth century and the Regency passed, White's became a club where members were chosen according to position and sociability. In the 1760s Edward Boodle became manager of a tavern within which a club soon formed when certain guests began to pay a fee to shut the doors to all others save

themselves. William Brooks was brought in to manage the club. And so some of the most famous names of clubland—White's, Boodle's, Brooks's—were established.

The British clubs of the eighteenth and nineteenth centuries represented the crystallization of the elite that had conquered half the world, built the British Empire and ruled it for over two-hundred years. That elite was composed of the aristocracy and landed gentry, the sons of ministers and officers, industrialists and the civil service. They were a homogeneous, dedicated and amazing class of leaders—the real *Herrenrasse* of the times. At their clubs these men could discuss the problems of running the Empire, meet former schoolmates and friends returning from the Hindu Kush or the Sudan, and exchange opinions and experiences. An anecdote, recounted by Anthony Sampson in *Anatomy of Britain Today,* illustrates the importance of the London club:

There is the Beefsteak, at the top of a dingy staircase off Leicester Square, opposite a strip-tease joint: its motto is "Beef and Liberty." The "Beefsteak" is very sociable, and generates remarkable dialogues. Members have to sit wherever the waiters (all called Charles) put them on the single long table, and they like to tell the story of how before the First World

*Fret*

1

War, the police, seeing old men emerging happily every evening, assumed it was a brothel and began watching the club; one night they raided it, and found four men sitting round the long table. The conversation went something like this:

"And who might you be?" asked the policeman of one old gentleman.

"I am the Lord Chancellor."

"Aha! And you, sir?"

"The Archbishop of Canterbury."

"Oh yes! And the next?"

"I am the Governor of the Bank of England."

"And I suppose," said the policeman to the fourth, "that you're the Prime Minister."

"As a matter of fact I am," said Arthur Balfour.

The heyday of English clubdom came in the nineteenth century when, in the decades after the defeat of Napoleon, the country reached the pinnacle of world power. London then had more than two hundred clubs. Whole streets—Pall Mall, Regent Street and St. James's—were practically lined with club buildings.

The clubs developed their own peculiar set of manners and customs which were avidly copied in other countries, particularly so in Britain's former colony, the United States. Leary of having guests brought into the clubhouse, clubs set up restrictions to limit how many or what kind of guests a member might invite, or they provided separate facilities, often called, "the strangers' dining room," for them. High hats were worn for luncheon. Some clubs prescribed the dress members had to wear at dinner and whether, and where, they could smoke. Clubmen definitely felt that women were not clubbable. They might raise their glasses at dinner in the toast, "Gentlemen, the Queen," but women were admitted, if at all, only on special occasions and most sparingly. Women tried to form their own clubs but they were never very successful due to their reluctance to spend their own money for food and drinks.

While the American clubs freely adopted all English manners, some found a compromise regarding the treatment of women—separate wings were built for them.

But for the rest, the peculiarly English institution of the gentlemen's club was closely copied in the New World. Clubs in New York, Boston and Philadelphia drew their membership almost entirely from the wealthy upper classes, then mostly of Anglo Saxon descent. These people felt at home in an English atmosphere. In New York during the middle of the nineteenth century it was assumed that no new club could be successful unless it patterned itself on the London clubs. Today many American gentlemen's clubs are still almost indistinguishable from the English originals.

Even the architecture of the New York clubs derives from that of the London clubhouses. Next to each other in Pall Mall are the buildings of the Travellers and the Reform, both built in the Italian Renaissance style which Sir Charles Barry brought to England. Fifty years later, this design greatly influenced Stanford White and Charles McKim when they became the foremost clubhouse architects in New York.

The buildings of the Reform and the Metropolitan may have similarities in design, but the latter's membership has always felt greater affinity with the members of the Carlton, that bastion of Toryism and the club of the Marquess of Salisbury, Gladstone and Disraeli. The Carlton was a neighbor of the Reform in Pall Mall until it was bombed in 1940; later it moved to St. James's Street. It merged with the Junior Carlton some years ago and is going through a regeneration led by the shrewdest traditional elements of the Conservative Party. Today the Metropolitan and the Carlton have reciprocal arrangements.

Although clubdom has been on the decline since the First World War, many clubs still survive. A recent book by Anthony LeJeune, *The Gentlemen's Clubs of London*, describes fifty clubs, all occupying beautiful houses. Trying to adapt to the times, more are managed by professional caterers than by retired colonels as they used to be. As LeJeune says, they are still "a refuge from the vulgarity of the outside world, a reassuringly fixed point, the echo of a more civilized way of living, a place where . . . people still prefer a silver saltcellar which doesn't pour to a plastic one which does."

In New York, the "flowering of clubdom"

was the period from the end of the Civil War to the first decade of the new century, as the city grew in population and wealth. The increasing congestion and greater distances from home to business, as well as the rise of a new class of worldly bachelors and men-about-town, made club life more and more attractive. The leaders of fashion and business had to belong not just to one but to many clubs, foreshadowing the clubman of the tabloids. Club membership became a matter of prestige, of social and of business importance. It became the badge of social rank. If one belonged to the St. Nicholas Society, everyone knew that one's ancestors had settled in the country before 1785. And what could be more select than to qualify for membership in the Mayflower Association?

The *Who's Who in New York* of that time was *Rossiter's Club Men of New York*, a publication of club membership begun in 1893 and published every two years for the next ten or twelve years. Its 1903 edition, containing 60,000 names, had become a tome of 1,100 pages and gave a short description of the more important clubs and the name of each clubman, with his club affiliations coded behind his name. Rossiter's

figures show that the number of clubs in New York City increased from 119 with 24,000 members (excluding some 32,000 repetitions) in 1893, to 157 with 38,000 names in 1901.

Some interesting sociological conclusions might be drawn from a study of the advertising pages of *Rossiter's*. Catering to the wealthy and socially prominent, the book was attractive to advertisers, and the 1903 edition carried fifty ads. Of these, ten were from men's custom tailors, not surprising in a period when men dressed meticulously and the ready-to-wear trade was in its infancy. Interestingly enough, the next largest group of advertisers were detective agencies, with eight listed. Next were five ads for banks and four for French and American champagnes.

This was the time when club news was really "news" and the dailies and weeklies devoted much space to reporting all the goings-on. *The New York Times* had a special daily section where the public could learn about such important items as the latest blackballing of a prominent man by a prominent club, or the expulsion of a member. The planning of a new club was headline stuff. Although almost all

The Clubs of Pall Mall; the Reform Club is the second building from the right.

3

clubs had a no-reporters-on-the-premises policy and no official would hand out any information or announcements, there were enough leaks or indiscreet members to keep reporters busy.

Several clubs were formed during the mid-1800s. In 1842, wealthy members of the increasingly important German population of New York formed the Deutscher-Verein. Like all the other clubs, it moved uptown; it went from its original quarters on Broad Street to Chambers Street and then to 24th Street. In March, 1891, the Deutscher-Verein moved into its own impressive home at 112 Central Park South, designed and built by Stanford White. It remained in this clubhouse until the First World War. Its 1895 Membership roster included the names of Henry Villard, Theo Havemeyer, Bernhard Beinecke, Theodor Weicker, Emil Pfizer, Hermann Oelrichs and many others from important families. Havemeyer and Oelrichs were also Charter Members of the Metropolitan Club. The Deutscher-Verein still exists, making it the second oldest social men's club in the city, and it now meets twice monthly at the Union Club.

In 1852, the wealthy German Jews—"Our Crowd" in writer Stephen Birmingham's phrase—founded the Harmonie Gesellschaft. It later became the Harmonie Club and in 1906 Stanford White designed and built its home across the street from the Metropolitan Club. Jacob Schiff of Kuhn, Loeb & Co., the friend and competitor of Morgan, was a member.

But the oldest and most important strictly social club still in existence today is the Union Club which was founded in 1836. Known as the Mother of Clubs, it gave birth to at least five other clubs in the next seven decades. The group of wealthy men who joined together to form the Union Club had traveled abroad and had become acquainted with the social clubs of the West End of London. They decided that they needed a club of their own in New York, and they discussed the idea over dinner at the Athenaeum Hotel at Broadway and Chambers Street. One of the founders, diarist and mayor of New York Philip Hone, wrote at the time: "If this club can be gotten up like the English

clubs it may succeed; little short of that will meet the views of the members."

The Union Club was two years old when, on April 23, 1838, two ships, the *Sirius* (nineteen days out of Cork) and the almost twice-as-large *Great Western* (fourteen-and-a-half days out of Bristol) arrived in New York, having crossed the Atlantic by steam power only. A new age was dawning. Between that time and the end of the century, the population of New York increased tenfold, from 300,000 to 3.2 million. Except for the grim interval of the Civil War, this was the age of Golden Dreams. Railroads were built across the nation; the telephone and electric lights were installed. Many great fortunes were amassed. Society dreamed of glittering balls and marble palaces. The Metropolitan Museum of Art was founded in 1869. And in 1891, the year the Metropolitan Club was conceived, Carnegie Hall opened at 57th Street and Seventh Avenue with a series of concerts in which Tchaikovsky himself conducted several of his own works.

At the beginning of this period, the Union Club was the only club catering to the old established and wealthy families of Dutch and English ancestry. The growth of New York, however, increasingly attracted citizens of other states. Many were found eligible for membership and were elected. But the Union Club's constitution limited the membership to one thousand and soon it had a long waiting list.

Rather than wait for years, many on the waiting list decided to form their own club, the Calumet, in 1879. Some wit called it the "Junior Union Club." It became known for its wonderful spirit of comradeship but it was to fall victim to the 1929 crash. In 1935 it was dissolved and its members taken into the Metropolitan Club. In addition, from time to time, dissention developed among the Union Club members and caused internal rebellions. Although, compared to their English counterparts, the American social clubs were less political and more business oriented, one political incident led to the formation of a new club after the outbreak of the Civil War. A number of hot-headed Union Club members were out-

In 1875, the Union Club had been in its premises on 21st Street at Fifth Avenue for twenty years. Increasing membership was already causing overcrowding.

raged when the Governing Committee permitted Judah P. Benjamin to resign instead of expelling him—not because he was a Jew but because he had become the financial brain and Secretary of State of the Confederacy. They seceded and formed the Union League Club in 1863 for the express purpose of maintaining the "territorial integrity of the nation." It became the stronghold of the Republican Party. Its rumored non-written rule was: "No women, no dogs, no reporters, and no Democrats." But similar unwritten rules could be said to have applied to a number of other men's clubs in New York.

The other political club—the Democratic counterpart to the Republican Union League Club—was the Manhattan Club, the bastion of swallowtail democracy. Founded in 1865 by Samuel John Tilden and Douglas Taylor, it became the center of activity of the Democratic Party, and it exercised great influence on both local and national levels. The composition of its membership changed as the support of the Party changed, reflecting the political views of recent immigrants.

In the late 1860s, a group of Union Club members demanded that new admissions be restricted to those of Knickerbocker descent. This opinion not being shared by the Governing Committee, the dissenting gentlemen banded together and formed the Knickerbocker Club in 1871. Despite its name, one of the more active among the founding fathers of the Knickerbocker Club was August Belmont, whose ancestry and birth was German-Jewish rather than Knickerbocker.

In 1903, two young members of the Union were expelled when, as a prank, they put a poached egg upon the snoozing head of the club's most revered patriarch. They formed another club and named it the Brook, after Tennyson's poem. "Men may come, and men may go/But I go on forever." The Brook remains today, a small but very smart club even more in the English tradition than the other New York clubs. It occupies a jewel of a clubhouse on East 54th Street.

Some thirteen years prior to the poached egg incident, another eruption occurred within the walls of the Union Club in 1890, which, added to a long-simmering dissatisfaction with the clubhouse accommodations, provoked several members to band together and to start a club more to their liking. J. Pierpont Morgan, then on his way to becoming the outstanding banker of America if not of the world, took the leadership. Their planning was grandiose and befitting gentlemen of their caliber. The result was the Metropolitan Club and its Clubhouse, the most beautiful in New York.

The Knickerbocker Club at 28th Street and Fifth Avenue in 1871.

# Chapter 2

# WHY ANOTHER CLUB?

In 1891, when the Union Club celebrated its fifty-fifth anniversary, it was not only the oldest gentlemen's club in New York but also the leading one. Run by a Governing Committee of twenty-four men, the club had 1,194 regular members, thirty-three Army and Navy members, ten life members, and a waiting list of 330 names. Its finances were sound, but its clubhouse was not.

After leasing several formerly private houses, the members built their own clubhouse in 1855, on Fifth Avenue at 21st Street. By the 1880s, the pre-Civil-War building had become inadequate. Not only had the membership increased, but members used the club more frequently and the facilities were crammed. The plumbing was antiquated, ventilation was poor and lighting equally so. As years went by, the building was increasingly considered not only unsanitary but actually unsafe.

The location down on 21st Street also became undesirable. In 1869, when Alexander T. Stewart built his town house on 34th Street, the area was still considered Upper Fifth Avenue. But New York quickly pushed up beyond the ugly Croton reservoir between 40th and 42nd Streets, which was finally razed in 1900 and replaced by the magnificent New York Public Library Building. In 1871, Mary Mason Jones built her Marble Row on land inherited from her father on Fifth Avenue between 57th and 58th Streets. The house was completely surrounded by empty lots for years and her friends warned her she would isolate herself from New York's social life. But when the Vanderbilts built their town houses all the way from 51st to 58th Streets in the early 1880s the rush to the Fifties and beyond started in earnest. Ogden Mills, the Goelet brothers, Levi P. Morton and William C. Whitney moved into the Fifties. W. Watts Sherman built a house in 1889 at 838 Fifth Avenue, where Mrs. Sherman gave her elegant and popular dinner parties. And a year after the Metropolitan's new Clubhouse went up at 60th Street, Henry A. C. Taylor had Stanford White build a magnificent townhouse for him at 3 East 71st Street. By the end of the century, Fifth Avenue had been surfaced in asphalt up to 90th Street, and the row of millionaires' mansions stretched over two miles, from Murray Hill in the 30s to 80th Street.

Dissatisfaction at the Union Club grew and the Governing Committee was forced to do something. In 1888 they appointed a committee of five members, none of whom were Gover-

*Egg-and-tongue*

7

nors, for the purpose of finding a site for a new building. The members of the committee were William Woodward, Jr., Levi P. Morton, D. Ogden Mills, Ogden Goelet and William K. Vanderbilt. They found two acceptable and available vacant lots, but the Board thought the prices prohibitive and so nothing came of the plan to build. A few years later, three members of this committee became Founding Fathers of the new Metropolitan Club and another, Levi P. Morton, became its second President.

Not only was the clubhouse inadequate, but the members grew increasingly dissatisfied with the leadership of the club. In the beginning, the Union Club had been essentially "an association of gentlemen." It was not incorporated, and until the 1870s there was no election of governors. When one of the governors died or saw fit to resign, his former associates on the board chose his successor, not for any factional or personal reason, but presumably with the intention of choosing the very best man to be had. But times had changed and a youthful element unconcerned with tradition crept into the club. They wanted to know why they had no voice in electing the governors as they were entitled to do by the constitution. Soon the pathway to the governor's table was made smooth and easy for popular men, even if they were not of the right cut for governors of a sedate old club like the Union. As the years passed, things went from bad to worse, until the younger element had secured a large representation on the board.

The atmosphere of the club underwent a decided change. There was more levity and less regard for old-fashioned courtesies and traditional ways of club life. Gradually the older and perhaps better element began to waver and lose active interest in the organization.

The governing committee had failed to include some men who were obvious choices for the position. It seems indeed strange that such a man as J. Pierpont Morgan, who loved the Union Club above all others as long as he lived, was never a governor, although he had been a member since 1865. Neither was W. Watts Sherman, although his father, Watts Sherman, who joined the club in 1838, had

been a governor. Neither were any of the Vanderbilts, Goelets, Iselins, or Roosevelts ever governors.

To make matters worse, in the late Eighties, the Union Club board began to experiment with its blackballing power. Within two or three years, the board had blackballed at least half-a-dozen eligible and desirable men on the most frivolous grounds. Two blackballs were needed to defeat a candidate, and certain governors had been known to remark jokingly after one of their blackballing exploits that they wondered how so-and-so "liked his pill."

Blackballing had long been a customary means of restricting and selecting the membership. Every club in England as well as in America had provisions for it. A long time ago, members were elected by ballots cast by the entire membership. As a result blackballing was very common. All clubs had cranks, embittered men, among their memberships who were ready on the slightest provocation to blackball a candidate. Some objections made to candidates were unbelievably whimsical. Take for example the attitude of novelist William Makepeace Thackeray when a man called Hill was proposed for membership in the Garrick Club. Mr. Hill was a self-made man with a cockney accent and the letter "H" was not his strong suit. "I pilled him because he is a liar," said Thackeray, "he calls himself 'ill' when he isn't."

But in the course of time in most clubs, the right to vote on admissions was taken from the membership and given to the board of governors or the governing committee—as the Union Club terms it—after the candidate had been cleared by a committee on admissions. Today if one or more members object to the admission of a candidate, the proposer is given a hint that it might be advisable to withdraw the name of his candidate and the whole affair is treated with utmost secrecy. Not so in 1890. The blackballing by a prominent club of a prominent man was quickly known to everyone and the news even appeared in the press.

The story that has clung most tenaciously to the name of the Metropolitan Club holds that J. Pierpont Morgan started the new Club out of resentment over a blackballing episode at the

Union Club. As E.A.L. Bennett (1884-1964), the late and beloved librarian of the Metropolitan, wrote in one of the early Club Bulletins:

The great J. P. Morgan, in a fit of pique because a candidate he had proposed for membership in a well-known Club was blackballed, summoned the famous architect, Stanford White, to his presence and said: "Build a Club fit for gentlemen. Damn the expense."

Had there not been substantial discontent among the members of the Union Club, to whom he had to look for the bulk of membership of any new club, Morgan would never have succeeded, nor would he have even attempted it. Yet the story is essentially accurate in that the blackballing episode was the last straw.

In mid-1890, J. Pierpont Morgan proposed a business associate and friend for membership in the Union Club. He was John King, president of the Erie Railroad Company, a man whose career and character had won the respect of all who knew him. King was blackballed and one of the men who had joined in the blackballing remarked that King literally ate with his knife, suggesting that his table manners were not as polished as they might have been. Since King had worked his way up from the shovel, so to speak, this was not altogether surprising, but apparently it did not disturb Morgan. As Anatole France's delightful abbé Jérôme Coignard said: "Il est plus malaisé de manger comme un gentilhomme que de parler comme lui."

The blackballing aroused a tremendous storm in the club. Not only was Morgan alienated, but dozens of other members were disgusted. To the embarrassment of Morgan and the humiliation of King, the story was leaked to the press, including *The New York Times*, *The Tribune* and all the scandal sheets. When invitations were sent out for the new Club some months later, John King received one and became one of the Charter Members of the Metropolitan.

Then, several weeks later, William K. Vanderbilt proposed his brother-in-law, Dr. William Seward Webb, who was married to William's sister Eliza Osgood Vanderbilt, for membership in the Union Club. Although his marriage to Eliza in 1881 had not won the approval of her father (she had to wait until she was thirty before she inherited ten-million dollars and the house at 680 Fifth Avenue), Eliza's brothers were fond of Webb and found a place for him in the Vanderbilt railroad empire. He was president of the Wagner Palace Car Company and of the Herkimer, Newport and Poland Railroad Company. Born in 1851 of a distinguished, old American family (his ancestor Richard Webb from Gloucestershire in England had become a freeman of Boston in 1632), Webb studied medicine at Columbia University, Vienna, Paris and London. Before entering business, he practiced medicine in New York. He maintained a magnificent estate and horse farm in Shelbourne, Vermont, where he entertained many famous guests. Shelbourne Farm is still in the hands of the Webb family.

Despite all these credentials for club membership, he too was blackballed. Allegedly Webb had joined a secret society at college and afterwards, on entering another college, joined a rival secret society. As the story goes, a Union Club member had been a college mate of his and harbored a hatred towards him for this treachery. New York's most popular scandal sheet of the day, *Town Topics*, published its own malicious version of the blackballing, saying that when Webb inherited the millions of his father-in-law, he had become even more unbearable than before.

Whatever the reason, the affair caused Cornelius and William K. Vanderbilt as well as Webb's brother, H. Walter Webb, all Union Club men, to join the malcontents. And soon the Goelets, Iselins, Roosevelts and many others were allied with Morgan in the attempt to form a new club. Not long after this episode became public, the Union Club blackballed lawyer Austin Corbin, causing the ranks of the disaffected to swell and ensuring the success of the bold new venture.

The Founders determined that they should make public their reasons for starting the new club. In the statement they released, they said that "in addition to the facilities where acquaintances and friendships might be fostered, a larger and more spacious clubhouse was needed, to provide for existing demand and future growth." This clubhouse required "the most essential element of permanency of location which circumstances and the pressures of commerce, presumably, might not disturb." It also required "the adjacency, if possible, to Central Park and the convenience, therefore, for the members in the pursuit of their outdoor activities—primarily riding, driving and bicycling." In other words, they wanted new and larger quarters and an uptown location.

Skepticism and disbelief greeted the announcement that a new club was being started with a spacious new clubhouse. A reporter from *The New York Times* asked one of the most prominent members—an ex-governor of the Union Club—if it were possible for a club to take in 650 members at a jump and still be as exclusive as a club that had a waiting list and could take in but one man at a time as vacancies occurred:

"Of course, it isn't," replied the autocrat of clubdom, "but the men at the helm of the new club are the most experienced clubmen and are proceeding very carefully, and I have no doubt whatever that the time will come, and at no distant day, when the Metropolitan Club will be recognized as the first social club of the city. I say this advisedly, having a pretty accurate knowledge of the list of men already taken in. Not all of them are millionaires, by any means, but all of them are clubbable men of A-1 social standing. With such men as a nucleus, there can be no question about the social status of the Club which they propose to build and develop.

Do I think there will be room for two clubs as nearly identical as the Union and the Metropolitan in the same uptown field? Yes, I do, for this reason. Though both clubs will appeal to essentially the same class of men, yet the two organizations will be very dissimilar in many ways. The Union is and always will be conservative and opposed to innovations. The Metropolitan is bound to be progressive. . . ."

Another reason for skepticism was the cost of building a clubhouse that would meet the founders' stated requirements. At the time the Metropolitan Club was being planned, the Century Club was building one of the great clubhouses of New York at 7 West 43rd Street. The cost of this building, designed by McKim Mead & White came to $212,908, an amount equal in today's purchasing power to from five-million to eight-million dollars. The Clubhouse the Metropolitan Founders were discussing would cost several times that amount. It was one thing to have an old established club with a secure membership and a long waiting list behind such an undertaking—and quite another thing to start from scratch.

But Morgan was a determined man. Once he decided on a new club, he committed himself to it, and for years he did not even set foot in the Union Club. Despite everything, however, the Union always remained his favorite club, and in his later years he started to go there again; his son, J. Pierpont Morgan, Jr., eventually became a governor of the Union Club.

Morgan also had the good sense to keep his friend W. Watts Sherman at his side. Sherman took charge of the project, and it was really he who did the organizing, planning, and tending to the innumerable details. Sherman had a particular qualification for this job. He had been one of the twenty-one prominent men who had drafted the Constitution for the Knickerbocker Club in 1871.

The first thing that Sherman did for Morgan's project was to draw up a list of twenty-five wealthy and desirable men and invite them to serve as organizers of the proposed new club. At the beginning of February, 1891, he sent them invitations to a dinner to take place at the Knickerbocker Club on Friday evening, February 20th.

# Chapter 3

# FROM CONCEPTION TO BIRTH: FEBRUARY 20, 1891, TO FEBRUARY 24, 1894

When New Yorkers woke up on Friday, February 20, 1891, the streets were white from a snowfall that had begun at three o'clock that morning. Twelve hours earlier, the snow would have been a calamity, because Thursday had been the day of New York's funeral procession for General William Tecumseh Sherman, who had died on Monday, February 16, at his home at 75 West 71st Street. At two o'clock on Thursday afternoon, the casket was brought down the steps of the house on the shoulders of six veterans and placed on the caisson. Behind walked a soldier leading a black horse, carrying General Sherman's saddle and riding boots. The mourners, led by President Harrison, followed the caisson down to Madison Square, through streets lined by hundreds of thousands of New Yorkers and draped with black shrouds and buntings, flags and pictures of the dead hero. Finally, the casket was put on the ferry to Hoboken and then on the funeral train which would take it to its final resting place in St. Louis.

Friday, February 20, was given over to removing the decorations and signs of sorrow. That evening nine men attended the dinner given by W. Watts Sherman (no relation to the general) at the Knickerbocker Clubhouse on Fifth Avenue at 32nd Street. They were the men who were to bear the main burden of starting the new Club. Present were Robert Goelet, William K. Vanderbilt, William C. Whitney, Henry A. C. Taylor, Adrian Iselin, George G. Haven, Samuel D. Babcock and George S. Bowdoin, in addition to host Sherman. After dinner, they were joined by John L. Cadwalader, Charles Lanier, Cornelius Vanderbilt and James M. Waterbury. Sherman also had on hand proxies from Ogden Goelet, Louis L. Lorillard, J. Pierpont Morgan, James A. Roosevelt and Frank K. Sturgis. A total of eighteen of the twenty-five men who had been invited were thus represented at that meeting. The remaining seven—James P. Kernochan, Henry J. Marquand, D. Ogden Mills, A. Newbold Morris, Sidney Webster, George Peabody Wetmore and Egerton L. Winthrop—joined within a few days.

After dinner, when the four latecomers had arrived, Sherman called the meeting to order. He had come well prepared: the Articles of Affiliation had been drafted; they were approved and signed by all those present. A tentative slate of officers was elected with Morgan as President and Sherman as Secretary.

Morgan, it seems, pushed his old friend Sher-

*Torus band*

J. Pierpont Morgan

Morgan's yacht, *Corsair II*.

man to the forefront in the work leading to the founding of the Club. Morgan was probably too preoccupied with his business activities; he was also known to be shy. Moreover, Sherman had a very distinguished family background and a much more secure social position. In 1890, Morgan had not yet organized J. P. Morgan & Company, nor won the approval of "The" Mrs. Astor, Caroline, mother of John Jacob Astor IV and ruling matriarch of New York Society. He was not invited until much later to Mrs. Astor's Annual Ball, which meant he was not yet one of the "Four Hundred," the term derived from the capacity of Mrs. Astor's ballroom.

Morgan and Sherman had been intimate friends for many years. In 1857 Morgan had joined the firm of Duncan, Sherman & Co., founded by W. Watts Sherman's father in 1851.

To whom should be accorded the honor of being the Founder of the Club? J. Pierpont Morgan, who undoubtedly had the idea and gave the impetus, or W. Watts Sherman, who did the preparatory work and gave the Founding Dinner on February 20, 1891? The Board itself, when Morgan died in April, 1913, sent to his family a eulogy in which Morgan is referred to as the man "to whose initiative The Metropolitan Club owed its foundation and to whose counsels its success had been largely due." Sherman, who had died a year earlier, was not mentioned in his eulogy as a Founder. Still, in retrospect, he should at least be considered the Co-Founder of the Club.

The guests at Sherman's dinner on February 20 were a formidable group. They were the richest and most powerful men of their time, the rulers of New York and the country. They had much in common, for the ancestors of most of them had come to America in the seventeenth century, and almost all were Episcopalian. If the most prominent family in New York was missing from the list, it was only because William Waldorf Astor had already decided to live in England and his cousin, John Jacob Astor IV, avoided as much as possible the New York social scene over which his domineering mother, Caroline, and his wife, Ava, presided. Both, however, became Charter Members.

A handful of the Founders was particularly active in the formation, the financing and the organizing of the new Club. They were—first—Morgan, the Goelet brothers and the Vanderbilt brothers. Among them they raised about a quarter of a million dollars, giving impetus to the sale of the junior debentures which provided the funds for the building. Sherman was the most active organizer and gave liberally of his time, but his financial contribution was smaller. Other large financial contributors were William C. Whitney, Charles Lanier and D. Ogden Mills.

J. Pierpont Morgan was born in Hartford, Connecticut, in 1837, studied abroad at the University of Göttingen and began his banking career in 1857 when he joined the banking firm of Duncan, Sherman & Co. in New York. In 1864, he became junior partner of Dabney, Morgan & Co., and then in 1871 of Drexel, Morgan & Co. Over the years, he built the family fortune into a colossal financial and industrial empire. He was an ardent sportsman and entered his yachts in many international races. The three yachts he owned successively were all named *Corsair*, reflecting perhaps Morgan's romantic and playful identification of himself with the famous pirate, Henry Morgan. He was a philanthropist and a renowned art collector. He was also an avid clubman and belonged to some thirty clubs; among them, at the time of his death in 1913, were the Union, Union League, Metropolitan, Century, University, Knickerbocker, Brook, Racquet and Tennis, Catholic, Riding, Players, Harvard, Whist, Turf and Field, Groliers and Automobile Club. It was said he could not decline a request to join a club.

Morgan's house at 36th Street and Madison Avenue.

Morgan was a towering personality in an age of towering personalities. He was not only a most resourceful investment banker, he was also a tower of strength in times of panic and financial uncertainty, a leader in some of the great financial and industrial enterprises of the century. The great fortune he made, he used in the ultimate luxury of royalty, the collection of superb art. He did not choose to build great

Morgan & Co. offices — The Drexel Building.

mansions like Biltmore House or The Breakers. His bequest to posterity was the Morgan Library, a center of the cultural life of New York. His taste was superb in matters of art and beauty and he collected nothing but the best. His discrimination extended not only to painting and sculpture, but also to his mistresses, one of them the fascinating and talented actress, Maxine Elliott. Such behavior may seem surprising on the part of the great banker, leader, family man and anchor of the Episcopal Church. But fate had injured him deeply. When a young man, he had fallen deeply in love with Amelia Sturges. Morgan had just established his own office at 54 Exchange Place and three years after he met her he asked for her hand in marriage. Mimi, however, had contracted a severe cold which settled in her lungs. Her cold got progressively worse, but Morgan insisted that the date of the wedding be fixed for October 7, 1861. Dr. Tyng married them in the Sturges' town house and Mimi was so ill she could hardly keep on her feet during the ceremony. It was a deeply touching sight when the twenty-four-year-old Morgan carried his bride in his arms down the front steps to a carriage which took them to the pier and the SS *Persia* bound for Algeria and sunshine. But it was too late; Mimi died in Nice on February 17, 1862. Morgan broke down. He stayed abroad for two months, joined by Mrs. Sturges, and then brought the body back to the United States for interment. She was the great love of his life.

His great desire was to have children and in May, 1865, he married Frances Louise Tracy. They had one son and three daughters.

Born five years after Morgan in Albany, New York, W. Watts Sherman attended private schools in Scotland and England. At the University of Heidelberg, he studied medicine, but in 1878 he joined his father's firm, Duncan, Sherman & Co. He was a public-spirited and cultured man of studious habits who spoke five languages and was a discriminating collector of books and art objects. He also was a prominent clubman and among his associations were the Society of the Cincinnati, the Society of Colonial Wars, the Sons of the Revolution, the St.

Nicholas Society, the Automobile Club of America, the Knickerbocker (of which he was a founder), the Century, the Racquet and Tennis, the Riding Club, and, of course, the Union Club.

Morgan knew the Sherman family well. His first job in business had been with Duncan, Sherman & Co. In the formation of the Club, he worked very closely with his friend Bill Sherman and delegated to him most of the task of sending out membership invitations to eligible men and also the innumerable details of organizing the Club.

Sherman died in New York in 1912. After his death, his family gave to the Club the handsome bust which stands on the landing between the second and third floors. Unfortunately the name of the sculptor is not known.

Two sets of brothers were among the most active of the Founding Fathers—Robert and Ogden Goelet, and Cornelius and William Kissam Vanderbilt. Like that of the Astors, the Goelet fortune was based on New York real estate. The Goelets were of Huguenot descent, as were many of the families that assumed the lead in the early years of New York. Francis Goelet had fled from Holland to New Amsterdam in 1667 with his son Jacobus. Grandson Peter P. Goelet (1764-1828) married Amy Buchanan, daughter of Thomas Buchanan, a leading merchant of the Revolutionary period, a member of the Committee of One Hundred and the owner of much New York real estate, including fifty-five acres of farmland between 45th and 48th Streets on Fifth Avenue. Their son Robert Goelet (1809-1879) married Sarah Ogden and their sons were Founding Members Robert and Ogden Goelet. Robert Goelet (1841-1899) managed the family real estate business. He was a great yachtsman and owned the 306-foot steam yacht *Nahma*. He was a connoisseur of wines and other good things of this life, and a friend of kings and queens.

Ogden Goelet (1846-1897) was also a great yachtsman. In 1882 he gave the Goelet Cups to the New York Yacht Club. He died in 1897 on his steam yacht, the *Mayflower*, at Cowes, on the Isle of Wight. Both Robert and Ogden took an immense interest in the construction of the

Robert Goelet

Wm. Watts Sherman

Clubhouse and the early management of the Club.

More than any other, the name of Vanderbilt is associated in most people's minds with great wealth. The two Vanderbilt Founding Fathers were sons of William Henry Vanderbilt (1821-1885), reportedly the richest man in the world at the time. When his father, "the Commodore," died in 1877, William Henry built three massive brownstone houses on Fifth Avenue and 52nd Street, one for himself and two for his daughters. His architect suggested they be built of marble, but Wiliam H. was afraid of marble. Had not A. T. Stewart and William B. Astor died shortly after their mansions of marble were built? He was to die three years after 640 Fifth was ready for occupancy anyhow, marble or no marble.

His oldest son and crown prince was Cornelius Vanderbilt II, born in 1843, chairman of the board of the New York Central Railroad and many other railroads. In 1882, he and his wife, Alice Gwynne, built the gigantic mansion

William K. Vanderbilt's "Marble House" in Newport, built at a cost of eleven million dollars.

on the west side of Fifth Avenue at 58th Street, which, unforgiveably, fell victim to the wrecker's pick axe in the 1920s. Their "cottage" in Newport was The Breakers, the seventy-room Italian Renaissance *palazzo* designed in 1893 by Richard Morris Hunt. Cornelius helped establish the Vanderbilt clinic and the Cathedral of St. John the Divine. When he died in 1899 he left a fortune of seventy-two million dollars.

His brother William K. Vanderbilt, another enthusiastic yachtsman, was born in 1849. He married the redoubtable Alva Smith from Mobile, Alabama. Not to be outdone by any other of the Vanderbilt builders, Alva hired Richard Morris Hunt to build her a house to outdo all other houses, right across from her father-in-law's mansion, at 660 Fifth Avenue on the northwest corner of 52nd Street. William K.— or rather Alva—also built the fabulous Marble House in Newport. He took great interest in the building of the Metropolitan Club and sent his own design to Stanford White from Paris. Frank Crowninshield considered William K. "the greatest supporter of sport, opera, yachting, racing, art, architecture, coaching and the theatre in American Social Annals." He also supported some of the most glamorous *grandes horizontales* on both sides of the Atlantic. When he died in 1920, he left a fortune similar in size to that of his elder brother.

Intensely interested in the Club in those early years was Founding Member William Collins Whitney, "Old W. C.," to his friends. Born in 1841 in Conway, Massachusetts, he was a descendant in the eighth generation of John Whitney, one of the leaders of the Puritans who settled in Watertown, Massachusetts, in 1635. Educated at Yale and the Harvard Law School, he came to New York in 1864 to practice law. In 1869, he married the wealthy Flora Payne, daughter of Senator Henry B. Payne of Ohio and sister of Charter Member Colonel Oliver H. Payne, the future Treasurer of Standard Oil Company. In New York, Whitney got involved in politics as a Democrat, was a supporter of Grover Cleveland and became Secretary of the Navy in Cleveland's first ad-

Consuelo Vanderbilt, after her marriage to the ninth Duke of Marlborough, dressed for the Coronation of Edward VII.

Consuelo's brother, Willie K. Vanderbilt, at the wheel of his German car.

Alva Smith Vanderbilt (Mrs. William K.) dressed for the impressive ball she gave in her new three-million-dollar chateau on Fifth Avenue in 1883.

ministration. He resuscitated a moribund Navy and created the Naval War College at Newport. In four years, he spent eighty-million dollars to add 94,000 tons to the fleet, one of the ships being the ill-fated *Maine*. He later made a fortune of forty-million dollars in street traction companies in New York together with Peter A. B. Widener and Club Member Thomas Fortune Ryan (April '02). Thereafter he devoted his time to society, horses and houses. Purchasing the old Robert L. Stuart Mansion at 871 Fifth Avenue in 1898, he had Stanford White turn it into a very elaborate residence with New York's largest ballroom. Its bronze gates came from the Palazzo Doria in Rome. He was a worldly man, one of the founders of the new Metropolitan Opera and host with his attractive first wife to artists, musicians and writers who frequented their salon as friends, not hired entertainers. He died in 1904, leaving an estate of nearly twenty-three million dollars.

Darius Ogden Mills was born in North Salem, New York, in 1825. Like many other easterners, he joined the gold rush in 1848 and became a very rich man when the Comstock Lode was discovered in 1859. With William Ralston, he founded the Bank of California. When he came to New York some years after the Civil War, he bought a brownstone mansion at 51st Street and Fifth Avenue. He became a contributor to the Metropolitan Museum and the New York Botanical Gardens, but also established the famous Mills hotels for indigent men. He died in 1910.

When John Washington, great-grandfather of the first President of the United States, came to America from England, he was accompanied by several friends, chief among them Thomas Lanier, a Huguenot refugee from France and ancestor of Founder Charles Lanier. Charles' grandfather was Captain of cavalry during the Revolutionary War in Colonel William Washington's regiment. Charles Lanier was born in Madison, Indiana, in 1837. After finishing school in New Haven, he became a partner in the Wall Street banking house of Winslow, Lanier & Co.

The other Founders were of similar caliber. There were members of old New York families like James A. Roosevelt and A. Newbold Morris. The legal profession was represented by John R. Cadwalader, Henry A. C. Taylor (son of Moses Taylor), and Sidney Webster. Others were men of wealth and patrons of the arts like Henry G. Marquand, James P. Kernochan, James M. Waterbury, Louis L. Lorillard and George Peabody Wetmore, whose father had made a fortune in the China trade. The brokerage and banking fraternity had the heaviest representation. There was George Griswold Haven, Samuel Babcock, and Frank K. Sturgis, for some years president of the New York Stock Exchange. Another Founder was Adrian Iselin, Jr., who was to make a loan to the Club when it was sorely needed. Egerton L. Winthrop and George S. Bowdoin, a partner of Drexel, Morgan & Co., complete the list of Founders.

At the Founding Fathers' Dinner on February 20, 1891, all those present entered their signatures in the new Membership Book, which has since been signed by everyone who has become a Regular Member of the Club. The Book contains the text of the Original Constitution, and, by signing, Members pledge adherence to its provisions. Sherman had done his homework; the Constitution had been drafted in advance, and all was ready except for one space which was left vacant—where the name of the new Club was to be filled in. The space is still vacant today.

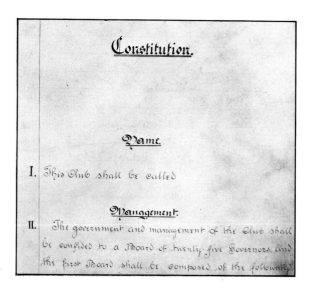

We the undersigned do hereby agree with one another to unite ourselves together in an Association for the purposes, and upon the conditions, set forth in the following Constitution, and by signing the same with our names we do jointly and severally undertake that the membership of each of us, and his rights of property, in the Club, shall be held, or surrendered, in such manner, and upon such terms, as this Constitution or its amendments shall prescribe.

John L. Cadwalader

G. S. Bowdoin

Sam. D. Babcock

Robert Goelet

Ogden Goelet

C. J. S. Martin.

Adrian Iselin Jr.

J. W. Kernochan

Charles Lanier

Henry G. Marquand

J. Pierpont Morgan

A. Newbold Morris

J. A. Roosevelt

W. Watts Sherman

F. K. Sturgis.

Henry A. C. Taylor

C. Vanderbilt

W. K. Vanderbilt

Egerton L. Winthrop

Sidney Webster

Geo. Peabody Wetmore

Some years before the building of the Club, this was the scene at Fifth Avenue and 59th Street. The old Plaza, at left, was unfinished when this engraving was made, and the artist's imagination added peaks to the roof that were never built. Note the horsedrawn streetcars and fashionable carriages.

The fact was that no name had been agreed upon, or, perhaps, there was an obstacle to using the name most of them had in mind. Another two-and-a-half weeks would pass before the curiosity of the press and the public would be satisfied. In the meantime, lacking a proper name, the new Club was generally referred to as "The Millionaire's Club" and the name has stuck as a subsidiary title ever since. As the mystery of the name continued, public interest seemed to heighten, and on February 28, *The Times* ran an article on its Club News and Society page headed "The Millionaire's Club."

The third meeting of the projectors of that Club of clubs which is generally talked of with bated breath as the "Millionaire's" was held yesterday af-

ternoon in the parlors of the office of the Goelet estate, at 9 West Seventeenth Street. W. Watts Sherman presided, and before him were nearly all of the twenty-five men in the project. . . .

They held a four-hour meeting but would give out little for publication beyond the fact that they had made out a list of men who were to be invited to join and that as soon as enough acceptances were received they would purchase the Hamersley Property at Sixtieth Street and Fifth Avenue and build thereon a house that will be as perfect as money and experience can make it. . . .

There was much discussion over the name yesterday for the new Club but none was decided upon, although many favor the title "The Park Club."

One gentleman proposed that as there would be a great deal of watching from the windows, at the superb equestrian and pedestrian parade which crosses

20

the Plaza every fine day, the organization might be called 'The Spectator' after the famous London Club and the suggestion will be seriously considered. The new Club certainly has backing enough to make it the most powerful social organization in the country, and the site it is considering can hardly be equalled both in point of beauty, or view and convenience to the three superb hotels that will face the Grand Circle.

The public had to hold its bated breath until March 8th when *The Times* ran another article, this one with the heading, "The Metropolitan Club."

The Club projected by numerous wealthy men who think that there is room for a club that shall give all clubs now established a hard tussle for supremacy, and which has been known for want of any name given by its promoters, as the "Millionaire's Club," yesterday took a long stride towards tan-gibility. It was given a name. "The Metropolitan Club" it will be known as hereafter.

Another long meeting ensued in the Goelet office with nineteen men attending. The officers were formally elected, the Constitution approved, and fees fixed at $300 for the Initiation Fee and $100 for Annual Dues for Regular and $50 for Non-Resident Members. These were higher than any other club dues in New York at the time.

The historian is handicapped because no actual records of any of these meetings have survived. The first volume of the minutes of the Board of Governors has been lost, but it seems that three names had been seriously considered—The Metropolitan, The Park and The Hudson. The voting was nine, six and four, in that order, and "The Metropolitan Club" it was. But did the men at that meeting know

In 1894, when the Club first opened its doors, the Members looked across an unfinished patch of road in the middle of Fifth Avenue (which later became Grand Army Plaza) to the Plaza Hotel, finished in 1899, only to be torn down and rebuilt on a grander scale in 1907.

In the mid-1880s, Fifth Avenue was lined by the mansions of the very rich. St. Thomas Episcopal Church is on the left.

that a club of that name had existed in New York since 1878, and that it was located two blocks down Fifth Avenue from the planned site? And, if so, had they somehow arranged to use this name or were they surprised by an article published by *The Times* two days later?

On March 10, *The Times* headline read, "Very Hard on the Postmen. It would seem that there is one Metropolitan Club too many." As a matter of fact, the New York Directory had had a listing for many years prior to 1891, "Metropolitan Club, 751 Fifth Avenue." After some expressions of sympathy for the postmen, *The Times* went on:

People who do not pass their time out of reach of the newspapers but try to keep fairly informed about what is going on (!) have long known that the marble house at the southeast corner of Fifth Avenue and Fifty-eighth Street is leased and occupied by the Metropolitan Club. The Metropolitan Club is, in its way, an exclusive organization. Its membership is confined to gentlemen of the Jewish religion, and it calls itself German-Jewish or Jewish-American, ac-

cording to preferences of nativity. Many of the members belonged to the Standard Club which was quartered at Broadway and Forty-Second Street until it disbanded in 1878. Then the Metropolitan was formed although no formal incorporation occurred until about five years ago. The new club had grown rich and worked to acquire some property and build a house. Articles of incorporation were filed with that view. . . . Property was actually acquired but by that time the majority had taken a strong fancy to the neighborhood in which most of the organizers of the new club reside.

They jumped at the chance to lease the house at Fifty-eighth Street which is but a stone's throw from ex-Secretary Whitney's and Cornelius Vanderbilt's.

The proximity of the homes of the millionaires to this clubhouse, and the fact that they passed it daily in their drives to the Park and were thus able to observe its merits alike of management and of location, throws a flood of light on Saturday's meeting. It need no longer be a matter of conjecture what it was that inspired the millionaires to adopt the name Metropolitan or to choose a location near the lower plaza of Central Park. The force of good example has rarely been more happily illustrated in this town.

*The Times* then proceeded to offer such advice as forming a joint club with two houses or calling one, Metropolitan Club, Sr., and the new one, Metropolitan Club, Jr.

And in the Sunday edition of *The Times*, March 15, a reporter, a Will Rogers of his day, continued the jibes in the column, "Phases of City Life":

Three or four patrons of a popular chophouse up town, a night or two ago, fell to discussing the question of a suitable name for the recently organized millionaire's club. "I see that their chosen title, The Metropolitan, belongs to another club," remarked one gentleman.

"That is so," said another, "and the money kings are all at sea for a name."

"Why don't they call their organization the 'Bullion Club,' or the 'Coupon Clippers and Ten Percent Club' or the 'Unearned Increment,'" inquired a young man, pausing in a spirited attack on a welsh rarebit.

"Oh, if they want something more aristocratic and more picturesque," said a fourth speaker, "something like the 'Croesus' or 'Monte Cristo' or: . . ."

"'The Aladdin,'" suggested the welsh-rarebit-eater. "Why would not the 'Midas Club' be a good name," asked the first speaker. "I supposed the 'Mammon' or 'The Plutocrats' would be considered too common. However, the new club might be very appropriately dubbed 'King Solomon's Mine.'"

New York's most famous scandal sheet, *Town Topics*, also had its say about the new name. By definition, they maintained, a metropolis is not only the largest and most prominent city of a country but also the seat of its government, as in the cases of London and Paris. So how, they asked, could a Metropolitan Club be situated in a place that is not a Metropolis?

But Metropolitan was the name decided upon, and somehow the new group headed by J.Pierpont Morgan ended up in possession of the name. What induced the older Metropolitan Clubmen to relinquish their name? The copy of the "Articles of Incorporation of the Metropolitan Club of the City of New York," dated June 11, 1885, is still on file at the County Courthouse. It was signed by five men, including David Solis Ritterband who was its president in February, 1891. Were they paid to give up the name? Or was the lease on the Marble House, to which they were much attached, somehow involved? The whole block on the east side of Fifth Avenue between 57th and 58th Streets was taken up by Marble Row. John Mason, a merchant, had bought the land in 1825 from the city for $1500. The property came into the hands of his daughter, Mary Mason Jones, who built Marble Row and lived in one of the houses. She was a prominent member of society at the time, almost an institution. Her cousin's daughter, Edith Jones Wharton, left us a masterly portrait of the poised old lady and her surroundings. She was the model for the redoubtable Mrs. Manson Mingott in *The Age of Innocence*. Perhaps Mrs. Jones was the one who induced the old Metropolitan clubmen to give up their name.

At the turn of the century, Fifth Avenue in the Fifties is crowded with the fashionable world, probably seen here on an Easter Sunday.

Within a month of the organization meeting, a sufficient number of Members had been secured. No doubt the name of J. Pierpont Morgan had been of great help in accomplishing this. The next order of business for the new club was to acquire the site on which they already had an option. There were a number of men among the Founders who were knowledgeable concerning New York real estate. Probably Morgan or Sherman, or even more probably the Goelets or the Vanderbilts, knew before anyone else of the Hamersley property, a choice piece of real estate at Sixtieth Street and Fifth Avenue that was about to come on the market. The land was vacant, surrounded by a brown wooden picket fence; some decrepit stage horses occasionally pastured there. The owner, Lily Hamersley Churchill, was abroad, and the price put on the land was relatively low. This knowledge undoubtedly contributed to the decision to start the new club.

This parcel of land first appeared in the land records of the City on May 1, 1799, when, "The Mayor, Aldermen and Commonality of the City of New York, in consideration of £195 and payment of 4 bushels of good merchantable wheat as quit rent, grant and convey to Hugh Gaine of the said City, Printer and Stationer, a piece or lot of land parcel of the Common Lands." The land is described as lying between the Middle Road and the East Road. This was long before Manhattan was laid out in its current gridiron plan. This structuring took place in 1811 when the Randel Survey arranged the mostly empty land north of Houston Street into a tidy series of right-angled streets and avenues. The farmland Hugh Gaine bought was in what would become the best and most expensive section of town, between 60th and 61st Streets along Fifth Avenue and facing what was to become Central Park.

In 1820, John Mason, the same merchant mentioned above and at one time president of the Chemical National Bank, bought the land for $2000. When he died in 1839, he was the owner of most of the land between Fifth and Park Avenues from 54th to 63rd Streets. He had not approved of the marriages his children had made, so he cut them off in his will with small annuities. They contested the will and a heated legal battle continued until 1853, when the court set aside the will and ordered the land divided among the children. The block running from Fifth to Park between 60th and 61st Streets went to Andrew Gordon Hamersley, the widower of John Mason's daughter Sarah who had died in 1848. The block between 57th and 58th Streets went to Mary Mason Jones (mentioned above), who in 1867-70 built the Marble Row on Fifth Avenue.

The Hamersleys were an old English family tracing their descent from Hugo le King, a native of Provence in France who went to England in 1366 and bought a large estate called Hamersley. Gordon Hamersley was a wealthy man and when he died in 1883, he left his fortune to his only son Louis Carré Hamersley, who married Lilian (Lily) Price, daughter of a U.S. Naval Officer. Louis died in 1884 and four years later his widow married the eighth Duke of Marlborough, uncle of Sir Winston Churchill, and moved to England. Within three years, part of the Hamersley property was for sale, perhaps because admission to the entourage of the most powerful sovereign of the time turned out to be rather expensive.

The Board appointed a Committee of eight, of which the most active Members were Cornelius Vanderbilt, Charles Lanier and William C. Whitney, with instructions to obtain an option on this land. The first option was for six lots, totaling 100 feet on Fifth Avenue and 150 feet on 60th Street for a price of $400,000. By the time of the following meeting at Goelet's office, they were asking for 175 feet on 60th Street, and when it was decided to erect a courtyard entrance on 60th Street with a ladies' annex in the back, they asked for 200 feet of the 250 feet available along 60th Street towards Madison Avenue. The final purchase price was to be $480,000.

For initial capital to purchase the land, the twenty-five Founding Fathers, who would constitute the original Board of Governors, each pledged to contribute $5000. This $125,000, added to $360,000 in initiation fees from the 1200 Members they hoped to enlist, was enough to buy the land. The cost of the building would eventually come from a first mortgage and from the subordinated debenture issue of $700,000 to be subscribed by Members, led by Morgan and the Vanderbilt brothers with $50,000 each. The $5,000 each Founding Father contributed does not seem much money now, but in 1891, the purchasing power of the dollar was much greater than it is today. For instance, in October, 1907, the new Plaza Hotel opened its doors diagonally across from the Metropolitan Clubhouse. It advertised the price of a room in "The World's Most Luxurious Hotel" as $2.50 per day for single rooms and $16 for a suite consisting of a parlor, two bedrooms and two bathrooms. And the price of a room at that time included real service.

The decline in the purchasing power of the dollar—or conversely the increase in wages and prices—has been enormous over this period of ninety years, but it has been uneven. Some prices, for example, for food products, rose only slightly; others, such as building costs, showed incredible increases. In the construction industry, fifty dollars buys today what one dollar bought in 1893. On the average, however, it is safe to assume that since the Club was formed the price level has increased between twenty-five and thirty times. In other words, the dollar is worth between 3% and 4% of what it was then.

As it turned out, the Metropolitan Club paid the right price at the right time for the land it acquired. Under the impact of the stunning news that the malcontents were starting a new club, the Union Club Board appointed a new committee in 1891 to find a site, but again nothing happened. Finally, in 1899, they bought a site on Fifth Avenue and 51st Street for $700,000, neither as large nor as desirable as the 60th Street lot. In May, 1896, the University Club acquired a site for a new clubhouse at 54th Street and Fifth Avenue. The club bought five lots measuring 100 x 125 feet for $675,000, a price of $54 a square foot. The site the Metropolitan acquired, a much superior one, cost $24 a square foot.

Cornelius Vanderbilt sailed to England a few weeks later to close the transaction. The deed was signed on May 9, 1891, at the American Consulate in London. The signature of Lily W. Churchill was witnessed by the American Con-

Cornelius Vanderbilt III and his wife, Grace Wilson Vanderbilt, entertained as many as 1000 guests at a time in the ballroom of their mansion on Fifth Avenue at 58th Street. The ballroom of the seventy-room house was an exact replica of Versailles.

25

sul general, John C. New, and the land was transferred into the names of Cornelius Vanderbilt, Charles Lanier and William C. Whitney, as trustees for the Metropolitan Club. Of the purchase price of $480,000, $100,000 was paid in cash and the balance in a two-year note personally guaranteed by the three trustees.

Incidentally, a fair portion of the money handed over to the Duchess by Cornelius, which had been partly contributed by him and his brother, returned later to the family when his niece, Consuelo, married the ninth Duke of Marlborough. Desperately in love with Winthrop Rutherfurd, Consuelo was forced by her formidable mother into marrying a title. To all her desperate protests, her mother had only one reply, "You do as you are told." While Lily's wedding to the eighth Duke had been a relatively simple affair, with a ceremony at the Tabernacle Baptist Church on Second Avenue, Consuelo's wedding on November 6, 1895, in St. Thomas's Church on Fifth Avenue was the most magnificent in American social annals. Winthrop Rutherfurd later married the daughter of the Metropolitan Club's second President, Levi P. Morton.

The land purchased was only a part of the Duchess' holdings. She owned another fifty feet of land on 60th Street which she also sold and which ended up in the hands of John E. and Eva K.D. McGowan, who erected a building on it. On December 4, 1911, the Metropolitan Club bought this lot, building and all, for $165,000.

In March, 1891, when the Board of the Metropolitan Club committed itself to buy the land from Lily Churchill, the whole block between 60th and 61st Streets was still vacant and

The second Plaza, built in 1907.

fenced in by a brown picket fence. But the northerly half of the Fifth Avenue frontage was bought at the same time by Elbridge T. Gerry who promptly commissioned Richard Morris Hunt to build a French château on the site and therefore two new houses went up side by side between 1892 and 1894. They looked out over a Central Park which was still relatively young and wild. Central Park South was mostly built up but still had *lacunae* of empty lots. Diagonally opposite the Club site was the old Plaza Hotel which was built just a few years earlier. The land was bought in 1883 for $850,000 and a four-hundred-room hotel erected on it. It was an ugly structure, looking more like a department store or a warehouse than a hotel. It did not last long. Sold in 1902 for $3,000,000, it was torn down and a French-American Renaissance style hotel was erected at a cost of $12,-000,000, with Henry J. Hardenbergh as the architect. From the day it opened, October 1, 1907, it rivalled the Waldorf as the smartest hotel in town.

Fortunately, the planners of the City had left an open space between the Hotel and Fifth Avenue between 58th and 59th Streets, then usually referred to as the Grand Circle. In 1891, there was nothing on it and it looked like a big sandlot. At the South was the hundred-room French château of Cornelius Vanderbilt. Standing in front of the old Plaza Hotel, one could see the Marble Row south of 58th Street with the first house occupied by the Jewish Metropolitan Club. Between 58th and 59th Street, two hotels were built, the New Netherland and the Savoy. The overall view was not, however, very elegant until the new Plaza was built. In 1908, the Grand Circle, now called Grand Army Plaza, was redesigned by Thomas Hastings who put a fountain in the center topped by an entrancing nude Lady of Abundance, her appealing backside turned towards Cornelius Vanderbilt's house. At the same time, the equestrian statue of General Sherman with his horse led by the Lady of Victory was moved to a little island between 59th and 60th Streets, in full view from the Club's windows. A story is told—probably apocryphal—of the Southern Gentleman on a visit to New York conducted

by his niece. When they came to Saint Gaudens' masterpiece, he looked at it for a few minutes and turned away: "Just like a damnyankee, letting the lady walk."

The eastern United States at the *fin de siècle* had an abundance of talented architects. There, were the firms of Carrère & Hastings and Warren & Wetmore, as well as individual architects such as Richard M. Hunt who had built the châteaux of William K. Vanderbilt, Elbridge Gerry and Mrs. William Astor, and Horace Trumbauer of Philadelphia who in 1901 built The Elms in Newport for E.J. Berwind. But the firm with by far the greatest experience and reputation, especially in the construction of clubhouses, was McKim Mead & White. By 1891, they already had three clubhouses to their credit. When Stanford White and Charles McKim received invitations from the Board to become Charter Members, their views had already been obtained regarding the proposed building. Once the land had been secured, Stanford White was promptly commissioned by the Board as the architect, and, fortunately, was given a relatively free hand to erect a building of rare beauty and dignity. His name will be forever linked with that of the Club. The last public appearance of any member of the White family took place in the Metropolitan Club in 1945. At the Annual Club Ball, Stanford White's octogenarian widow, escorted by then-President Lee Warren James and by her son, made a majestic progress from the Dining Room to the Great Hall down the staircase; she took up her position in front of the fireplace where she received the homage of the Members and guests.

While the Clubhouse was being built, the Club's Board of Governors set up temporary headquarters in the Madison Square Bank Building on 23rd Street, and from there they continued to select Members, collect initiation fees, and sell bonds for the payment of the new Clubhouse. The work on the plans made slow progress. The first spurt of enthusiasm had brought in 650 Members, about half the ultimate goal. But then interest lagged, partly because of skepticism about the success of such an ambitious undertaking.

There are persons (*The Times* wrote on August 9) who fancy that the Metropolitan Club, or the "Millionaire's Club" as it is better known, had died in infancy, its obsequies have been quietly performed, and that it must be numbered in the list of projected clubs that never got any further than mere projection. They are wrong though. To be sure, the projected club is not making the welkin ring—if indeed any club or individual can perform that feat—but it is still alive and slowly growing, and in the Fall it will probably be heard from in no uncertain way. In fact it has a good deal more life in it than the Union Club men wish it had.

The article went on to give an up-to-date report on the status and present plans of the building, and mentioned that W. Watts Sherman "who is preeminently the organizer of the club" was currently doing Newport and the other summer resorts.

In those early days, the curiosity of public and press was excited by rumors that the new Clubhouse would have accommodations for the ladies of the Members' families. The idea had been in the key planners' minds from the beginning, and for that reason the number of lots they considered buying had several times been increased. Nobody in his right mind at the time would even think of having ladies share the Clubhouse with men, or be admitted to it except for special—and rare—occasions. But the idea of having separate facilities, in a separate building, had been tried before and seemed appealing.

Despite ten months of discussion and counter-suggestions from Members, White's original plans came pretty close to the final plans accepted by the Board. They provided for a courtyard on 60th Street on which the Main Entrance to the Clubhouse was balanced to the east by the entrance to a Ladies' Restaurant. The first public announcement of this innovation came on September 20, 1891, in *The Times*:

The rumor that the Metropolitan Club would give its endorsement to the idea of providing quarters for the wives and daughters of members in their husbands' and fathers' clubhouse turns out to be true. It is officially announced that a suite of apartments for the ladies of members' families will be fitted up in the easterly end of the clubhouse now in course of erection on the corner of Fifth Avenue and Sixtieth Street. This suite will comprise dining rooms, boudoirs, and parlors, and will, of course, be distinct from the clubhouse proper. The rooms will be so arranged that they can be utilized for club purposes in case the experiment proves unsatisfactory. There is no danger of such an outcome, though, for such aristocratic club organizations as the Somerset of Boston, the Lawyers' and Riding Clubs of this city and other equally well-known clubs in other parts of the country have thoroughly tested the idea and made it one of their most attractive features.

Boston's Somerset was a prominent enough club at the turn of the century to have no less than fifty members who confidently listed their occupations as "gentlemen."

Another article of the same date reported:

The Metropolitan magnates say that the announcement of the completion of their plans for the new clubhouse is a little premature. They have, to be sure, decided upon the interior and the foundation plans, but they still have not made up their minds whether the exterior shall be of stone, marble or brick. Consequently they cannot tell what the building will cost, although $750,000 would probably be a tolerably good guess.

The article went on to say that there were now almost seven-hundred Members, plenty of money in the treasury and that there would not be the slightest difficulty in placing the construction bonds.

Finally, on February 12, 1892, almost a year after the dinner of the Founding Fathers at the Knickerbocker Club, *The New York Times* published a long article headed "The Metropolitan Club—It will have the handsomest Clubhouse in the world." The article went into great detail, giving the measurements and purpose of each room throughout the entire building.

The story in the adjoining column of *The Times* that day was headed "Great Day for the Bulls. The Record of the Stock Exchange Broken as to Sales—Wall Street Full of Excitement—Many Tales of Lucky Brokers." Sales that day totaled 1,446,874 shares. It was a good omen. This and the certainty now that the building would proceed helped the membership drive and before long almost a thousand Members had signed up.

On February 8, 1894, a letter was received by the Board from the architect stating that the Clubhouse would be delivered to the Superintendent (as the Manager of the Club was then called) on February 17, 1894. Three years had been required to design, build and furnish the Clubhouse in those leisurely times.

On April 17, 1894, the Finance and Building Committee discharged itself, reporting that the cost thus far and fully paid was $1,777,480, and that the Committee had $122,519 in the bank. At the turn of the century, this was a staggering figure, and it did not include the cost of the Annex which was added twenty years later.

The cost was financed by a first mortgage of $900,000 from the Bowery Savings Bank taken on July 31, 1893; it carried an interest rate of 5% and was due in twenty-five years. On top of it was a second-mortgage income debenture of $700,000 dated October 2, 1893, carrying 5% interest and due in April 1923.

It was originally hoped that it would be sufficient to raise $600,000 from the Membership but finally it was necessary to increase this to $700,000. The $5,000 each of the Founders had pledged raised $125,000 of this sum. As could be expected, Morgan and the two Vanderbilt brothers led the parade by subscribing $50,000 each. They were followed by Ogden Goelet, Robert Goelet, Mills, Marquand and Lanier with $25,000 each. This brought in a total of $400,000, over half the sum needed. Taylor, Whitney, Babcock and Sherman put up $10,000 each. Most of the others subscribed in sums of $5,000 each.

The balance of the cost came from the initiation fees of the Members, which amounted to about $300,000, making a grand total raised of $1,900,000. The second mortage had a sinking fund and holders wishing to sell tendered their bonds at prices from par down. As a result, the issue was bought back at a discount of 25% to 40%. By February, 1906, the issue had been reduced to $464,000. No interest was ever paid on the second-mortgage income bonds, since the earnings of the Club, with the exception of one year, were never sufficient for that purpose. They were exchanged in 1923 for a new 3% bond and all interest arrears were waived.

The opening days of the Clubhouse brought a new sensation to delight the press and the public. Rumors abounded that the Reverend Dr. William S. Rainsford, rector of St. George's Church where J. Pierpont Morgan was a member, had been blackballed by the Metropolitan Club Board of Governors. Technically this was untrue, as Dr. Rainsford had previously withdrawn his name. Dr. Rainsford, originally a revivalist minister from Toronto, had become a pillar of the Episcopal Church in New York and its leading spokesman. *The Sun* broke the story and *The Times* took it up in its edition of February 24, just four days after the first dinner given in the new Clubhouse for the Founding Fathers. *The Times* reported:

Dr. Rainsford's name was proposed a few months ago. There has been a meeting of the Governors since then, and Dr. Rainsford is not elected. This does not show that the well-known Clergyman has been blackballed, however, and a member of the Committee on Admissions said the reports were totally untrue. He said that Dr. Rainsford had written to the Governors before their last meeting asking them to withdraw his name from the list of proposals for various reasons of his own. For this reason he remains unelected.

The article continued to say that there was much excitement over the reported blackballing at the Riding Club, 7 East 58th Street, of which Dr. Rainsford was a member, and that Dr. David H. Greer, who was a Charter Member and rector of St. Bartholomew's Church, said the report was true beyond a doubt. Some members, apparently, had a special aversion to Dr. Rainsford because of his anti-liquor stance and his general broadness in church matters. *Town Topics* reported its own version in its issue of March 1:

The interest in the opening of the clubhouse has been intensified by the publication of the story of the blackballing of that eminent divine, Dr. Rainsford. It also brought out the rather paradoxical feature of an opposition to the election to the club of the rector and personal friend of its President J. Pierpont Morgan. Mr. Morgan is generally credited with having made the first move toward the organization of the Metropolitan Club in consequence of and as a protest against the rejection of his other warm friend, Mr. John King, by the Union Club. Those who best know Mr. Pierpont Morgan's characteristics and temperament say that the first half hour after he first heard that Dr. Rainsford might not be elected must have been a squally one in his vicinity.

Certainly no kow-tow-ing by these fellows. When J.P. died he took care of Dr. Rainsford for life with a legacy.

The first official dinner in the new Clubhouse took place on the third anniversary of the Founding Fathers' Dinner, February 20, 1894. Given for Governors only, it was held in what is now the Manager's office on the first mezzanine and what was then the Strangers' Dining Room. It was a joyous occasion, the crowning of three years' hard work. Four days later, Saturday, February 24, the Clubhouse was opened to the press and the following day the Sunday *Times* announced the news with big headlines:

METROPOLITAN CLUB'S PALACE NOW BUILT AND EQUIPPED IN UNRIVALLED SUMPTUOUS FASHION—THE ORGANIZATION AND ITS HOME ACCOMPLISHED FACTS—TWO YEARS AGO THEY WERE DESCRIBED AS FABLES—GALLANT PROVISION FOR THE COMFORT OF WOMEN GUESTS—FEATURES OF CLUB LUXURY THAT SURPASS THOSE OF OTHER SOCIAL ORGANIZATIONS.

There followed a detailed description of the exterior and interior with a four-column artist's drawing of the Clubhouse, a copy of which now hangs in the Office. Oddly enough, the illustration shows large sconces between the first-floor windows which do not exist now and did not then. Another few days passed before the Clubhouse was ready for the inspection of the Members, their wives and guests, who were invited to an open house on Tuesday, February 27.

On the day before, New York was hit by the worst storm of the season. Snow and sleet fell for over thirty hours and forty-mile winds blew through the streets which were covered with fifteen inches of snow and sleet. Four cable cars went out of control at Broadway and Seventeenth Street and travelling on the streets was not very pleasant. But nothing could keep the Members and their ladies, friends and guests from coming to see the new Clubhouse. This was their only chance because from the next day on only Members would be permitted inside. So everyone came.

*The New York Times* waxed poetic in its column next morning reporting the event:

Like the barons of old who opened their castle gates and dropped their drawbridges for the embrace of knightly cavalcades, the hospitable Members of the Metropolitan Club threw open the immense iron gates in front of their spacious courtyard yesterday for the admission of the New York Social World. True, there was no drawbridge, but in every other respect the great clubhouse far outshone the castles of the ancient barons.

Visitors began to arrive in the early afternoon and kept coming and going until late in the evening. All were most enthusiastic in their admiration and overwhelmed those Members present with congratulations upon their good fortune in belonging to so princely an organization. From the bowling alley in the basement to the thirty-four bedrooms in the attic, the delighted guests wandered. They stood in little groups discussing the furniture and decorations of the different rooms.

Most of the Members had taken their wives and daughters and friends from out-of-town. Lunch and supper were served in the dining room on the third floor and in a number of the private dining rooms. But the Clubmen did not want the opening spoken of as a reception. One said, "This is only a little private view for our friends." Nor was it a formal reception, for, though hundreds attended in the afternoon and evening, most of the women went in walking costume and wore hats.

Among those present were Mrs. J. Pierpont Morgan and Mrs. W. Watts Sherman, Mrs. John Jacob Astor and Mrs. Ogden Goelet, Mrs. William K. Vanderbilt and Mrs. James A. Roosevelt. *The Times* listed 148 names.

The Metropolitan Club in 1898, with Elbridge T. Gerry's house to the left. Note the columns and hedge along the Fifth Avenue side of the Club, later removed.

Finally, on Thursday, March 1, 1894, three years and ten days after the Founding Fathers' Dinner, the Clubhouse was opened officially to the Membership. There were no formal ceremonies that day. Members constantly entered the Clubhouse and wandered through the rooms. They dined in parties of two and three. The Executive Committee had hired a first-class chef. *The Times* again wrote poetically: "Even Lucullus would have thought himself fortunate had he been invited to dine with a member of the millionaire's club last evening."

In the evening little groups of Members might have been seen chatting here and there in the corners, smoking their favorite cigars. Among those who dined there that evening were ex-Secretary of the Navy Whitney, George H. Holt, William E. Iselin and Clarence S. Day.

The long line of cabs waiting on the corner added to the club-like appearance of the building. Cabs could not be driven into the Courtyard, a privilege reserved for the private carriages of the Members. Luckily there were no broken slumbers caused by the calling of cab

The Front Gate in its original form. The outermost columns were removed in 1912.

numbers, as the houses opposite the Club on 60th Street were occupied by tradesmen who were there only during business hours.

At that time, 60th Street was not a one-way street and no evil-smelling trucks and cars roared by. The old Fifth Avenue stages, with their dark panels, jolted and rumbled slowly up and down over the rough granite cobblestones, and the hansom cabs, the victorias and, in winter, the sleighs still drove around the Park and along the Avenue.

The impression the clubhouse made on the press is indicated by the article which appeared in *Town Topics* of March 1, 1894:

As to the clubhouse itself, it is probably the most complete and most gorgeous in appointments and furnishing of any in the world. The first and last impression of the visitor will be that of the atmosphere of exceeding wealth which will fasten to the institution the title of the "Millionaire's Club" without chance of removal. Millions look down on one from every side. From the cellar to ceiling every appointment is of the most sumptuous possible nature, and the architects have shown a thorough knowledge of the needs of clubmen. The sleeping rooms are alone open to criticism, being somewhat too low of ceiling and rather too small. Other slight defects may, of course, be developed when the club comes to be used, but this was the only one noticeable on first inspection. The magnificent entrance hall, with its superb marble main staircase, 15 feet wide, and its own fine proportions, being 52 feet long by 55 wide and 45 feet high, with its walls of Numidian marble and its frescoed and gold ceiling, is the handsomest hall of its kind in the country. That the house will be an enormously expensive one to run is evident at a glance, but the furor among clubmen that its opening will occasion will doubtless soon increase the present membership of 800 to a number which will, at $100 a year annual dues, cover at least the running expenses.

The observation that the house would be enormously expensive to run turned out to be prophetic, as all subsequent administrations can testify.

# Chapter 4

# THE ITALIAN RENAISSANCE REVIVAL AND McKIM MEAD & WHITE

A half a century before the founding of the Metropolitan Club, the organizers of London's Reform Club decided that convenience and prestige demanded that they build a new clubhouse. Their choice of the architect turned out to be a momentous one. It was ultimately to have a tremendous influence on the designers of New York's club buildings of the *fin-de-siècle*.

The men planning the Reform Club building in Pall Mall in 1839 invited seven architects to submit plans. Four did: one suggested an Elizabethan Renaissance mansion, the second a Corinthian temple and the third a richly modeled Graeco-Roman palace. The Board chose the fourth plan, submitted by Charles Barry, whose design was inspired by the Italian Renaissance Palazzo style which was beginning to influence all of English architecture.

The Renaissance was a period of transition from medieval to modern times. It was a conscious return to classical ideas and forms, and reached its highest flowering in Italy during the fifteenth and sixteenth centuries, or, as the Italians say, the quattrocento and the cinquecento. Its towering figures were Leonardo da Vinci and Michelangelo. Brunelleschi was the earliest of the great architects of the Renaissance and produced its first fruits in the dome of the cathedral in Florence begun in 1420, in the church of San Lorenzo and in the Pazzi Chapel built in 1430. Deeper understanding of the monumental Roman works resulted in grand and unified designs with pure and well-integrated details. Numerous palaces and churches in Rome and other cities were erected by Peruzzi, da Vignola, Michelangelo, Palladio and Antonio da Sangallo the younger, whose Palazzo Farnese in Rome embodies the period's highest standards.

Charles Barry, born in 1795, the son of a successful stationer, studied in Paris, Rome and Athens and traveled extensively in the Near East and up the Nile. He became one of the outstanding architects of his time. He triumphed in many competitions, including one for the design of the Houses of Parliament when they were rebuilt after the fire of 1834. More than any one else, it was he who replaced the Greek Revival of the Regency with High Victorian Italianate style. Beginning as a Greek Revivalist, he quickly discovered the greater richness and flexibility of cinquecento Italy. The Traveller's Club began this architectural revolution, and the Reform Club completed it. Barry was knighted by the Queen in 1851.

His inspiration in designing the exterior

*Rosettes*

of the Reform Club building was the Palazzo Farnese in Rome, built by da Sangallo the Younger, Michelangelo and della Porta. And although the Reform Club has only three rows of windows compared with the Metropolitan's four, and has the main entrance on the longer front side, it clearly inspired the architects of the Metropolitan Club Building. The Reform building is smaller—its dimensions are 142 by 120 feet compared with the Metropolitan's 200 by 100 feet—but the two resemble each other strikingly.

The interiors of the two clubs also have a number of similarities. The Reform had a special Smoking Room and a Strangers Room for guests. So had the Metropolitan Club Building. Both have enormous dining rooms. That of the Reform measures 117 by 26 feet and that of the Metropolitan, 95 by 40 feet. The classical Roman influence, however, is dominant in the interior of the London building, whereas the French influence and that of Robert Adam are dominant in the Metropolitan Club interior.

Stanford White—like his contemporaries—was familiar with the works of Sir Charles Barry and Robert Adam as well as those of other mid-nineteenth-century London architects such as Decimus Burton. He had visited London many times: the first time in September, 1879, on the way back from a long stay on the Continent, and then again with his young bride in 1884. He wrote to his mother enthusiastically on August 22 about the architectural

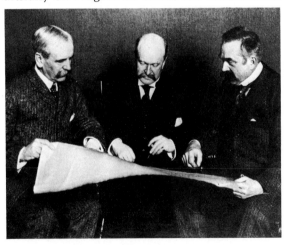

Mead, McKim and White in 1905.

wonders he had seen in London. He also let her know that she would soon be a grandmother.

White and his partners quickly recognized the particular suitability of the Renaissance mode for urban structures, especially clubhouses. They used the style in the Villard Houses designed in 1882. But it was the success of the design for the Boston Public Library (1887-95) which most clearly marked McKim Mead & White's commitment to the Italian Renaissance mode. Shortly after this success, White used a Renaissance design to transform Edwin Booth's house in Gramercy Park for the Players Club. But the first clubhouse in New York to be completely designed in the neo-Italian Renaissance manner was that of the Century Association (1889-91). The façade of that clubhouse takes some of its inspiration from San Michele's Palazzo Canossa in Verona.

Like Barry's before him, White's method was essentially mimetic, that is, based on the principle of creative imitation. White's influence on the architecture of New York became so strong that following Le Corbusier's visits to the city in 1935, the great Swiss architect noted, "In New York, then, I learned to appreciate the Italian Renaissance. It is so well done that you could believe it to be genuine. It even has a strange new firmness which is not Italian but American."

It was therefore no wonder that, when the Founding Fathers of the Metropolitan Club discussed the choice of the architect for the new building, they unanimously agreed on McKim Mead & White. Morgan knew White's work from his connection with the Madison Square Garden project. For Sherman, White as a young man worked on his Newport estate. For Henry A. C. Taylor, he had built a luxurious mansion in Newport in 1885. For Robert Goelet, he had built Southside, his villa in Newport, and a commercial building at Fifth Avenue and 37th Street. For all of them, the choice was obvious.

At that time, the firm of McKim Mead & White was on the way to becoming the most famous American architectural partnership. White had been a close friend of Charles Follen McKim and joined the firm upon his return from a long stay in Europe in June, 1879. The firm prospered from its beginning and its staff grew steadily, reaching a peak of about 110 employees during the 1891-3 period. By 1900, it had become the largest architectural firm in the world. Altogether, they received almost a thousand commissions during the half century in which they were active, ranging from public and office buildings to private residences to mausoleums and the interiors of yachts.

In 1891, they were already considered specialists in the design and construction of clubhouses and had three important ones to their credit, the Algonquin Club of Boston, designed in 1886, and the Century Association and Deutscher Verein buildings in 1890. To follow were the Harvard Club in 1893, the University Club in 1898 and the Harmonie Club in 1904. But no two of them were alike. The Century building was gracious and festive, the facade based on north-Italian-Renaissance style; the Metropolitan Clubhouse was simple and severe, its splendid colonnaded courtyard reflecting the opulence of its Membership.

The firm was fortunate in that it operated during the period of intense business and building activities from 1880 to 1912, before the enactment of the graduated income tax by Congress. Within a decade of its passage in 1913, the source of private munificence that had been such an important part of the firm's patronage began to dry up.

Of the three partners, Stanford White was the flamboyant one and to this day is the best known and remembered. Born in New York city in 1853, he came from as old and distinguished an American background as any of the Founders. His first American ancestor was a selectman in Cambridge, Massachusetts, in 1635. His great-grandfather was an Episcopal clergyman and his grandfather a shipping merchant. His father, Richard Grant White, was a distinguished music and drama critic whom the London *Spectator* called "the most accomplished and best-bred man that America has sent to England within the past generation." Stanford's mother was Alexina Black Mease, daughter of a cultivated Charleston family who had moved to New York. After an education in private

schools and by tutors, the boy briefly attended New York College. His father's increasing financial difficulties forced him not only to abandon his dream of studying to become a painter, but also required him to become self-supporting as soon as possible. It was finally decided that he study architecture in the Brookline office of Henry Hobson Richardson while the latter was completing Boston's Trinity Church. Richardson was one of the new generation of architects trained abroad in the great Paris school, the Ecole des Beaux-Arts, to which the empire of Napoleon III had given fresh prestige. White worked for Richardson for six years. The precocious youngster learned quickly and soon was given important assignments. Here he worked for the first time with Augustus Saint Gaudens, John LaFarge and Charles Follen McKim.

White was anxious to train his eye and taste on the great creations of the French and Italian Renaissance and of ancient architecture, and in 1878 he left for an extended stay in Europe. Part of the time, he stayed in Paris with his close friend Saint Gaudens, exploring the environs of that city. Charles McKim joined them there, and the three gifted young men—all redheads—became friends and collaborators. They made one memorable trip through romanesque Provence. From Lyon, they took a boat down the Rhône to Avignon, stopping off at all the towns along the river's bank which were full of Gothic and Roman architecture. It was then that Saint Gaudens made the caricature of the three, a bronze medallion now in the possession of the Century Association.

Later Stannie (White's nickname) toured southern France and Italy alone with his sketch book, studying the marvels of Roman, Gothic and Renaissance art he adored, and schooling his taste on the masters of Western culture. While staying in Venice, he walked one day on the Campo Santa Maria Nuova and discovered the lovely church, Santa Maria dei Miracoli, an early Renaissance creation of Pietro Lombardo. Built in the 1480s to house the miraculous image of the Virgin Mary and encrusted with precious marbles inside and out, it was his inspiration when he designed the Great Marble

Stanford White

Hall of the Club. This visit and others to come made a deep impression on his style and future work. He returned to New York in August, 1879, and shortly thereafter joined McKim and Mead in a new partnership, McKim Mead & White.

At about that time, White met and fell in love with Bessie Springs Smith, daughter of Judge J. Lawrence Smith, a descendant of Colonel Richard Smith, the original patentee of Smithtown, Long Island. Among the Smith forebears had been Olaff van Cortlandt, Burgomaster of New Amsterdam. Bessie and Stanford were married in 1889. They had one son, Lawrence Grant White.

As a perverse fate would have it, White was shot and killed on June 25, 1906, on the roof garden of one of his famous creations, Madison Square Garden, by a worthless millionaire playboy, Harry K. Thaw, because of trouble over Thaw's beautiful wife, the actress Evelyn Nesbit Thaw. Actually Evelyn had graduated from artist's model to chorus girl in the hit *Florodora* which was the sensation of the day and ran for 547 performances. The reason for the murder, revealed at Thaw's famous trial, was the extreme detail in which Miss Nesbit described her three years of friendship with Stanford White. Whatever Thaw had heard, he made desperate efforts to imitate and to surpass. Finally, perhaps in despair over the high standards set by White, he flew into a jealous rage and shot the architect.

Thaw's subsequent trial was a farce. The victim became the defendant; the murderer, the hero. A well-financed campaign of slander against White was fed by the growing resentment of the middle classes towards the privileged and their extravagances. Today, the objective historian knows that White's marriage to Bessie was a happy one despite their divergent natures. His interest in the ladies of the stage and demi-monde was more visual than sexual; he worshipped youth and beauty. It was to men like White that the Swiss poet Heinrich Leuthold wrote the immortal lines:

Uns aber lasst zechen! —und krönen
Mit Laubgewind
Die Stirnen die noch dem Schönen
Ergeben sind.

Und bei den Posaunenstössen
Die eitel Wind,
Lachen über Grössen.
Die keine sind.

Charles Follen McKim was six years older than White, and was born in 1847 in Chester, Pennsylvania. His father was one of the leading abolitionists; his mother, a Quaker. He was named after Karl Follen, the German professor at Harvard who had been summarily dismissed because of his outspoken abolitionist sentiments. Young McKim was one of the first Americans to study at the Ecole des Beaux-Arts in Paris. He came to New York in 1871 and soon established himself as one of the leading architects in the country. He met White while he was working in Richardson's office, and they became life-long friends. McKim was the quiet brains of the firm. He later became the first president of the American Academy in Rome, to whose founding he devoted years of zealous effort. He died in 1909.

William Rutherford Mead was born in 1848 at Brattleboro, Vermont. He studied at Amherst College, joined an architects' office in 1868 and studied for a year and a half in Florence at the Accademia de Belle Arti. Sparse in conversation as a Vermonter, practical, financially astute, he was the balance wheel and stabilizer of the firm.

In the nineteenth century, the Ecole des Beaux-Arts in Paris exercised great influence on architectural thought throughout Europe, including Russia. The Ecole stressed the harmonious combination of traditional, classical elements with utility. Richard Morris Hunt was the first American to study there before and after the Civil War. He later designed some of the most opulent mansions of America's first gilded age. H. H. Richardson followed him as the second American, then Charles McKim; Joseph Morrell, Wells, Kendall, Carrère and many other aspiring architects of the time went to Paris as well. Stanford White never entered the Ecole, but his son, Lawrence Grant White, studied there later.

Founded by Cardinal Mazarin in 1648, the Ecole enjoyed a great revival under Napoleon III when Paris was rebuilt by Baron Haussmann. Art students between the ages of fifteen and twenty-five could compete for the prestigious Grand Prix de Rome. The successful competitors received an annual allowance from the French government for three or four years of study, two of which had to be passed at Rome.

The three men, before forming their partnership, had taken a famous trip along the New England coast in the centennial year and as a result launched a short-lived colonial-revival movement. But then White took his long trip to Europe, partly in the company of McKim, and became enamored of the Italian Renaissance. On trips to England, he came to know the work of Sir Charles Barry and studied the finest examples of the decorative art of Robert Adam. White discovered in Adam an inspiration and was greatly influenced by him.

Maybe unconsciously, White had followed the footsteps of another great American who exercised a profound influence over the course of American architecture. When Thomas Jefferson was American Minister to France from 1790 to 1795, he traveled extensively in the same countries which White visited almost one-hundred years later. Jefferson chose the Italian architect Andrea Palladio as his first inspiration, later turning directly to the Greek and Roman originals. In Nîmes, Jefferson gazed for long hours—"like a lover at his mistress"—at the Maison Carrée, that lovely, beautifully-perserved Roman temple built in A.D. 14 which became the model for many later structures in Europe and America.

Jefferson inspired the classical design of the Virginia State Capitol and the superb Greek design of the Bank of the United States building in Philadelphia (destroyed, alas). When the visiting French architect Beaujour saw it, the only words he could find were: "Si beau, et si simple." Jefferson's influence on American architecture lasted almost a hundred years, as any visit to Washington will prove.

The three partners were radically different and yet perfectly complementary personalities. McKim and White were the major designers, and White had the special responsibility for interior detailing. Mead did little preliminary designing, but often offered timely criticism of his partners' plans and arrangements. Stannie was a dynamic, indefatigable worker. Virile and overflowing with energy, he revelled in rich materials, in color and ornaments. His tall figure, crowned with red bristling hair, was visible above the crowd in every artistic assemblage. Not holding to conventional office hours, he might appear in his office before seven in the morning, his arms full of rolled drawings or he might bound in after the opera, in full dress, throw his cloak aside and set to work. When the draftsmen arrived in the morning, the room might be festooned with garlands of tracing paper filled with his rapid sketches and cryptic notes.

White knew most of the Members of the Building Committee and had worked for some of them. Robert Goelet, the Chairman of the Committee and the most active Member, was not only a client but a close personal friend. When the date of White's marriage to Bessie

Smith was fixed for early Februrary of 1884, his close friends wanted to give the usual bachelor dinner for him. The arrangements were made and the invitations sent out by a small group which included not only close friend "Gustibus" Saint Gaudens, but also Bob Goelet. The dinner is interesting as a chronicle of all of White's most intimate friends, and his friends always said that he never lost a friend. Present, of course, were his partners McKim and Mead, and also Hunt and Wells. There were many painters, sculptors and intellectuals, including David Maitland Armstrong, who had returned a few years before from his study period in France and Italy and was later commissioned by White to do the five stained-glass windows in the Great Hall of the Metropolitan Club. Emlen Roosevelt was there and Daniel R. Newhall of the Pennsylvania Railroad, as well as Professor William R. Ware of Columbia University who later selected the winning design for the Madison Square Garden competition—the award went to McKim Mead & White. In all, over forty men attended the dinner.

When McKim Mead & White appeared on the scene, they immediately became a powerful influence in replacing the various neo-classical traditions in architecture by that of the Italianate Renaissance. It was largely under the impetus of McKim, White and their gifted designer Joseph Morrell Wells that the new style was introduced in America. It used classical elements but was not imitative. It reaffirmed the supremacy of form and worked in the spirit of unity, uniformity and balance. The first building to embody the new manner was the group of four Villard Houses in New York, built in 1885.

The Chicago World's Columbian Exhibition of 1893 brought this new American-Renais-sance style to the attention of a wider public. During the planning period, a quarrel developed between the modern wing led by Louis Sullivan and the traditionalist Beaux Arts adherents led by Hunt, McKim, White and others. The latter carried the day and for the first time the Italianate-American-Renaissance style was presented to the eyes of millions accustomed to the prevailing Classic, Gothic, Queen Anne or Colonial forms. Construction of the Fair grounds was started at exactly the same time as the Metropolitan Clubhouse, early in 1892. In October, 1892, two Charter Members, Levi P. Morton, then Vice-President of the United States, and Chauncey Depew gave the dedication speeches in Chicago. Twenty-seven-million people from all over the world visited the Exhibition during the six months it was open, from May to October, 1893. McKim Mead & White built the Agriculture Building and the New York State Building, the latter a striking Italian-Renaissance edifice inspired by the Villa Medici of Rome. Observers at the time felt that there was a resemblance between the New York State Building and certain rooms at the Clubhouse. The *New York Times* reported on February 27, 1894, "In the main the decorations (of the Clubhouse) recall the New York Building at the World's Fair, especially the central hall, with its rich columns and bold flight of stairs, as well as its grand chandeliers hanging from the coffered ceiling." But judging from the photographs, the exterior and the interior decorations in the Clubhouse are much simpler and more restrained and aristocratic.

For the next generation, the American Renaissance became the primary animating force of American art, architecture and culture. The Building of the Metropolitan Club represents the purest expression of the new trend.

# Chapter 5

# BUILDING
# THE CLUBHOUSE

Very soon after the firm of McKim Mead & White was selected to design the Metropolitan Clubhouse, they submitted their first sketches to Robert Goelet, the Chairman of the Building Committee, with a letter dated May 14, 1891. White had been put in sole charge of this project, with William M. Kendall assisting him as staff architect. White proposed that the main entrance be on 60th Street, "the Club entrance and the Ladies' entrance balancing, with a carriage court 30 ft. x 60 ft. between." He added that "the plan has been very hastily drawn and must not be considered as at all definite in matters of detail." This was tactfully phrased since the gentlemen White had to deal with were all cultured and knowledgeable, with architectural ideas of their own. They had the means and the leisure to devote their lives to that most intoxicating of amateur occupations—building. The files of McKim Mead & White, now at the New-York Historical Society, are full of letters and memoranda from Robert Goelet, with suggestions and hints. One dictum only seems to have been laid down from the beginning: that a large Lounging Room be located on the Fifth-Avenue frontage with large windows so that Members could watch the carriages entering the

Park or the strollers along Fifth Avenue. Such a stipulation would determine a good part of the architects' plans for the rest of the building.

But the Founders also wanted a big building, one that could accommodate at least 2,000 Members. They meant active Resident Members who would make frequent use of the facilities. Unfortunately for the economics of running the Club, the Resident Membership never came even close to 2,000 men.

On May 19th, 1891, the deed to the land was signed and the same day the ground breaking for the building took place. John D. Crimmins (who became a member in 1898) was the contractor for the excavation. Founded in 1848 by John D. Crimmins' father Thomas, this is one of the few privately-owned firms involved with the Building which is still in existence. On May 5, 1891, Crimmins had written the following letter of proposal for the excavation:

Dear Sir:

We have looked over the property, NE co 61st [sic] & 5th Av., the location of the new Club House. The excavation will be principally rock. There is a very small percentage of earth. Instead of classifying the prices of excavation for each, rock in cellars, rock in sewers or rock in vault, we will make

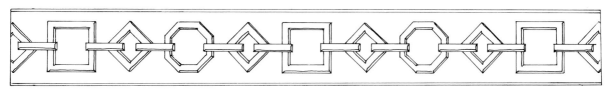

*Decorative chain band*

39

an average estimate of $2.25 per av. yd., for which we will perform all the excavations necessary in connection with the foundations of the proposed club building.

Very truly yours,
J. D. & T. D. Crimmins

This was accepted at $2.25 for rock and $1.30 for earth, and the work commenced. Robert Crimmins, current owner and grandson of John D. Crimmins, estimates present costs to be $7 a cubic yard for earth and $30 for rock, using excavating machinery. Back then it was a wheelbarrow job. In August, 1891, *The Times* reported that there was a good deal more rock in that part of New York than was necessary from the builder's standpoint and blasting was slow work. Consequently, not much apparent progress had been made, but the contractor felt that the foundation would be completed before the cold weather set in.

By the end of September, the work on the excavation was finished and work on the foundation was begun. The ground plans had been filed with the Department of Buildings on September 17, and a tentative interior arrangement had been worked out. But the design of the façade was left unresolved. White, who was known for his rapid sketching ability, and his assistant Kendall, produced some fifty different sketches for the façade and the pick of them was presented at a Board meeting on September 29.

The time spent over the decision on the final design of the façade is one proof of the interest these well-travelled gentlemen had in architecture. Another Board meeting was called for November 20, 1891. The Members of the Building Committee, taking separate cabs to avoid publicity, met at the McKim Mead & White offices on West 12th Street. Here, over drinks, they amiably discussed the question of the façade. One of the early sketches which had been given serious consideration included "a large and beautiful stoop" leading to doors and a vestibule on Fifth Avenue. Apparently Morgan swayed the Board away from the idea of an entrance on Fifth Avenue to one on 60th Street. An entrance on Fifth Avenue would necessarily have limited the size of the great

Lounging Room overlooking Central Park. So the Board returned to the plans White originally submitted to Robert Goelet on May 14, 1891, which suggested a courtyard and entrances on 60th Street.

As late as January, 1892, Board Members were still offering their design suggestions to White. From Paris, William K. Vanderbilt proceeded along his own lines. In a long handwritten letter dated January 31, 1892, he sent White plans based on a French house with a central courtyard. White could hardly take the plans lightly, in view of Vanderbilt's confession, "I have worked hard on them for the past week and you can imagine they have taken some time for a novice to make." Vanderbilt insisted, "I prefer individually these plans to any I have yet seen. They do not embrace some of the grand features that yours do but for practicability I think they will answer every purpose."

But early in February, 1892, White's plans with the asymmetrically-placed courtyard were released to the press.

When releasing the plans, White said:
The Clubhouse will stand unrivaled in its size, and although the style will be in the severest and simplest character of the Italian Renaissance and the feeling of severity and solidity will be carried through the interior, the scale of the building and the nature of its materials will give it an appearance unlike that of any building in New York.

In April of 1892, McKim Mead & White signed on David H. King, Jr., as the general contractor. King, who had been invited to become a Charter Member of the Club, was one of the most prominent contractors of his day and, as with most of their commissions, the architectural firm sought the finest workmanship rather than the lowest bidder. They had previously worked very successfully with King, their most notable project to date having been the construction of the old Madison Square Garden.

When White received the commission for the Metropolitan Club building, he was working with King on the construction of the Washington Arch at the southern end of Fifth

Avenue. To celebrate the centennial of George Washington's taking of the oath of office in 1889, the city erected a temporary wood-and-plaster memorial arch designed by Stanford White. It was such a success that the cry went up for a permanent arch. Charter Member William Rhinelander Stewart led the campaign to collect the needed funds and both White as architect and King as builder waived all fees or profits. Built of white Tuckahoe marble, the Arch was completed in 1892.

On April 22, 1892, David H. King wrote to White:

I intend to start the Metropolitan Club Monday morning next and will wish you to send me copies of all the estimates from the different contractors.

The contract with King was for $660,000 plus 7.5% profit.

As the Club Building went up, New York was more and more astounded at the beauty of its exterior. *Town Topics* wrote in its August, 1893, issue:

The exterior of the new Metropolitan Club at 60th Street and Fifth Avenue, is now practically completed and is being generally pronounced the neatest and most imposing club structure in town, both by connoisseurs and by those not usually interested in architectural effect. In the opinion of everyone I've met, it is declared to be even more attractive than that other creation of Stanford White's, the Century Clubhouse on West Forty-Third Street. By the way, Mr. White is something of a clubman himself, his list including the New York Yacht Club, the Century, the Metropolitan, Racquet, Union, Players, Grolier, Riders, City and University.

It took one year and ten months to finish the building. The architect's files are full of memos and letters from Robert Goelet and Henry A. C. Taylor, who was chairman of the Building Committee in Goelet's absence, testifying to the myriad details which required a decision. An interesting aside is given in an unpublished account written by one of the architects, Egerton Swartwout, who worked on the Metropolitan Club, and who later established his own firm with Evarts Tracy, whom he met while working for White. Swartwout wrote:

This reassuring talk with Mr. Mead came at a time I most needed it, for I had just had a narrow escape from a serious entanglement with Mr. White. Dicky Hunter had been for some time making sketches for a large interior, the central hall of the Metropolitan Club, a big marble building on Fifth Avenue, Sixtieth Street, as I recall it, and had been having a lot of trouble with the main stairs which ran up in a double flight at one side of the great square hall opposite the entrance. It was to be very elaborate and monumental, Dicky said, all of Pavonazzo marble, handsome stuff according to the large sample he showed me. Back of the stairs was a corridor on the second floor cut off by a screen of columns with wrought-iron rails between, and the trouble seemed to be in the spacing of these columns. There were a dozen or more sketches drawn freehand one over the other, and one day when Dicky was out at lunch I got looking them over. I didn't know what it was all about but none of them seemed right to me and I made a quick sketch of what seemed the obvious arrangement and just when I had finished I saw Mr. White coming in with Hunter. I popped back on my stool and was busily at work when they came up. White pawed over the sketches hastily, found my sketch which I had unconsciously made in imitation of Dicky's way of indication, and said—Here, this one, do that—and dashed off. And poor Dick spent the rest of the afternoon trying to remember when he made that sketch and how he came to make it.

For you see, he explained, the whole trouble is those two damned little steel columns at the start of each end of the colonnade, the marble columns will have to be split and hollowed out to cover them. But can't they be moved, I ventured. The damn things are in place and the engineers say they have to stay where they are. It's all a fool way to do an important building I think, and Dicky puffed surreptitiously on his pipe, this letting constructionists work up the plans from sketch plans that are just a general indication of what's wanted and before the interiors have been really designed. It always makes trouble. Van der Bent is a good man and does his best but how can he get things properly centered when he doesn't know, and damn it nobody knows, what the finish is to be. Look at these stairs now, the rough stairs are all out and in place, personally I think they're too steep. I think McKim will have a fit when he sees them if he ever does, but I suppose they're sort of stage scenery anyway, every one of those rich fat members will take the elevator, but it's the wrong way to do it.

How do we develop the drawings? Well, take this

building; I don't know how they got the job, handed to them on a silver platter probably, we've done a lot of clubs you know, the firm or some of them are members of most of the good ones, though there may have been some spade work, if so White for it's his job here. Then it's talked over with the building committee and they get a general idea of what's wanted and the cost usually, though I don't believe that matters much here, it's a rich men's club, but what we know out here in the drafting room about such matters is just guesswork.

In this case there was first a set of sketch plans at eighth scale, very simple drawings. I think they made three or four different schemes, and Kendall worked up some sketches of the exterior and Frankie Hopping rendered a perspective, colored, blue sky and trees where there aren't any, and flying shadows, cloud shadows on the building you know, a real snappy piece of work. And soon we got the word to go ahead, fast. That's the way with jobs like this, the building committee putters around for months and then wants to start work on the building overnight.

It was a rush getting out the working drawings. Van der Bent and Koen on the plans and our outside engineers on the mechanical part, and Kendall on the exterior, Weeks and I did some work on it, too. They pushed it hard on the job, the foundations were in before our drawings were all finished. Had some trouble with the marble. Quarry gave out or something, and they had to use stock from a different quarry for the plain ashlar. Looks all right now, but I wonder if it will show when it is weathered, different quarries weather differently you know. Still it's a swell job. Seen it yet? Well I'll take you up there some time.

Oh yes, about the trouble I'm having now. It's this way. The interiors weren't started when they began construction and there was some delay here, other things came up I suppose, and when I got the job of designing this hall, the shell of the building was nearly completed. And so a couple of men and I went up there and measured everything up, steel columns and stairs, and by golly some partition blocks were cut.

Yet it does seem funny to have to do that checking up, but we've found it has to be done. The steel work is never quite as it shows on the engineer's plan, sometimes changed in the shop drawings and sometimes set wrong, beams sticking down in the ceiling and connections stick out where they shouldn't. And when you start to lay it out carefully things don't center as they should. It's not the right way to do, I'm sure of that and Bacon thinks so too. All the interiors, the important rooms should be designed and carefully figured when the general working drawings are made, and then we could give them figures to the finished work and they have to keep within them. And they could let the whole thing in one contract. But maybe that's why they don't do it because they never seem to know at first just how much money they have to spend on the interiors, or they don't want to know perhaps. We're great people here to start in with simple interiors and before we're through it's as elaborate as hell. But the clients seem to like it, don't kick much as far as I know, and when it's finished they're proud of it.

The finishing touches were added to the building in February, 1894. Morgan, during the entire construction period, had followed the progress of the building from behind the scenes. A letter written to him by Stanford White, dated February 21, 1894, shows to what extent he was consulted even on minor problems:

My Dear Mr. Morgan:

The few things yet remaining to be done at the Metropolitan Club will be done by tomorrow, with the exception of the carpet on the main stairs. The accompanying letter will explain this matter, and Sloane & Co. are now awaiting orders from me as to which carpet they will lay. As the original carpet contracted for can be laid by tomorrow, I write to ask if I may have your permission to wait for the English carpet, which probably cannot be laid until Friday or Saturday.

As Sloane & Co. will have to work their men over time in order to sew the carpet, and as they are waiting word from me to start sewing on the American carpet, I will be greatly obliged if you will send me an answer by bearer.

Stanford White

Finally, in February, 1894, the architects turned the building over to the Membership. *The New York Times* at that time gave full coverage to everything concerning club life. The opening of the Metropolitan Club's "Marble Palace," its architecture and its interior were fully described and analyzed in five separate articles on February 24, 25, 27, 28 and March 2.

# Chapter 6

# OF DECORATIONS, ORNAMENTS AND MARBLE

If the Italian Renaissance style has one characteristic above all others, it is the simplicity of its decorations. Deriving ultimately from Greek and Roman antiquity, columns and pilasters, moldings and consoles, caryatids and· atlantes, ornaments and murals are clearly articulated. Eternal gratitude is due to the Italian architect Giacomo Barozzi da Vignola (1507-1573) who codified the rules of classical architecture for the Italian Renaissance and posterity. Despite the fact that the best interpreters of the Roman styles, such as the Englishmen Robert Adam, and Charles Barry and the Americans Thomas Jefferson, Charles McKim and Stanford White, went to the source, Italy, for their schooling, the tradition actually came to England and America via France where, for better or for worse, it was refined during the period of the Louis. During the two centuries of their splendid reign, innumerable châteaux and hôtels were commissioned by the nobility as well as by nouveau-riche financiers and *fermiers généraux*, the hated tax collectors who were among the first victims of the guillotine. Inevitably, many of these houses were decorated in a florid and bombastic style but others were like beautiful jewels. Understandably, the interior decoration of most of the great mansions built in America during the Gilded Age was entrusted to French experts.

White had the good taste not to overload the Metropolitan Clubhouse with decorations, murals, columns, and the like. He used columns sparingly and only for the purpose for which they were created, to support weight. His ceilings were light and pleasing, not heavy and oppressive. His decorations are spare and delicate, with a wealth of variety.

What White created here, with the help of Cuel, Herter and others, is a true treasure house of Renaissance decorative art, a feast for the student, the layman and the connoisseur. This chapter offers the layman a description of the design elements available to the architects, some knowledge of which will enhance the enjoyment of visiting the building and of reading about it and its art.

*Supports*

The various orders of columns are well known and require only brief mention here. The Greeks created three Orders, the Doric, the Ionic and lastly the Corinthian. Of these, the Doric is the simplest and the most majestic. The shaft is slightly convex and fluted with about twenty channelings; it has no base and

*Festoons*

43

the capital is simple. In its severity and frugality, the Doric Order is masculine and reflects the character of Sparta. Not surprisingly, White did not use any Doric columns in the Clubhouse. The Ionic and Corinthian Orders are more elegant. They have flutings, usually twenty-four, separated by fillets and are of greater height and slenderness. To conform to the classical ideal of beauty, the height of the Ionic column should be about eight times the diameter, and the Corinthian, about ten times. The entablature, starting from the lowest element and consisting of Architrave, Frieze and Cornice, is generally one fourth as high as the column; the pedestal is one third as high. The shaft rests on a molded base. The principal difference between the two is in the capital. The Ionic Order capital has paired scrolls, also called volutes, under the abacus, connected by a baluster. The echinus is usually carved with eggs-and-darts, three of which show between the scrolls. The Roman version may also have a wide necking with a honeysuckle ornament below the echinus. The total impression is one of grace, elegance and beauty. The most striking characteristics of the Corinthian Order are richness and magnificence and therefore it became more popular with the Romans than it had been with the Greeks. Its main difference is in the capital which is bell-shaped and in typical examples is enveloped with rows of acanthus leaves, with volutes under the projecting angles of its abacus. In the Club Building, White used the Ionic Order in the Card Room and the old Billiard Room on the Second Floor—and in the Foyer on the Third Floor. The Corinthian theme is used only on the pilasters, principally in the Dining Room.

The flutes of a number of the columns and pilasters are filled, mostly on the lower portion but also to some extent on the upper part, with a convex molding known as reeding. The origin of this is to be found in an effort to preserve the arrises and fillets from damage but it has become a form of decoration of itself.

To the above Orders, the Romans added the Tuscan, a simplified Doric with unfluted columns on bases, few but bold moldings and a general lack of ornament; and the Composite, a modified Corinthian, having a capital with eight volutes, adopted (with egg-and-dart bands between each pair) from the Ionic and grafted on the Corinthian bell. It lacks the simple beauty of either the Ionic or the Corinthian capital but has great richness.

White used Tuscan columns in the Great Marble Hall, where the two mottled red ones supporting the Palladian entrance as well as the twelve white ones on the Gallery are monolith marble columns. He also used them on the outside, the gates and the portico, where a band of leaves and another one of rosettes are the only decoration on the capitals. In both instances, they are flanked by square columns called piers and stand on pedestals.

Pilasters are used frequently throughout the Club Building. They are upright supporting members, attached to and projecting slightly from the face of the wall and equipped with a base and a capital like a column. In general, they follow the rules and proportions of the classic orders. They may be fluted or not but have no entasis or taper. During the Renaissance they became a purely decorative device and were often paneled and ornamented.

The ancients also used human figures as supports. The male figures are known as "atlantes," after Atlas who, Greek mythology tells us, at the end of the earth supports the vaults of heaven on his shoulders. They are also known as "telamones," Greek for "bearers." The female figures are known as "caryatids" after the priestesses who danced at the feast of Diana in the temple at Caryae in the Peloponnessus. According to the early Roman architect Vitruvius in his book *De architectura*, these maidens were punished for aiding the Persians, were carried into captivity and compelled to serve as carriers of burdens. The perfect example of caryatids at their most beautiful is on the porch of the Erechtheum in Athens. Judging from their smiling faces, the weight they are condemned to carry cannot be too burdensome. They are frequently used nowadays as supports on fireplaces. They are also used as half-figures, as they are at the Clubhouse in the West Lounging Room supporting the oval medallions of Hercules' Labors.

*Modillion*

The decorated ends of wooden beams can probably be regarded as the original models for consoles, also called modillions or mutules. The S-shaped double volute with a large and a small spiral is the standard form. Space for decoration is afforded by the sides while the front is usually ornamented by scale motifs and leaves. When used to support a balcony or cornice, its attitude is described as recumbent; when used on cornices over doors or windows, its attitude is erect. A most impressive view of the consoles supporting balconies, cornices and windows at the Clubhouse can be obtained from the middle of the Fifth Avenue sidewalk, looking up. The acanthus leaves are especially beautiful.

### Moldings

Moldings in decorative art are bands on a surface, usually continuous, the cross section or profiles of which are always the same. They are plane or cylindrical surfaces, convex, concave, or of double curvature. Some of them are plain, but most are enriched by carvings.

A small plane surface is called a band, face, or fascia; if very small, a fillet, raised or sunk. A convex molding is called an ovolo, torus, or three-quarter molding. A small torus is called a bead, astragal, or reed. Concave moldings are called cavetto, scotia darkness, or three-quarter hollow.

A molding with a double curvature is called a cyma or wave molding. If the tangents to the curve at top and bottom are horizontal, it is called a cyma recta; if vertical, a cyma reversa. A small cyma is called a cymatium.

These and other moldings are used in the entablature of columns, on frames for windows and door panels, on walls, under cornices, on stringcourses, and elsewhere.

A favorite decorative motif, outside as well as in, are dentils, bands of toothlike rectangular blocks. They are often found in the lower section of a cornice and can be seen to good advantage in the Courtyard.

Moldings, either plain or decorated, are lavishly used throughout the Clubhouse. On the exterior they may be found in the stringcourse and the cornice, in the frames of the windows and on the balconies. On the interior, covered with gold-leaf, they are everywhere. Their study is a rewarding experience.

Most decorative band patterns were developed during the flowering of Greek culture, but some have Assyrian and Egyptian origins. Further developed by the Romans, they had another period of growth during the Renaissance. The most frequently used patterns in the Clubhouse are the following:

The *fret* was a favorite decoration on the ceilings of Egyptian tombs from the Fourth Dynasty on. In later examples it is combined with rosettes, scarabs and lotus into patterns of great richness. It had its greatest development among the Greeks (hence the common name, Greek fret), who used it not only on the abacus of capitals, but on panels and even in pottery. It is also known as the Meander Border after a river in Asia Minor, the Meandros, which flows in sinuous curves. Beautiful examples of frets can be found in the Clubhouse in the coffers on the ceiling of the Great Marble Hall or on the dividing bands in the ceiling of the Third Floor Hall.

Particularly attractive are the enrichments of the *torus* molding, the frequently large moldings of semi-circular sections often used in framing wall or ceiling panels or on door or window arches or on ceiling moldings of the Renaissance. They may resemble a bundle of rods around which ribbons are twisted or they may be surrounded by leaves, for instance, oak leaves with acorns.

A popular band is the *guilloche* or interlacement band which is formed by a number of

45

lines interlaced or plaited together. This pattern was used in Antiquity and in the Middle Ages. In the so-called northern styles—Celtic, Anglo-Saxon and Norman—one finds extremely complicated and richly combined interlacements.

*Bead* or *astragal* is the name given to those small half-round moldings which are often enriched by ornaments, like pearls strung together or as turned bands or cords. Beads may be enriched with balls, discs or reels.

The term *rosette band* is a general name for rosette, spray or other band when the rosette, an artificial rose, is the principal chracteristic. The single rosettes which are similar to conventional roses seen in front-view, are either in immediate juxaposition or divided by channels, by calices, or by stalks and sprays. A large rosette, as in the center of the ceiling coffers in the Great Hall, is called a *patera*.

One of the most frequently observed patterns is the *egg-and-dart* or the *egg-and-tongue* pattern on ovolo moldings. These are said to be of Egyptian origin, the egg denoting life and the dart, death. They are commonly found on the capitals of Ionic columns. On the outside of the Building they form part of the cornice and

*Acanthus leaf*

are placed above the row of dentils. On the inside, they are everywhere—over doors and windows, fireplaces and panels. A variation is a *leaf-and-dart* band called the *water-leaf*. These are also frequently used in the Clubhouse.

One more of the many bands should be mentioned since it or its variations are seen frequently in the Clubhouse. It is called the *vitruvian scroll*, or sometimes the *running-dog band*. It usually appears decorated with leaves, rosettes and flowers.

Many of the decorative patterns discussed here are shown on the pages opening each chapter.

### Ornamental Plants

Nearly all forms from the plant world have been used in architectural ornamentation—leaves, sprays, flowers and fruit. The preference for comparatively few in this luxuriant field was partly determined by beauty of form and partly by belief in their symbolic meanings. The most popular of all plants in ornamentation is the acanthus leaf. The acanthus is the morphological symbol of the West, as the lotus is of the East. Since its introduction by the Greeks, it has recurred again and again in every western art form. No symbolic significance has ever been attached to it. Its frequent and varied use is due to its ornamental possibilities and the beautiful serration of its leaves. Many varieties of the acanthus grow wild in the south of Europe, but the leaf used architecturally is a purely artificial creation, and bears very little resemblance to the natural growth. The Greeks

*Patera*

preferred pointed leaf-edges. In the Roman style, the tips of the leaves become rounder. The Renaissance developed the acanthus form and particularly its tendrils to the highest degree of perfection. There are many beautiful examples in the Clubhouse.

Many other leaves are used, however, among them the anthemion (based on the honeysuckle flower and leaves), the laurel, the olive, vines and oaks, ivy and wheat, the papyrus, and the palm.

Flowers have in all ages been exceedingly popular in ornamental art. Preferred above all is the rose, but also favored are the chrysanthemum, lily, hellebore and bluebell.

Fruit, tied in a bunch with leaves and flowers, was a popular decorative motif of the Roman, Renaissance and later syles. Clusters hanging in a curve and known as festoons can be seen on the exterior of the Building between the attic windows and hanging clusters are used as decoration on pilasters, and around panels or divisions.

There are too many decorative emblems or devices for all to be mentioned. For instance, there are trophies, like the ones in the panels of the Main Dining Room. It was the custom of the Greeks to hang on tree trunks the weapons which the fleeing enemy had left behind on the field of battle. These tokens of victory, or trophies, have also found a place in decoration. They can be seen not only in arsenals or guardrooms of palaces, but they have been used for purely decorative purposes, as elegantly arranged and prettily grouped weapons of war. A grouping of tools and instruments to symbolize some special theme leads to the design of symbols, such as symbols of music, painting, sculpture, science, etc. Ribbons are also frequently used as a decoration.

Always a favorite of the artists are the nude figures of children, floating in the air, peeking over door frames or holding festoons. They represent the god of love, Cupid, son of Venus. Also called "amoretti," they are usually shown as naked, winged boys, with bows and arrows. "Putti" are also naked boys, but they do not have wings. Both are often shown as half figures, and examples may be found in David

Maitland Armstrong's stained-glass windows in the Great Hall.

Every great artist, whether an architect or a sculptor or a painter, treats the choice of materials with profound respect. Michelangelo is said to have spent weeks in the marble quarries of Carrara to select the slab for his David. Cortissoz said of White and McKim that they handled the choice of their materials "with the same intensely personal feeling that a great technician of the brush brings to the manipulation of his colors." When White was working on the Tiffany house on Madison Avenue, the brick he used in the upper stories was made under his own personal direction, the best commercial pressed brick being too hard and close to accomplish his purpose.

The original designs for the Metropolitan Club Building provided for the wall surface above the first story to be of white brick. Soon an intense difference of opinion arose among the Committee members and the architects, about whether the exterior should be of stone, brick or marble. This debate even reached the press as has been reported above.

This kind of disagreement was by no means unusual and has occurred many times before and since. It was fought not only on economic grounds—marble was enormously expensive—but also on philosophical grounds.

Marble, the aristocrat of building materials, was extensively used by the Ancient Greeks. The Parthenon and other famous buildings were constructed of white Pentelic marble from Mt. Pentelicus in Attica. Divine statues, such as the Venus de Medici, were made of the remarkably lustrous Parian marble from Paros in the Cyclades. These same quarries were used by the Romans after their conquest of Greece. Among the famous marbles of Italy are those from Carrara and Siena in Tuscany, but marble is quarried all over the country. The Italians have used it so extensively that it has almost become a symbol of their culture.

An interesting discussion of the importance of marble is presented by H.V. Morton in *A Traveler in Italy*. He describes a trip from Verona to Vicenza in the company of an Italian marble dealer, to whom marble was more than geological fact or commercial product: it was a theory of life. To him, history was a simple matter of stonemason or carpenter. Stone represented civilization; wood, barbarism. He argued that the Teutonic tribes which invaded Italy in the Dark Ages were forest men who were scared of the magic world of marble that, to their amazement, had fallen to them; so scared in fact that they preferred to live in the open country like the beasts. This enabled the Latin spirit to survive within the stone walls of the cities, and to reassert itself during the Middle Ages in stone cathedral and palazzo, and to develop into the full marble splendor of the Renaissance.

But in nineteenth-century America, the struggle was between aristocratic, expensive marble and other lesser stones. There had been a fashion for Marble Palaces on Fifth Avenue for some years. The first one worthy of the name was built in 1869 by the department-store magnate Alexander T. Stewart on the northwest corner of Fifth Avenue and 34th Street. It was considered at the time the most costly and luxurious private residence in America. Sometime later, Mary Mason Jones put up the Marble Row of eight residences on the Fifth Avenue block between 57th and 58th Streets; such elegance at the time looked most incongruous amid the surrounding open lots.

When William H. Vanderbilt planned his mansion at Fifth Avenue and 51st Street, he decided against marble out of superstition. But his son was free of such nonsense and created his Marble House on Bellevue Avenue in Newport. Merrill Folsom writes of it: "Its elegant spectacular splendor is worthy of the Arabian Nights. Visitors approach it through massive wrought-iron gates, which open onto a white marble ramp. The mansion is a temple of white marble with pilasters and capitals modeled after those of the Temple of the Sun at Baalbek—although considerably larger."

A similar division of opinion occurred during the preparation for the ultimate design of the Villard Houses, the first of the structures in the neo-Italian-Renaissance style built by McKim, Mead & White. The brilliant architect Joseph Morrill Wells (1853-1900), who was in charge, strongly argued in favor of marble for the exterior, or at least for white limestone. Villard, however, insisted on brownstone which was considerably cheaper even than limestone. Looking today at the somber exterior of this charming building, even after its recent cleaning, one regrets Villard's decision. Edith Wharton was right when she called the brownstone of the New York houses of the period "the most hideous stone ever quarried." But then, the Villard Houses were essentially a real estate speculation.

A few years later, when Morgan the Magnificent wanted to build the great monument to his career, the Morgan Library, designed by McKim, the exterior was of carefully laid marble blocks with no mortar in the classic Greek manner. The most recent instance in this struggle is told amusingly by Behrman in his book about Duveen. When Member Andrew Mellon wanted to build the National Gallery in Washington in 1937, he planned to have the exterior constructed of limestone, as he had done with so many office buildings in the District of Columbia. Duveen was horrified at the idea. His "Duveens" could not hang in any edifice unless it was built of marble. To achieve his goal, he had to employ all his not inconsiderable persuasive talents. He took Mellon on a taxi ride through Washington to show him what the ravages of time, weather and pollution had wrought on limestone exteriors. Finally Mellon yielded. "This," he said plaintively, "has been the most expensive ride of my life." Duveen generously let Mellon choose the kind of marble to be used. He decided on Tennessee Marble because it was, like himself, unostentatious and austere. The additional cost of using marble instead of limestone for the Gallery was five million dollars. The cost of the exterior marble work of the Metropolitan Clubhouse in 1892 was $270,000, one quarter of the total cost of construction. In present day purchasing power, this would mean anywhere between five million and ten million dollars.

The cost of splendor is high!

Unfortunately, no information has survived about the discussions which took place among the Members of the Club's Building Committee and Stanford White in 1891 on this question of marble *versus* a cheaper stone. Marble would considerably increase the cost of the Building. But in the end, splendor carried the day. It was decided that the outside of the entire Building be of marble except the north side, now hidden by the Pierre Hotel, which was to be of white brick. The final specifications called for the entire first story and all groins, stringcourses, window trims and main cornices in the upper stories to be of tooled Rocky Creek, Maryland, white marble. The ashlar wall surface in the upper stories was to be of rubbed Vermont white marble. When later it proved difficult to get the Rocky Creek marble, it was decided to use White Tuckahoe marble instead.

Marble is a limestone composed in large part of calcite crystals, the crystalline texture being the result of extreme metamorphism by heat and pressure. Its beauty lies not only in its lovely smooth surface, but particularly in its wide range of colors, from snow white to gray and deep black, many varieties being shades of

red, yellow, pink or the deep green used on the Church of Santa Maria Novella in Florence. The colors, the result of impurities, are frequently arranged in bands or patches and enhance the beauty of the stone when it is cut and polished.

In the United States, the finest marbles come from Vermont. That state produces more marble than any other one locality in the country. But Maryland, Massachusetts and Tennesee, among others, are also important producers.

The supreme use of marble is in statuary and monuments. In buildings and residences, its largest application is in the interior for pillars and columns, for panelling and wainscoting, in bathrooms and for floors. It is also used for the outside of buildings as a facing material. Like all limestones, it is corroded by weather and acid fumes and is thus ultimately an uneconomical material for use in exposed places and in large cities. But contrasted to the drab sandstone, brick or granite buildings of the time, marble facings were the object of admiration and wonder.

The Villard Houses in 1918 when the Hon. and Mrs. Whitelaw Reid lived in one of them.

# Chapter 7

# THE EXTERIOR

Four stories high, with a five-bay western and a seven-bay southern facade, the Building is asymmetrically balanced on the east by a three-bay two-story wing fronted by a courtyard closed off by a one-story columnar screen. It is crowned by a prominent elaborately-modelled marble and copper cornice. The first impression is one of classic severity and simplicity. There is not a single circular motif as there is in the Century Association Building. Nor are there any arched windows as in the University Club Building or pedimented windows as in the Reform Club Building in London. The stringcourses separating the first and second floors reinforce the horizontal elements which are further emphasized by a series of balconies. The only relief is provided by the decorations which are especially abundant on the fourth floor and the cornice.

The dimensions of the Main Building are 90-feet wide on Fifth Avenue, 142-feet long on Sixtieth Street, 104-feet high from curb to cornices and 120-feet high from cellar floor to roof garden. At the eastern end is a courtyard 57-feet long and 57-feet 9-inches wide which serves as the main entrance to the Club. The colonnade, 34-feet high, continues the stringcourse of the main façade of the building to the

subsequently acquired Annex. A passageway on the north side affords a service entrance.

The ground-hugging first floor is made of large marble blocks in banded rustication, reinforcing the horizontal lines. It seems to provide a base which gives support to the other three stories. The rectilinear windows have plain moldings. The stringcourse delineating the top of this floor consists of a plain upper part similar to the cyma recta of the classic entablature and a lower part embellished by a band carved with rosettes and leaves. The material used on the first floor is white Tuckahoe Marble.

Whereas the marble blocks used on the walls of the first floor were laid showing horizontal lines and no quoins, the wall surface above the stringcourse is held together by strong quoins which seem to set this part of the building apart. The windows have more elaborate moldings. Those on the second floor are framed by a narrow acanthus-leaf band. A medallion with the letter M is in the center. The window ensemble is completed by a cornice with a band of dentils on top of a rectangular unadorned panel which seems to increase its height. There are balconies the length of the three center windows on both the Fifth-Avenue and the Sixtieth-Street sides. The balustrades have double

*Acanthus cluster and rosette band*

balusters (two small balusters set together base to base). The consoles, serving as brackets of the balconies, are recumbent, and the S-shaped double volutes resemble those used on the temple of Jupiter Stator at the Vatican in Rome. A huge acanthus leaf is placed beneath the double scrolls. The center window on the Sixtieth-Street side has inscribed on it the year in which the construction was started—1892—in Roman numerals.

The third-floor windows are similar except that the band framing them has the bead-molding motif, and the cornice, with an egg-and-dart molding below again over a plain panel, is supported by erect consoles. The center windows on either side of the Building each have a smaller balcony with solid sides, the front having a wreath in the center flanked by two hydria, the vessel which young Greek maidens took to the spring, filled with water and then bore home on their heads. The sides have a large rosette or patera. The center window on the south side is flanked and topped by medallions with the letter M on top, surrounded by a wreath.

The fourth-floor windows appear to be part of the cornice. They are much smaller than the others. There are nine on the Fifth-Avenue side and thirteen on the Sixtieth-Street side. They are linked together by fruit festoons.

The most prominent feature of the general design of the Building is the elaborately-modelled marble and copper cornice which projects six feet beyond the plane of the façade. It is built up of a series of classical moldings patterned after the cornice of a Corinthian entablature, the first being a band showing a series of separate rosettes alternating with decorations which are here called acanthus clusters, for lack of a more precise term. It is topped by a band of dentils, and that in turn by an ovolo molding with the Greek egg-and-tongue design similar to the one on the Erechtheum on the Acropolis in Athens.

From there, the cornice is extended out again by another marble slab supported by a series of recumbent modillions with large acanthus leaves similar to those supporting the balconies; between the modillions are large pa-

terae. The whole is crowned by the copper cornice in the cyma recta shape, which is decorated with a string of lion heads similar to Greek water spouts. There are about seventy of them. Among the fauna in ornamental art, the King of the Beasts was always the most popular. Particularly in favor was the lion head as a waterspout on the temples of antiquity, as a spout on vessels, with a ring in the jaw as a handle or a knocker, as on the bronze door at the entrance to the Annex, or as a purely decorative element on rosettes.

The Greek temples were roofed over with wood and covered with flat tiles of terracotta or marble. Over the joints of the tiles was a pointed tile running up and down the roof to prevent water from seeping in. To conceal the lower edges from sight, they were covered by antefixae. On the Clubhouse cornice, these look like a reversed egg-and-tongue design.

The entrance court is located to the east of the 60th-Street facade. The bold molding at the *piano nobile* extends to form the straight cornice of the columnar screen which is carried on a series of paired columns linked by elaborate wrought-iron gates of the finest workmanship. There are three gates; the center one, sixteen-feet wide and twenty-five-feet high, is for carriages. The year construction began—1892—is in the center in Roman numerals. On each side is an entrance for pedestrians eight-feet wide and twenty-feet high. The slightly tapered, unfluted columns of the Tuscan order as developed by Rome—four pairs of them—stand on pedestals about six-feet high and are unadorned except for a band of leaves on the abacus and a band of rosettes on the echinus of the capital. Originally each pair had another similar column in front of it which the City Administration ordered removed to widen Sixtieth Street

in 1922. The end columns or piers are square and untapered.

There are a further four pairs of columns in the Courtyard to support the portico. Each pair consists of an inner round shaft and an outer square one standing on pedestals. All the columns used here support weight, which is the purpose of columns. White had the good taste not to use columns just to fill a blank space on a wall, for no visible practical purpose, as has been done so frequently. A row of strong dentils serves as a stringcourse on the architrave.

The Courtyard is large enough to contain an ample driveway with a footway on each side; the left footway leading to the Main Building and the right, to the Ladies' Restaurant. At the back of the Courtyard is a two-tiered wing containing the Ladies' Restaurant and private dining rooms on the second floor and above it the Library. The center of the wing is recessed into

The Metropolitan Club in 1894.

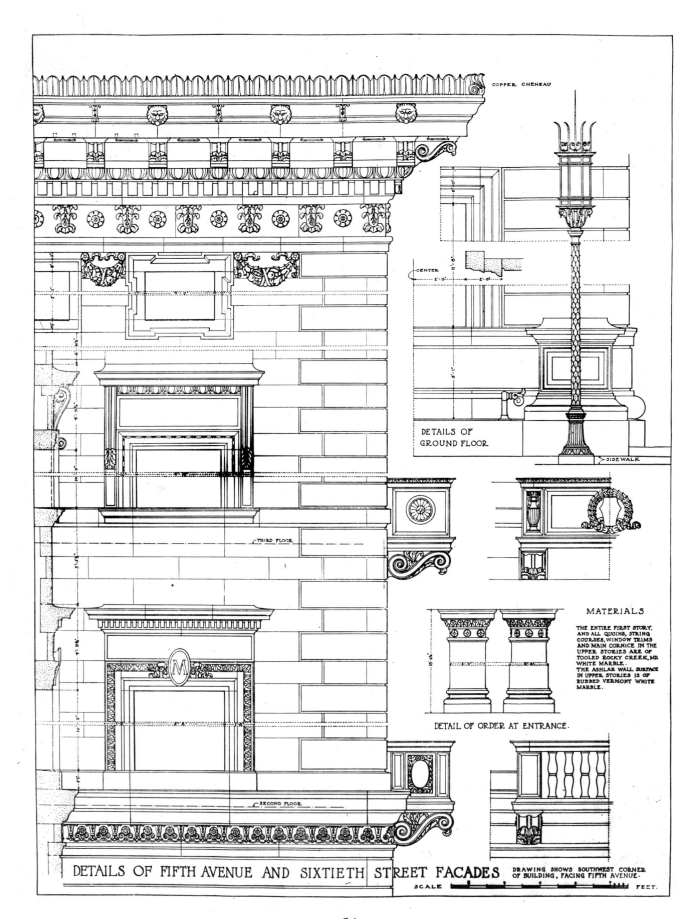

COPPER CHENEAU

DETAILS OF
GROUND FLOOR

CENTER

SIDEWALK

THIRD FLOOR

SECOND FLOOR

## MATERIALS

THE ENTIRE FIRST STORY,
AND ALL QUOINS, STRING
COURSES, WINDOW TRIMS
AND MAIN CORNICE IN THE
UPPER STORIES ARE OF
TOOLED ROCKY CREEK, MD.
WHITE MARBLE.
THE ASHLAR WALL SURFACE
IN UPPER STORIES IS OF
RUBBED VERMONT WHITE
MARBLE.

DETAIL OF ORDER AT ENTRANCE.

DETAILS OF FIFTH AVENUE AND SIXTIETH STREET FACADES

DRAWING SHOWS SOUTHWEST CORNER
OF BUILDING, FACING FIFTH AVENUE.

SCALE                                      FEET.

54

a shallow niche to give more space for carriages to turn.

Although no longer used for carriages, the Courtyard sets the Metropolitan Club apart from any other club building and adds to its majestic appearance.

As mentioned above, two different marbles were used in the exterior, Tuckahoe marble and Vermont marble. Since different marbles weather differently and since automobile fumes have dirtied all building exteriors, the Clubhouse was cleaned and painted a monochrome in 1965, making the marble unrecognizable.

Originally, the building had a strip of lawn and hedges with two columns on either side of the Fifth-Avenue front. One of the Charter Members, Elbridge T. Gerry, was at the same time building his château on Fifth Avenue between the Clubhouse and Sixty-first Street. Richard M. Hunt was the architect. Construction was started in April, 1892, and finished in November, 1894. On November 14, 1893, Hunt wrote to White that Elbridge Gerry objected to "the ugly square marble pillars which will obstruct the view of the Conservatory." But they went up all the same. As the streets of New York were widened, however, this embellishment, shrubs and all, fell victim to progress, as did the outer columns of the Main Entrance on 60th Street.

The cornice.

The dignified appearance of the Building is due to the fact that the main stories are twice as high, about twenty-five feet, as the normal story in New York domestic architecture. Cleverly hidden and hardly noticeable are the windows of some of the mezzanines, such as the former Stranger's Rooms, now the Manager's Offices, above the ground-floor windows at the corner of the Courtyard, or the small windows of the mezzanine bedrooms above the third-floor windows.

The iron front gates were designed by White and executed by the well-known firm of John Williams of 556 West 27th Street. Williams began his career as an employee of Tiffany and Company in its brass and bronze department. In 1872, he established his own firm. The growth of his reputation coincided with the increased use of architectural bronze in public and private buildings during the 1880s. In 1887, he established a department to handle the demands for artistic wrought ironwork, which came to rival that of bronze. Besides the gates of the Metropolitan Club, the firm produced the entrance gates to Harvard University and the Mapes Memorial Gates to Columbia University.

The upper sections of the cornice were rendered in copper and made by the Jackson Architectural Ironworks of 315 East 28th Street.

There are many opinions on which palazzo in particular served White as the inspiration when he designed the Metropolitan Clubhouse. Some consider that the use of an asymmetrically-located Courtyard indicates that the honor belongs to Raphael's Palazzo Pandolfini in Florence. Others suggest the Palazzo Farnese in Rome, designed by da Sangallo, Michelangelo and della Porta, although the building may have served merely as the model for the use of the quoins and the absence of pilasters, such as the front façade of the Century Association has. Probably the safest assumption is that the inspiration—undoubtedly of Italian-Renaissance-palazzo origin—came via the English interpretation created by Sir Charles Barry, particularly in the Reform Club building. In designing the Metropolitan Clubhouse, White emphasized horizontal strength, avoiding the pedimented window tops of the Reform in favor of rectilinear ones and increasing the classical severity of the design.

In 1894, the Building was not surrounded by high hotels and commercial structures. The Gerry mansion to the North was a lower building. In the dazzling whiteness of the new marble, it was no wonder that it overwhelmed the public and the press by its austere beauty. It has not lost this beauty in the intervening nine decades.

# Chapter 8

# THE
# INTERIOR

While the exterior of The Metropolitan Club was purposefully restrained, dispelling any charges of ostentation, great time and money were lavished on the interior.

The first set of front doors leads into a small outside vestibule, 10 by 14 feet, lined with white marble. On the right and left are two blind guard windows. The old Florentine palaces, being fortresses as well as dwellings, had guard rooms on either side of an entrance hall so that no intruder could hide, crouched below a single window to escape detection.

The vaulted ceiling of the Vestibule is delicately beautiful. The construction of the vaulting was made possible by means of the thin-shell masonry construction method of Rafael Guastavino who had come in the 1880s from Spain with his son to introduce this remarkable method to America. White was quick to see the advantages of this method and used it freely. Its most sensational use is in the dome of the Cathedral of St. John the Divine.

Of pristine beauty, the ceiling of the Vestibule bears a delicate tracery of stucco-work on a background of Wedgwood blue. In the center of a large oval framed by a stucco torus band hangs a simple lighting fixture. Allegorical scenes decorate the Vestibule; one shows an Amazon riding a goat, while another shows Europa on the back of a leopard or a tiger. Of antique Roman origin, the design is derived from studies made in the ruins of Pompeii in the eighteenth century.

Going up the stairs and passing through the next door, one enters the inner vestibule or Entrance Hall, panelled in white marble, 20 by 27 feet in size. At the left by the door is a covered seat for the porter, in the form of a gigantic sedan chair. The outstanding feature of the Entance Hall is the magnificent vaulted Adamesque ceiling, eggshell in tone, with elaborate gold decorations in low relief.

Robert Adam, born in Scotland in 1728, revolutionized architecture and interior decoration in England. From 1754 to 1758 he toured Italy where he studied under the great French architect Charles-Louis Clerissau (1722-1820), the friend and teacher of Thomas Jefferson. In Italy he met the most advanced artists of the day, including the great Giovanni Battista Piranese (1720-1770), whose influence on him was pronounced. A few years earlier, in 1748, Pompeii had been rediscovered. Although little had been excavated, Robert Adam and his brother

*Egg-and-dart*

James visited both Herculaneum and Pompeii. Until that time, knowledge of Roman architecture had been based largely on temples and public buildings, or rather, the ruins thereof. The new excavations revealed an entirely different aspect of the interior of the houses of ancient times: gay, luxurious, delicately enriched in various colors. Adam also studied the Etruscan manner with its arabesque arches, urns, medallions and garlands. On his return trip to England, he stopped in Split in Dalmatia and studied Diocletian's Palace; he published the results of his studies, *The Ruins of Spalatro*, in 1764.

On returning to London, Adam, assisted by his brothers James and William, quickly became known to the nobility and gentry and soon his services were in great demand. His fame rests on the brilliant neo-classical interior designs which he executed for many of the great English mansions such as Osterley Park in Middlesex, Syon House, Kenwood and many others. Over the years, he refined his style and created works devoid of tension, linear and elegant, of infinite variety.

Robert Adam died in 1792 and he is buried in Westminister Abbey.

The ceiling was the key to Adam's decoration of a room, as it had been in Antiquity. When reporters were admitted for the first and only time into the Club Building in February, 1894, the *Times'* man voiced the opinion that pictures on a ceiling "which have to be looked at by dislocating one's neck or viewed in a mirror" are ridiculous. But the ceiling is the largest uninterrupted area in any room and is therefore a prime field for decoration. How ridiculous the ceiling in the Main Dining Room would look were it whitewashed! Living in a room and visiting a room are two different things.

Stanford White was familiar with Adam and his work and was greatly influenced by him. When he designed the Club's Entrance Hall with its stark, pure-white marble walls, he needed a light, elegant touch which only the ceiling design could give him. He chose the Etruscan decorative manner made popular by Adam.

The Entrance Hall.

The ceiling in the Entrance Hall is barrel-vaulted. In the center is an oval enclosing a rectangle from which a beautiful Renaissance chandelier is suspended. Surrounded by a ring of candles are four putti. More electric candles are in the center. Garlands run from one corner of the ceiling to the next, curving toward the oval. The whole is richly embellished with delicate lines, circles, squares and cages, figures and medallions. There is great unity in the composition of the ceiling. It holds together a Hall which would otherwise be chilling.

The progressive refinement of the art of White and his collaborator during those years becomes apparent in a comparison of the ceiling in the Entrance Hall with the one in the Entrance Hall of the Henry Villard House designed about six years earlier. The mosaic ceiling in the Villard House is a charming, delicate work by David Maitland Armstrong, but one associates the mosaic he used more with Byzantine churches than with opulent men's clubs or the mansions of the rich.

Since it is the center of the building, the Entrance Hall leads to the Reception Office, the Waiting Room (now the Ladies' Lounge), and the Telephone Room, formerly the Stranger's Waiting Room. Members' mail boxes are on the south wall. Opposite are the cloakrooms and the elevator.

The Entrance Hall is separated from the Great Marble (or Main) Hall by a Serliana or Palladian archway supported by two Tuscan columns with monolithic shafts of mottled dark reddish-yellow and lavender marble, 13-feet high. The white marble arch is decorated on the soffitt with rosettes and the archivolt has bead-and-reel and egg-and-dart decorations.

Andrea Palladio (1518-80) is one of the most celebrated of all architects. He studied the remains of Roman architecture in Vicenza and later in Rome itself. He is most famous for the many palaces and country villas he built for the nobles and rich merchants of "Venezia terra firma." His characteristic façade displays superimposed pilasters or columns of often colossal order where a single column or pilaster embraces several stories. In the seventeenth century, Inigo Jones imported into England Palladio's classic and grandiose design, thereby deeply influencing English architecture.

Palladio's typical arch-and-column composition, with two flat-headed side openings under the architrave, has become known as the Palladian motif. The most noble example of it is found in the Basilica of Vicenza, which he designed in 1548. A two-story series of arches and columns give the structure a grandeur and elegance that made it immediately famous. The portal connecting the Entrance and the Great Marble Hall of the Club is very much like the arches of the Vicenza structure, down to the medallions, of a darker marble or onyx, over the architrave in the trapezoidal spandrel. The full beauty of the archway is best appreciated from the vantage point of the Great Hall.

Nowadays there is a screen between the two columns with a long-case clock in the center, blocking the view into the Main Hall which is used as a lounge where Members and their guests have their aperitifs before lunch or dinner. But on special occasions, such as the An-

The Marble Hall in 1895.

nual or Debutante Ball, the screen is removed and the view sweeps unobstructed from one Hall to the other as in the days of yore.

Through this Palladian archway, one enters the lofty Main Hall, also called the Great Marble Hall. It is the most imposing hall in the Building. Reaching up two stories, lighted on the north side by five large stained-glass windows, the Hall measures 53 by 54 feet and it is 45-feet high. The severe architecture of the exterior is reflected here. The walls are covered with Vermont marble, white mottled with black, relieved here and there by round and square panels of white marble. The floor is a checkerboard of gray and white squares of Vermont marble now covered by a rug. At one time there was an enormous Ardebil rug in the Hall, but in 1974 it was replaced by the present one which was purchased from the White House during the Nixon Administration. Nine bronze electric lights, in shape of ornate torches, jut from the walls. In the early years, they had flame-shaped glass tops.

White was inspired in this treatment by his admiration for a church he frequently visited while in Venice, the Church of Santa Maria dei Miracoli. This exceptionally fine Renaissance structure was built from 1481-1489 from a design by Pietro Lombardo to house a miraculous image of the Virgin Mary which belonged to a rich merchant, Angelo Amadi. The image received increasing veneration and was enriched with alms and gifts. The exterior of the church is entirely covered with fine marbles, which, according to an old tradition, were left over from the work on the Basilica of St. Mark. The single-nave, barrel-vaulted interior has smooth marble-encrusted sides, embellished by ornamental motives. The altar is raised above the floor where the worshippers sit and is reached by a stairway with fifteen steps. Here the exuberant imagination of the very skillful stonecutters of the time is almost more important than the architectural inspiration. This lovely church, which has all the delicacy and refinement of an ivory and crystal jewel box, represents the peak of Venice's first stage in classicism, the quattrocento.

The white-marble steps on the north side of the Great Hall sweep in two flights of stairs, fifteen-feet wide, to a high landing, where musicians may play or young debutantes make their curtsies. Two forged-iron candelabra with foliage designs flank the landing. Until recently, the bulbs were covered with milk-glass globes. From there, two other stairways mount right and left to the second floor where the galleries around three sides of the Hall are supported by twelve white monolithic Tuscan columns of Pavonazzo marble about twelve-feet high with richly-gilt Ionic capitals. Close examination of these exquisite columns discloses that most of them have been sawed in two, vertically, right through the middle. This puzzling phenomenon has been explained in the story quoted earlier written by the young architect Egerton Swartwout, who was on the McKim Mead & White staff. The Club Building was constructed of reinforced concrete. This form of construction was patented in 1857 by the French inventor, F. Joseph Monier, and its first use in America was in a private house in Portchester, N.Y., in 1875. As it was perfected, it was to exert a profound influence on the structural techniques of modern building. But in 1891, this method was still new. The working drawings prepared by the office of the architect lacked the precise information now considered standard and many of the details were left to the judgment of the builder. So it was here. When the white marble shafts arrived, the steel beams supporting the roof were already in place. So the marble shafts had to be split to encase the steel sections of the supporting columns.

The stairways and galleries have exquisite classic iron balustrades with a gilded letter M on plaques. They were executed after the designs of the great French master of ironworks of the seventeenth century, Jean Tijou.

The art of decorative ironwork has existed from the early Middle Ages to the present day. Its origin was utilitarian. Heavy wooden doors were reinforced—and incidentally decorated—with ironwork mounts, hinges and bolts. Windows were protected by grilles made of iron bars. In time, the blacksmith's art developed an

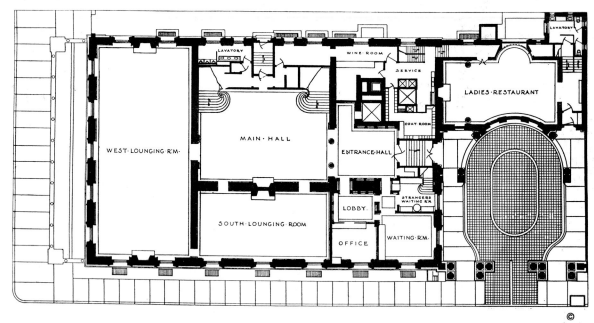

Plan of the First Floor.

amazing virtuosity and ironwork began to be used in churches for screens across the choir and around chapels and tombs. Châteaux and palaces were embellished with iron gates and railings. The creative imaginations of the iron craftsmen are wonderfully illustrated in the grand sweep of many Baroque staircase railings.

The blacksmith's art had been refined particularly on the Continent. In England, it had been unpretentious until the arrival in 1689 of Jean Tijou, a French Huguenot, who came in the trail of his life-long patrons, William of Orange and Mary. He became the most important figure in English wrought-iron work, both in terms of his achievements and his influence on native craftsmen. His style—purely French Renaissance in its embossing and lavish interlacing and leafwork—is best illustrated in the Fountain Garden at Hampton Court. Tijou covered the gates and railings with a mass of acanthus leaves, heraldic emblems and masks. His work for Sir Christopher Wren at St. Paul's Cathedral in London is more restrained in design, reflecting Wren's sober taste. His choir, aisles, gates and altar rails at St. Paul's rank among England's finest specimens of ironcraft.

Tijou's influence was perpetuated by the many apprentices he trained and, even more, by his *New Booke of Drawings Invented and Desined by John Tijou*, published in 1693. It contained the designs for his English works. The dates of his birth and death are unknown, although he may have died in 1711.

The ironwork on the stairway of the Metropolitan Club, and particularly on the loggias on the second floor, is of unusual beauty. It repeats the acanthus leaves and heraldic emblems—here decorated with the letter M—so typical of Tijou's work. The railings were built by the New York firm of William H. Jackson and Co. at a cost of $16,000, perhaps $500,000 in present purchasing power.

The railing of the stairway and around the gallery is effectively underlined by a prominent gilded band one-foot wide. It is made up of an ovolo band, a string of acanthus leaves, a running-dog design and a leaf-and-dart band. The stained-glass windows and the coffers on the ceiling are framed by gilded torus bands. In effect, gilding is the leitmotif of the entire building. It finds its greatest expression in that riotous symphony of gold, the Main Dining Room. Gilding is the crowning touch of mag-

62

nificence in decoration.

The art of gilding is of ancient origin. It was lavishly employed in Egypt, Greece and Rome and during the Renaissance and has been used continuously in the Orient. Gilding is the process of applying to a surface a thin layer of real or imitation gold. It can be used on almost any surface prepared to receive it by a treatment of size, mercury, acid or heat. The applied leaf is burnished or left matte.

Real gold leaf has been used throughout the Clubhouse and the gilding has been amazingly well-preserved except for a few places of heavy use.

On the south side of the Main Hall is a wide fireplace of white marble with a high mantel which has the year when construction began—1892—in Roman numerals on the frieze of the entablature supported by scrolls with lion feet. The flutes are beaded. A garland hangs from the eyes of the volute and it is capped by an acanthus leaf. The arch repeats the form of the Palladian Entrance doorway. All three arches in the Hall are crowned with acroteria. In the lunette of the fireplace arch is a marble-faced clock. The marble dial matches the medallions of the Palladian arch and the Roman numerals are bronze. The large onyx gilt-mounted urns at either end of the shelf have stood there since the year 1894. They were bought from Duveen.

A spectacularly unique hall like this needed a spectacularly unique ceiling. White chose the only one possible—a coffered ceiling. The coffering, caisson or sunk panel construction was first used by the ancient Romans; the Renaissance artists then adopted it and embellished it to their taste. Brunelleschi's fabulous Church of San Lorenzo in Florence has a coffered ceiling, with a gold eight-leafed patera against a white background.

Deep coffering is found in many of Palladio's porches. In the Palazzo Chiericati, they are decorated with bead, dentil, bead-and-reel, and leaf-and-dart moldings with a central patera, each being of a different design. In American buildings, they are usually all of the same design as they are here. In the atrium of the magnificent library of the University Club,

however, each one of them in the coffered ceiling is slightly different.

White chose a rectangular coffer framed in gold. In the center of each panel are large paterae, all of the same design, flanked by acanthus leaves and surrounded by festoons. The background color of the panels is dark red, reminiscent of the *sang-de-boeuf* color of Ming porcelains. This is framed by a Greek fret with a blue background. Next is an egg-and-dart band, and each coffer is separated from the next by a richly decorated torus band. There are thirty-eight rectangular coffers above the Great Marble Hall. Above the galleries, the coffers are square and of a different design. A smaller patera is placed on a circular gilded cushion. The square frame is placed against a blue background. A riot of bands, egg-and-dart, guilloche, bead, dentil, and others completes the frame.

From the center of the ceiling hangs an enormous Venetian lantern, twelve-feet high. No other fixture would have suited the Renaissance background of the Hall.

Venice's wealth and power were founded on its fleet, and the arsenal where the ships were built was the city's showplace. Not Henry Ford but the Venetians invented the assembly line, according to a visitor to the arsenal in the cinquecento. He was shown a keel being laid in the morning. He then described how the galley was towed past a number of sheds, and as she proceeded from shed to shed received parts, cordage, then cannon, lastly food. By the time the ship reached the end of the dockyard, the crew was lined up ready to go aboard. In the evening the visitor saw a completed galley floating in the water. At one time, sixteen-thousand well-trained workers were building the pride of the Republic, the armed galleys that defeated the Turks at Lepanto and the merchant ships that supplied Europe with pepper, cinnamon and cloves until the Cape route to India short-circuited the spice trade. Even the humblest accessories on the ships of the Serenissima bore witness to the refined taste and love of luxury which permeated all classes of Venetian society.

This fine taste was expressed also in the large

lanterns that graced the stern of every ship. Many were simple hexagonal cylinders, a larger lamp flanked by two smaller ones, each having a wax candle which was the only light for these ships sailing the dark seas. Other lanterns had a more artistic shape like the one now in Venice's Correr Museum. At one time, around 1750, it graced the stern of the galley of Girolamo Maria Balbi. From a round bottom and supported by putti, the six glass panes broaden from a narrow base and widen to the elaborately-decorated cover, again with putti resting between shields. The entire lantern is perhaps eight-feet high, with a candle lighting it. The lantern hanging in the Great Marble Hall may be not as ornate but it bears a great resemblance to Captain Balbi's "Fano." About the same height, it has six graceful half-figure atlantes on the edges of the panes, seeming to hold up the cover. It is the only style that would fit into the Club's Renaissance surrounding.

The lantern hanging in the Great Marble Hall has had an interesting history. It hung originally in the old State House, and was brought to the World's Columbian Exposition of 1893 in Chicago. Conceived to commemorate the 400th anniversary of the discovery of America, the Exposition was one of the most impressive and beautiful ever built. Its opening was the greatest national event since the Civil War and it heralded the role of world leadership the country would soon take on. One of the loveliest of the hundreds of buildings was the New York State Building designed by McKim Mead & White. It was variously described as resembling an old mansion of the Van Rensselaers or the Villa Medici in Rome. After the closing of the Exposition in November, 1893, the building was razed and some of its elements shipped away to find other uses. Stanford White bought the lantern, which probably had been hanging in the central hall. Another item to appear in New York was the mosaic pavement of the entrance hall; it had brass reliefs of the signs of the zodiac inlaid in marble and it was designed by George Maynard. This pavement is now in the Seth Low Library at Columbia University. For his own estate at St. James on Long Island, White picked up a bamboo shelter from one of the other exhibits at the fair.

Illumination in the Clubhouse is provided by chandeliers and lanterns suspended from the ceilings but also by a variety of wall candelabra (wall brackets or sconces), what the French call Bras Appliqué. The size of the rooms demands this treatment. The ones on the marble walls in the Great Hall resemble the wall torches of the Florentine palazzi. Most of the others derive their inspiration from the designs developed in France during the second half of the 17th century and during the 18th century by such great artists as André Charles Boule, Pierre Patti, de la Forre and others. The candelabra in each room have their own distinctive design, all of great beauty. The spirit of Louis XV, more elegant and delicate, prevails over that of Louis XVI. The candelabra are made of brass or bronze, originally equipped for both gas and electric current; each would repay careful study.

Very fashionable during the Belle Epoque were milk-glass (or frosted) globes; old photographs show that they were used in great numbers when the Clubhouse was built. The forged-iron candelabra on the landing of the marble staircase had them, and they hung on the ceilings of the West Lounge, the Library and the Main Dining Room. They can still be seen on the ceiling of the Hall on the Third Floor. One can argue about the beauty of these globes, nowadays associated with the restaurants and bars of the period. The crystal chandeliers which replaced them in the Main Dining Room can be pronounced a great improvement; the same cannot be said of the spotlights now disfiguring the Library Ceiling.

The Clubhouse has a great many fireplaces—some forty of them. Those in the large social rooms are of great beauty. In design they are carried right up to the cornice in the classical architectural harmony approved by Codman in his book *The Decoration of Houses*. The most beautiful, such as those in the West Lounge, the Dining Room and the Men's Bar, follow the French tradition introduced by Mansard; they have mirrors over the mantel, clocks on the shelf, and often candelabra on the frame.

Clocks were still new during the reign of Louis XIV; the pendulum clock was invented in 1655. Those in use before were spring or weight driven and not very accurate. Those operated by weight had to be placed on a wall to allow space for the hanging weight. But after 1655 a special mantel clock was being developed for use on fireplaces. At the same time, with the developing art of cabinet making, greater attention was paid to the clock case. The great clockmakers of that period—Martinot, Bidault, Boule—were fêted personalities. Louis XIV gave them lodgings in the Louvre. They might dine in the palace at the table of the gentlemen of the Chamber, and they had the right of entry to the King's presence along with distinguished members of the Household. In return, they created clocks flattering the monarch, such as one which showed the King enthroned and offered homage by all the princes of Europe.

The mantel clocks in the Metropolitan Clubhouse belong mostly to that period. The record shows that one Louis XIV clock was bought in 1893 from Duveen for $350, three Louis XV for $100, $145 and $175, and two Louis·XVI for $85 each. Gilbert Cuel furnished the Beurdeley clocks for the West Lounge for $520 each; he specialized in Beurdeley. A Louis XV clock was bought from H. B. Herts and Sons for $200, and C. Wernicke furnished a Louis XVI for $150. To translate these prices into present-day values, they should be multiplied by fifty.

Of the mantel clocks left today, there are two clocks by A. Beurdeley in the West Lounge, one by Darville in the Men's Bar, two beautiful large gold clocks by Rödel in the Main Dining Room, one by Goudin in the Library, one in the Men's Grill on the Second Floor, one in the Card Room (English with chimes) which was bought from Wernicke, and one in the Manager's office, inscribed T. TH. Dereberie & Cie, rue des Fosses du Temple No. 47 à Paris.

There are also two long-case clocks, one in the Entrance Hall and the other in the Hall leading to the Dining Room on the Third Floor. This variety of clock first appeared in England shortly after the Restoration in 1666, and in Europe where they quickly soon thereafter became popular.

The Great Marble Hall of the Club receives light during the day through five large stained-glass windows on the north wall above the Grand Stairway. Four-feet eight-inches wide and eight-feet four-inches high, framed in a gold border twelve-inches wide, they are the work of the American artist David Maitland Armstrong (1836-1918).

Lawyer, diplomat, author and finally manufacturer of stained glass, Armstrong is again gaining recognition. His formative years reflect the only course open to a talented young American in the years following the destructive Civil War and the absence of any artistic stimulation at home. Born at Danskamer, the family home near Newburgh, his paternal ancestors included Scottish chieftains and army officers; his mother came from an old Southern family. After graduating from Trinity College in 1858, he spent the next year touring Italy, France and England where he received his first artistic stimulation. He returned home to study law and then entered the Foreign Service. From 1869 to 1872, he was U.S. Consul to the Papal

David Maitland Armstrong; bronze plaque by Augustus Saint Gaudens.

65

States and when these were conquered by the new Italian monarchy, he became Consul General in Rome. But then he decided to leave diplomacy and to "go in for art at last," a bold decision for he had married Helen Neilson in 1866 and was to raise a family of seven children.

Most of the next few years were spent in Europe, the dream then of any budding young artist. "My God, I'd rather go to Europe than go to Heaven," young William Merrit Chase was to cry. In Paris Armstrong met Stanford White and shared an apartment with Augustus Saint Gaudens for a time. It was here in 1877 that Saint Gaudens made the bronze plaque of Armstrong which until her death in 1972 was in the possession of his granddaughter Gwendolyn Ella Armstrong Rives, the last owner of Kingscote in Newport (now owned by the Preservation Society of Newport County).

In Paris he studied under the academician Luc-Oliver Merson (1846-1920) and became director of the American Division of the Paris Exposition in 1878. Returning to New York, he began to work in stained glass with Louis Comfort Tiffany (1848-1933), a Charter Member of the Club. In 1887, he left Tiffany and started his own stained-glass company. His daughter, Helen Maitland Armstrong, worked with him and eventually became his partner. She excelled in making flesh-colored glasses such as the putti in the Club windows.

The art of making stained-glass windows is of great antiquity. It reached its height in the twelfth and thirteenth centuries. In France, the Cathedral at Chartres is an unrivalled treasury of thirteenth-century glass.In England, fine examples may be found in the Cathedrals of York, Lincoln and Salisbury. Nineteenth-century romanticism and the Gothic revival brought fresh study and works of glass. The arts and crafts movement under William Morris and Burne-Jones in England was especially productive. Great contributions to American stained glass were made by John La Farge whose many windows include those in the Church of the Paulists in New York. Louis Comfort Tiffany, the greatest of all American glassmakers, developed, with a German chemist, a new expression in irridescent glass called "favrile."

The manufacture of stained glass achieved new heights of quality and popularity in the United States in the 1880s. Craftsmen such as Tiffany, La Farge, Lamb, Armstrong and others, working closely with glass manufacturers, revived and renewed the craft and created the new American or opalescent glass. As Armstrong explained it: "In America we use two kinds of stained glass: 'opalescent,' also called stained glass because the color, light and shade are *in* the glass; and 'painted' glass, also called antique, because it is an imitation of old glass, where the light and shade are painted *on* the glass. . . ."

The new interest in glass making has inspired the Corning Glass Works to erect a stunning new museum in Corning, N.Y., the first devoted exclusively to detailing and displaying its long history. The main attraction at its opening in June, 1980, was sixteen stained-glass windows which Tiffany treasured above all others and had installed in his lavish house at Oyster Bay. The house burned to the ground in 1957, but somehow these windows survived. Also on display were solid representations of Tiffany's famed lamps and lampshades (one recently brought $360,000 at auction).

The best known of Armstrong's windows are those in Trinity Church downtown and in St. Michael's, Holy Communion and Ascension Churches in New York. One of his major accomplishments is the glass work done in 1899 for the U.S. Appellate Court Building in New York. The frescoed courtroom is surmounted by Armstrong's glass dome and pierced by his stained-glass windows in the side walls.

The Armstrong windows in the Club are of opalescent glass. They are light in tone with gold and green predominating. A shield is at the center, with garlands surrounding it and flesh-colored putti painted by Helen Armstrong. In a paper on the life and work of Armstrong prepared in 1980, Lynne Ambrosini said: "The row of flatly-patterned, ornamental windows are quite appropriate to the luxurious McKim Mead & White interior; they fit into the eclectic ensemble of veined-marble walls, red-velvet carpets, Ionic columns and coffered vaults.''

In the fall of 1980, these stained-glass windows were repaired and cleaned by Rohlf's Stained and Leaded Glass Inc., the outstanding experts in the field. On December 2, 1980, Peter A. Rohlf wrote to the author: "It has been a thoroughly rewarding experience rehabilitating and conserving the fine stained-glass windows designed by D. Maitland Armstrong. . . . These windows are some of the finest examples of stained glass in the United States today. . . . The detailing of the ribbons, wreaths and fruit which take shape from the juxtaposition of the different pieces of opalescent and antique glass are typical of the American Renaissance mood of design. . . . The fine Armstrong windows are of Museum quality and should be regarded as one of the finest examples of secular stained glass in America today.''

Classical architecture does not as a rule offer a very warm welcome to stained glass. There is none in Italy. It remained for the American Renaissance to reconcile classicism and stained glass.

Here again is the influence of the Church of San Lorenzo. Brunelleschi's intelligent spacing of the large windows high up permitted the light to spread calmly and uniformly through the interior. White's treatment produced a similar effect during the early years visible in the old photographs. Unfortunately, in 1929, when the Gerry Estate sold the property on the adjoining block to Louis Pierre, the forty-story Pierre Hotel was erected. This effectively cut off the daylight.

Stanford White spent many hours in the Church of San Lorenzo while he was in Florence as a youth. He absorbed the beauty, symmetry and harmony created by the artistry of Brunelleschi and the money of the Medici. Not unlike some Members of the Metropolitan Club, the Medici had risen from humble beginnings to enormous wealth and power as merchants, bankers and politicians. To the Church, the Medici gave three Popes, to France, two Queens, and to the world, the fruits of their passionate patronage of the arts which made Florence the most stupendous repository of European culture since the Athens of Pericles.

San Lorenzo is the church of the Medici. The harmonious basilica is a triumph of Brunelleschi's perspective vision. The gray stone columns, with their elaborate capitals, support the round arches and harmonize perfectly with the white walls. The ceiling of the main nave has coffers centered by gold rosettes against a white background framed in gold. Light spreads calmly and uniformly in the interior thanks to the intelligent spacing of the windows high up. Similarities in concept with the Club's Great Marble Hall are apparent.

San Lorenzo was built on commission from Cosimo the Elder who was buried in front of the altar when he died in 1464. Next to him lies Donatello whom he admired above all other artists. What greater honor could patron pay to genius? Adjoining the church is the New Sacristry with the Michelangelo sculptures and the Chapel of the Princes, the most overpowering Mausoleum of any ruling family in the world.

Two of the most important rooms of the Clubhouse converge at the Main Hall. To the west is the enormous West Lounging Room and to the south the Men's Bar, formerly known as the South Lounging Room or the English Reading Room. Both are elaborately decorated.

The famous architects during this active period of building lavish private houses and clubhouses were also knowledgeable interior designers and decorators. The styles of decoration of the Italian Renaissance or of the French monarchy were imitated countless times in costly rooms and halls. Still, when they were asked to build the grandiose palaces of the very rich, or their clubhouses, the architects leaned heavily for the interiors on the expertise of the *decorateurs*. These skilled professionals understood the nuances and treacherous subtleties of scale, refinement and orthodoxy. They were much more than the interior decorators of today who usually only buy furniture, curtains or pictures for their clients. The *decorateur* of old was responsible for the actual design of the in-

The West Lounge in 1895.

terior—the walls and the ceilings, the cornices, the coves and the chimneypieces. They also designed the furniture and bought clocks, busts, porcelains, tapestries and paintings.

The most renowned *decorateurs* were from Paris, where they had embellished the palaces and country mansions of the monarchy and nobility for ages. Not surprisingly, the French professionals were preferred in America. The favorite of the great Richard Morris Hunt was Jules Allard et Fils of Paris, the best known of his profession at that time. Allard opened a shop and office in New York in 1885 at 304 Fifth Avenue in partnership with Eugene Prignot. Hunt employed him for the Marble House built for William K. Vanderbilt in Newport in 1892, for Cornelius Vanderbilt's Breakers

(1895), for E. J. Berwind's The Elms (1901) and many others. Lucien Alavoine acted as subcontractor for Allard who shipped the finished interiors from Paris and sent over teams of expert craftsmen to install them here. In 1905, Alavoine bought out both the Paris and New York operation of Allard.

Allard et Fils may have been the best of the *decorateurs*—they were certainly the best known—but there were others. London's great decorator was Charles Garrick Allom, later Sir Charles Allom. He achieved international fame when King George V was crowned and Queen Mary summoned Allom to redecorate some of Queen Victoria's somewhat stuffy rooms at Buckingham Palace and Windsor Castle. In 1905, he opened a branch in New York. Lord

68

Entrance Hall with Adamesque ceiling and Palladian archway.

*Above*: Marble fireplace in the Main Hall.

*Right*: Great Marble Hall, also called Main Hall.

*Below*: Graceful curve of marble stairway with iron balustrade.

*To the right*

One of Armstrong's stained-glass windows in the Main Hall.

Venetian lantern in the Main Hall.

Ceiling coffer above the Gallery.

*Above*

Iron balustrade on Gallery.

Ceiling coffer in the Main Hall.

Fireplace in the West Lounging Room.

The West Lounging Room.

Panel showing one
of the labors of Hercules
in the West Lounging Room.

The Ladies Lounge
on the Main Floor.

Beurdeley clock
on chimney piece
in the West Lounging Room.

Ambrose Cucinotta

Ceiling painting
with Mercury in the center,
in the West Lounging Room.

Duveen, who had enormous influence with some of the greatest spenders of the time, recommended him to many of his clients. His most noble effort was for Member Henry Clay Frick during the building of the mansion at Fifth and 70th Street in 1913. Allom came to America when Frick offered him the job of doing not only the Fragonard Room but most of the other rooms as well. For Allom, a prima donna, "most" was not enough and he sailed back to England in a huff. Frick recalled him, however, and put the whole job in his hands. Among the other major decorating jobs Allom did was Member Stotesbury's mansion, Whitemarsh Hall, and Member Huntington's San Marino home outside of Pasadena, California.

New York's best known American *decorateur* at the time was Christian Herter, who had studied painting in Paris in the atelier of Pierre-Victor Galland. On his return, he formed the firm of Herter Brothers and became the leading American-born *decorateur* of the day. Among the innumerable houses he was commissioned to do was William H. Vanderbilt's massive tripartite house on Fifth Avenue for which he designed both the exterior and interior. He also did work for the Metropolitan Clubhouse, having received the assignment to decorate the Library.

And then there was the house of Duveen. Today the name Joseph Duveen, First Baron Duveen of Milbank (1869-1939), is linked mostly to his dealings in paintings as the purveyor par excellence of priceless treasures to the plutocracy. His father, Sir Joseph Joel Duveen, however, was a dealer in antiques and a *decorateur* in London and New York for many years. He decorated Westminster Abbey for the coronation of Edward VII in 1902. Around the turn of the century, the younger Duveen was still known primarily as a *decorateur* and dealer in fine furniture. To the Metropolitan Club building, Duveen supplied furniture, andirons and clocks.

But there was at that period another outstanding French *decorateur* who is less well known today. He is Gilbert Cuel and he did most of the magnificent interior designs for the Metropolitan Club. Cuel was born in 1848 in Senlis, North of Paris. After studying at Saint Vincent college in Senlis, he went to Paris where he opened a shop as "tapissier" and "ébéniste." The business prospered and he employed three workmen. He decorated houses, made and repaired furniture, chairs and sofas, curtains, gildings, and so forth. According to his daughter, Madeleine, who was still living in 1980 at the age of 102, Madame William K. Vanderbilt—the redoubtable Alva—happened to pass Cuel's shop at 210 rue des Capucines and was so impressed by the quality of his fine work and services that she encouraged him to come to New York. This he decided to do in the mid 1880s. He opened a shop at 510 Fifth Avenue with one of his Paris employees named Robert, and he travelled back and forth between Paris and New York every three or four months.

His first commission in New York was to decorate part of the house of William K. Vanderbilt at Fifth Avenue and 52nd Street. Later he also worked for Cornelius Vanderbilt on his 58th Street mansion. In 1890, he designed the interior for the Vanderbilt yacht being built in Liverpool, and also decorated the Vanderbilts' Paris mansion. On his stationery, Cuel had the coat-of-arms of Spain with the imprint, "By special appointment to H.M. the King of Spain." He gave his trade as "Artistic Furniture, Works of Art," then "Ébénisterie and Bronzes de Beurdeley."

Early in 1892, Stanford White started negotiations to hire Allard et Fils to be the *decorateurs* for the new Clubhouse. In a letter to White dated April 25, 1892, Jules Allard reports that he has visited the Chairman of the Building Committee, Robert Goelet, and tells White that he "would be pleased to know that I had been given the order for the decorations and furniture of the Metropolitan Club." He continues, ". . . will you please send me the plans for ground floor consisting of different rooms drawn on small scale, and upon my arrival in Paris I will commence work on the models." Many meetings occurred and much correspondence was exchanged. A letter from Allard dated October 21, 1892, informed

White as follows: "[I] intend to sail for France very soon and would be gratified to carry with me the assurance that my proposition for the decorations and furniture of the Metropolitan Club have met with your approval." And another letter dated November 28, 1892, says, "Our designs for the Metropolitan Club have arrived on yesterday's steamer" and asks for an appointment with White to present them.

What neither Allard nor White knew was that secret negotiations had been going on simultaneously with Gilbert Cuel for the same contract and that Cuel had received a written agreement dated December 20, 1892, to handle virtually all the decoration with the exception of that for the Library.

What happened? The only clue to this turnabout is given in a letter Robert Goelet wrote to White from Paris dated December 15:

Dear Stan:

Just after I had sent my letter to you, I received yours of November 30. I do not understand what you say about Allard. I saw him read a copy of his note to you. I understood he had made a price, carried out certain parts of your design. Made an entirely different one (his own idea) for Ladies part. I also had him make me out cost of extras, curtains, etc., which I sent to G. G. Haven. I should have thought the Building Committee would have seen you or at the least Haven. Also why has W.K.V. kept Cuel's designs to himself?

As far as I know I shall not go up the Nile as I shall meet the Yacht I have chartered at Malaga. . . ." [He goes on to tell of his further plans for the trip and ends:] My wife sends all sorts of affectionate messages to you which I won't bother to write. Take good care of yourself and be a *good* boy.

Yours truly,
Robert Goelet

William K. Vanderbilt was not a Member of the Building Committee, but could it be that he put great pressure on certain Members of the Committee on behalf of Cuel? Or even more probable: was it the "redoubtable Alva," still married to W.K. at that time and domineering him "something awful," who put on the pressure? She was responsible for Cuel's establishing himself in New York, and he un-

doubtedly would welcome the business. Did she insist that the Vanderbilts do something for her protégé? The two Vanderbilts had each subscribed $50,000 of the construction bonds, together more than any single subscriber including J. Pierpont Morgan, who had also taken bonds for $50,000. The next largest subscribers were Robert Goelet, Ogden Goelet and Ogden Mills with $25,000 each. It seems reasonable to assume that this is how Allard was dumped and Cuel was hired. Fortunately there is no reason to doubt that Cuel was just as competent as Allard. No doubt either that White was not pleased that such a decision was made without consulting him.

In the contract of December 20th, Cuel was commissioned to do the "Cabinet Work, Ornamental Work and Decoration, Painting, Gilding, etc. of Ladies Vestibule, Main-outside Vestibule, Private Vestibule, Entrance Hall, Main Hall, First and Second stories, South and West Lounging Rooms, Ladies Restaurant and Main Dining Room."

Cuel imported French craftsmen for a great deal of the work, and used many imported fabrics, materials and products. The six ceiling paintings, three in the West Lounge and three in the Main Dining Room, were painted on canvas in Paris by a painter by the name of Perili, rolled and shipped to New York and finally mounted there by French craftsmen. This same method was used about ten years earlier when Allard decorated the boudoir of Mrs. William H. Vanderbilt in her palace at 640 Fifth Avenue. The boudoir had a ceiling painting, *Aurora*, commissioned from Jules Lefebvre, who painted it on canvas in Paris and shipped it to New York—where it was mounted backward, the sun traveling from West to East.

The extensive use of French labor for many of the construction jobs aroused the indignation of the Ornamental Plasterers' and Shop Hands' Society. On February 13, 1894, they sent a printed protest to McKim Mead & White protesting the use of foreign labor and threatening to refuse to handle any material not made in New York.

The final and total cost paid to Gilbert Cuel when the building was finished was $46,609 for

Gilbert Cuel.

the wall decoration, $6,210 for gas fixtures and $29,500 for furniture and hangings for a total of $82,319. In present-day dollars, this would be equal to between $2,057,000 and $3,300,000. Cuel continued his business in New York until he died in 1915 on one of his trips to Paris.

The West Lounge is a superb example of the work of Gilbert Cuel. In dimension, it takes up the entire length of the building on Fifth Avenue, about 85 feet in total. The width is 40 feet and the room is 25 feet high. Five large windows on the east wall permitted early members to watch the progress of the carriages into Central Park, as they permit current members to watch the St. Patrick's Day Parade in comfort.

The walls and ceilings are decorated with extreme richness. Here, Cuel has carried out an elaborate scheme of Louis XIV decorations. Basically, the walls are covered in stained oak, but, except for the dado, their prominent features are the rich decorations in light colors and gold. Here are the famous medallions showing the twelve labors of Hercules from Greek mythology. The design of the five windows on the west wall is repeated on the opposite side by the entrance flanked on each side by two mock windows covered with mirrors. The large cream-colored panels between the windows frame octagonal medallions. All of the figures are in mezzo-relief, with a muscular Hercules the most prominent in each. The panels are perhaps twelve-feet high and framed with torus bands; the medallions, with gold egg-and-dart bands. The octagonal medallions are held up by amoretti seated on consoles; but alternate medallions are held up by sphinxes, each leaning on a cornucopia. All of the panels are crowned by small plaques with the letters MC. The four corners of the West Lounge have two medallions each, oval in shape and framed by a heavy gold band. They are supported by half-figure caryatids in high relief.

All of the windows have heavy red brocade curtains, and early photographs show that the mirrors once also had draperies. When they were removed, no one knows. Illumination is provided by sixteen elaborate bronze wall candelabra, each with five lights, flanking the medallions.

There are a total of sixteen medallions, so the hero had to repeat four of his labors.

Alcmene, the wife of Amphytrion, was seduced by Jupiter and gave birth to Hercules who became famous for his extraordinary strength and courage. Hera, Jupiter's jealous wife, sent two serpents to the infant's cradle. He strangled them. Later, Hera again vented her everlasting hatred and cursed him with madness, whereupon he killed his wife. For purification, twelve labors were imposed upon him: to kill the monstrous Nemean Lion, the nine-headed Hydra, and the man-eating Stymphalian Birds; to capture the fleet-footed Cerynean Hind, the mad Cretan Bull, the flesh-eating mares of Diomed, the Erymanthean Boar, and the Cattle of Geryon; to clean, in one day, the stables of Augeas and to procure the golden apples of the Hesperides. The next task would make any brave man hesitate, and even Hercules needed the help of his friend Telamon—he had to procure the girdle of Hippolyta, the Queen of the Amazons. Lastly, he had to capture the three-headed watchdog of Hades, Cerberus.

Hercules is presented as a large and muscular man, either naked or draped with the Nemean Lion's skin and armed with a huge club. After his death, he was deified and admitted to Olympus where he became the husband of Hebe.

The short sides of the Lounge have identical large fireplaces. Each chimney-piece, six-feet high, is made of mottled gray and reddish marble, as are the entablature and the shelf which is supported by five small erect consoles. On the over-mantel is a slightly narrower rectangular mirror ending on top with an arch cartouche. It was during the period of Louis XIV that mirrors were first used in this fashion and it was Mansard who brought about this innovation. The mirror is framed by a thin ovolo band with festoons below the cornice, all gilded. On the shelf is an ornate Louis XV clock by Beurdeley, flanked by brackets with five lights each. The fire-back is of cast iron; the andirons of bronze.

The Club Building has some fifteen fireplaces in its social rooms. Those in the Lounge and Main Dining Room are of unusual artistry. The standard classic work on the art of interior decorations is *The Decoration of Houses*, written jointly by Edith Wharton and Ogden Codman, Jr., and published in 1897. It contains a separate chapter on fireplaces. One of the *dicta* of Codman is that the chimmey-piece should be extended up to the cornice. In 1978, a reprint of this book appeared with introductory remarks by John Barrington Bayley and William A. Coles. At the end, they give "a portfolio of pictures of interior details," done according to the canon of *The Decoration of Houses*. One of the thirty pictures shows the fireplace in the West Lounge.

The portfolio has another photograph of the Club interior, a beautiful view of the north half of the West Lounge with special emphasis on the ceiling paintings. Codman's classic also has a chapter on "Ceilings and Floors." In it he categorically states that "of all forms of ceiling adornment painting is the most beautiful" and he waxes enthusiastic about the massive goddesses and broad Virgilian landscapes of the Caracci and the piled-up perspectives of Giordano's school of prestidigitators, culminating in the great Tiepolo. Bayley and Coles feel the Lounge ceiling qualifies for inclusion in this list. It is truly magnificent. It has one large rectangular painting in the center, flanked by two smaller, circular ones. They are oil on canvas by Perili of Paris from designs by Cuel. The inspiration is the school of François Boucher (1703-70), the favorite of Mme. de Pompadour. Painted in Paris, the completed canvases were packed and shipped to New York where they were installed by French workmen.

The big central canvas is *Morning:* Phoebus Apollo urges his three white chargers through rolling clouds, attended by amoretti, and Selene (or perhaps it is Aurora) points out the path for him. Cupids and a few doves are in the field where more light and fewer clouds are seen. The southerly circle contains a figure of Mercury wearing his winged hat (petasos) and sandals (talaria), a caduceus in one hand, a garland in the other. Mercury, or Hermes, was the god of commerce and trade, of cheats and thieves, of luck and of eloquence. The northerly circle shows Fortuna, the oracular goddess of chance, with one knee on clouds, holding a torch in one hand, resting the other on her wheel. The allegorical symbolism is not difficult to interpret.

Lighting in the West Lounge is provided today by bronze wall brackets, sixteen in number. Early photographs show that originally there were four fixtures suspended from the ceiling, each consisting of a cluster of milk-glass globes. They were removed and now there is no overhead lighting.

Where the ceiling is covered down to the wall, Cuel has interposed an elaborate range of panels decorated with figures and groups of still-life in monochrome alternating with reliefs in colored plaster and foliage festoons hanging from cartouches which encircle and enrich the main ceiling. Most of them show reclining nudes, surrounded by putti and such. The monochrome is of pinkish tinge. The spirit of the West Lounge is that of a throne room, and it needs to be filled with people to look its best.

Cuel also made the furniture for the West Lounge to the specifications of the architects. The contract provided for twenty armchairs, fifty easy chairs, six large sofas, three large tables, six writing tables and twenty wine tables, reflecting the various uses of the Lounge at the time. From contemporary photographs, we know that the chairs were covered with dark, heavy velvet, typical of the dull taste of the period. This is rather out of keeping with the tasteful, light-hearted Renaissance decorations of the walls and ceilings.

The inspiration for the decoration of the West Lounge is the celebrated Galerie d'Hercule of the Hôtel Lambert on the Île Saint-Louis in the heart of Paris. (This beautiful room is described in *The Great Houses of Paris* by Fregnac and Andrews.) The Hôtel Lambert was built by Louis LeVau in 1640 for the son of a wealthy financier. It has changed hands many times during its history. Madame du Châtelet, mistress of Voltaire, owned it from 1739 to 1744. A hundred years later, in 1843, the Polish Prince Adam Czartorisky, exiled from his native land for having pleaded with Czar Alexander I to restore the kingdom of Poland, bought it. The family sold the Hôtel recently to Baron Guy de Rothschild who has filled Le-Vau's great rooms with a truly fabulous collection of paintings, furniture, enamel, faience, Renaissance jewelry, and other antiquities.

The Galerie d'Hercule is a more elongated room than the West Lounge of the Club. It has five floor-length French windows to the right as one enters. Seeing those magnificent windows one wishes that White had used such a design in the Clubhouse instead of the large, undivided, double-hung windows.

On the intervening wall sections on both long sides, flanking the five windows and arcadian landscapes, are medallions, alternately oval and octagonal, representing the Labors of Hercules. Together with the stucco atlantes, sphinxes, amoretti and other decorative emblems sustaining or crowning them, they were executed by van Obstal.

Cuel adopted the medallions pretty closely, even down to the half-figures below the oval ones. But the stucco figures, particularly those on top, which may be rather pompous and overloaded in the Louis XIV period, are much simpler in the modern version in the Club. The octagonal medallions here have a simple wreath with the letters MC in the center.

There is a more intimate atmosphere in the adjoining South Lounging Room. The style here is that of the Régence, that brief period between the death of Louis XIV and the maturity of his great-grandson and heir, Louis XV. The Regent Philippe II, duc d'Orléans, squandered away his life by riotous living. Régence, the style in architecture and decoration which originated during his regency from 1715 to 1723, introduced curved lines and many motifs such as shells, masques, and sinuous foliated scrolls which were to be further developed in rococo design. The use of gilt bronze was extensive and walnut, rosewood and other woods largely replaced ebony in veneers.

The South Room is smaller (27 by 54 feet), but since the ceiling is as high as the one in the

West Lounge, the room gives the appearance of great height. At the time of the opening in February, 1894, the walls were covered with big stretched panels of dark-red silk, the woodwork framing them being of a pale chocolate enlivened by thin gold lines. The plain, coved ceiling had a monochrome pinkish tinge. At the time, the furniture was covered with dark-red cut velvet. The small fireplace is charming, the chimney-piece a yellowish marble. Above the shelf is a large mirror framed in gold molding, with festoons below the cornice.

The chimneypiece was inspired by the designs of the French Régence architect and *decorateur* Charles Etienne Briseux (1680-1754), the author of several books on architecture. His interiors were mostly carried out in oak, and painted a light gray, the carvings being set off with gilding treated in various ways, both in matte, and burnished. The mantel, made of many varieties of marble, was beautifully shaped and polished. By the end of the reign of Louis XIV, colored marbles had been introduced from Italy and Africa and some of the old French quarries reopened. The use of large mirrors over the mantel was introduced by Mansard, encouraged around 1688 by the French invention of a new process of casting glass. These attractive new mirrors account for the great richness of some of the gilt frames made to enclose them. The fireplace designed by White is simpler and more delicate than those of Briseux.

A French brass clock stands on the shelf with its face in white enamel, Roman numerals for the hours and Arabic for the minutes. The name Darville, Paris, is inscribed on the face. The fire-back is of cast iron. On cold days, a few logs are kept burning, giving off a cozy warmth.

The room is lighted by ten bronze sidebrackets of elaborate design, each having five bulbs. The brackets in each room throughout the Clubhouse are of different design; no two rooms have the same kind. A delightful crystal chandelier hangs from the center of the ceiling. It is Waterford hand-blown-and-cut crystal with bronze mountings and probably dates from the late eighteenth century. The three windows have red brocade portières and look out on 60th Street. Since the end of prohibition, the east wall has been taken up by a large men's bar, with a mirror behind it. The story—probably apocryphal—is told of two of our illustrious forebears reading through the *Morning World* or *Times* in this room. Said one, "I see in the paper that you have just buried your wife. What a pity." Said the other with his head still deep in the financial section, "Not at all—had to—died, you know."

An anonymous gift in 1965 permitted this Room to be redecorated. The old silk panels were replaced with a burgundy color, and the wood work was painted a mocha shade, probably darker than the original. The ceiling is an off-white monochrome.

In the last few years, the Bar has filled the void left by the decline in card and billiard playing. Men assemble there sometimes before lunch, but especially before dinner between five and six o'clock to talk, renew friendships or make new ones. A real club atmosphere, unusual nowadays, exists here again.

The second floor is dominated by the gallery which goes around three sides of the Marble Hall, the fourth, or north, side being taken up by the stairway topped by the five large stained-glass windows. Two sides, the east and west, have six white monolithic Tuscan columns of Pavonazzo marble, crowned by Ionic capitals. The balustrade between the columns is formed like opera boxes and here the beautiful Tijou ironwork displays its design to greatest advantage. Nine sidebracket candelabras provide illumination. The ceiling has square coffers the details of which have been described above.

Looking at the gallery, Robert Goelet was concerned that the railings were dangerously low and on January 20, 1894, wrote a letter to White suggesting that the height of the iron balustrade be increased by at least twelve inches. As a result, a secondary rod of clear glass extending about one foot above the railings was installed, an unusual feature, not to be found, to one's knowledge, elsewhere on similar buildings.

Another unusual touch, intriguing to the

The South Lounging Room (also called The English Reading Room) in 1895.

historian, is the wind indicator on the east side of the gallery between the third and fourth white columns. It was installed by the Jackson Architectural Ironworks Company. Why such an indicator here? Was it that many Members were mariners owning yachts and sailboats and might be interested in wind changes? Or was it just the natural need of Members to know from what corner the wind was blowing?

The rooms opening on the west and south sides of the Gallery were given over to the entertainment of the Members. The first was the Reading and Writing Room (30 by 36 feet), for a time the Governors' Room and now the Card Room. Then came the small Card Room, now holding two billiard tables, and adjoining, the large Card Room.

At one time this was the most important room in the Club. One wishes that the walls could talk. They would tell of nightlong games of bridge or backgammon or poker, of talks and quarrels, of high stakes despite rules setting maximum stakes, of friendships made and broken, and decisions about how the Club should be run and who should be the next President. Drinks and snacks were served from the adjoining kitchenette—if wanted, all night long.

The Card Room is of an imposing size. The width on the west side is twenty-nine feet and there are two windows, one floor-length, opening on a balcony. The south side is sixty-two feet in length and has three windows, one also floor length, opening on the south balcony. The view over the Grand Army Plaza, with the Plaza Hotel as a background, down Fifth Avenue and over Central Park is the best from any Club window. Between the second and third windows, below the Dining Room east wall, is a beam-like architrave, supported by two col-

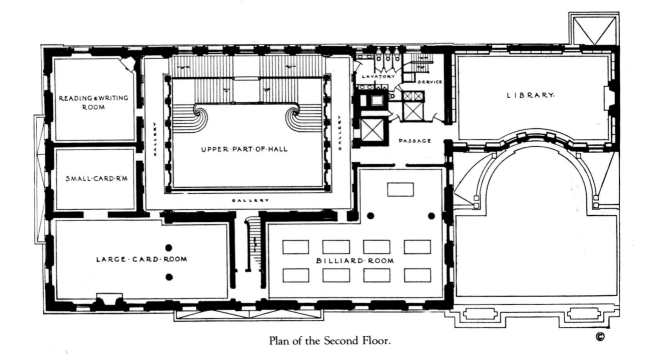

Plan of the Second Floor.

umns in purest Ionic style. The capitals are closely modeled after those of the Erechtheum built on the Acropolis in 420 B.C. Although not made of marble, but of painted wood, they are the most beautiful columns in the Club Building. The capital is heavily gilded. The volutes are prominent and gracefully curved. The echinus has an ovolo egg-and-dart band and below that a necking with an anthemion band in the Roman fashion. The shaft is fluted with reedings about a foot long at the top and about three feet long at the lower end. The base is traditional.

The space on the south side between the first and second windows is completely filled by a large fireplace, floor to cornice in height. The fire opening is cut into a yellow mottled marble plate, framed by brick. It is lined with a cast-iron fireback. The andirons are conventional. The mantel is of carved wood, deep cream in color. The festooned entablature rests on grace-fully-curved columns decorated with acanthus leaves. On the middle of the shelf stands a clock flanked by porcelain vases. The over-mantel has gilded stucco decorations of a simple design in bas-relief. In the center of the panel is a wreath in torus form, framed by a square of gold rosettes. Under the cornice is a gold-embellished shield. In the early years, a stuffed

deer's head was affixed to the circular panel. The whole room is a cream-colored monotone, sparingly adorned with gold bands and rosettes; the large sliding doors are black.

On the walls of the Card Room are tablets giving the names of winners in tournaments, and also several poker hands of royal flushes, with the name of the winner and date.

There is also an interesting and valuable collection of some two-hundred photographs of old New York, a gift from Frank A. Roe presented in January, 1927. A number of the pictures are undated, but the oldest one, a scene of Broad and Wall Streets, goes back to 1869. Another picture shows Broadway looking south from 32nd Street, *circa* 1870. One photograph of particular interest shows the original Madison Square Garden of 1871. And a 1903 photo, taken looking down Fifth Avenue from a point just below the Club, shows an almost unbroken line of fine residences, each some three to four stories tall, and it is not until the spires of St. Patrick's rise above them that the skyline is interrupted.

In addition, there are fine pictures of the old Daly's Theatre at Broadway and 30th Street, of the old Customs House, of the New York Stock Exchange at the turn of the century, of Castle Garden in 1884, and of the first of the Astor

Houses. One can go on and on, admiring the old horse cars, the elevated railway, Grand Central Station in its early days.

Next, separated by a small kitchen facility, comes what is now the Lee Warren James Room, formerly the Billiard Room (30 by 60 feet).

For a good part of the Club's existence, this was one of the most active rooms, crowded every afternoon and evening. At that time it held seven billiard tables. The room was then very English in character, with dark mahogany doors set in enframements capped with entablatures. There was a white wainscot, a deep cornice set with rosettes, and a leafy continuum bordering the ceiling. The walls were covered with buff and dark green leather or a lincrusta made to resemble leather. The Ionic columns resemble those in the cardroom. Since the decline of interest in billiards, the room has been redecorated and its character changed. Now it is used for special parties, dances or meetings. The portrait of past President Lee Warren

James hangs there.

In the wing, above the Ladies' Restaurant (now the Canadian Club Lounge), is the Library, one of the most charming rooms in the Clubhouse. It is entered through a passage between the elevator and the James Room, in the middle of which hangs a Venetian lantern, similar to the lantern in the Great Hall, although much smaller.

The Library is a large harmonious room, thirty-four by fifty-two feet and twenty-one feet high, the odd shape due to the inward curve of the wing to allow carriages in the Courtyard to turn. The room was decorated by Herter Brothers of New York. Its five windows on the south side overlook the Courtyard and give a superb view of the large iron front gates. Bookshelves of stain-grained oak line the walls. On the top of the bookcases are lighting fixtures, globes of milk-glass held by half-figures of bearded men, worked in heavy brass.

The space above the bookcases, up to the

The Billiard Room in 1895.

cornice, is covered with a neutral brown, grain-patterned wallpaper. It is a good background for the increasing number of President's portraits which are finding their final resting place there. The original covering was an embossed leather or lincrusta Yandell fabric, also apparently of a neutral, brownish-golden shade "to create a sober, rich, chastened atmosphere" as described by the *Times* reporters when the building was thrown open to their inspection for a few hours. Early photographs show a bold damask pattern. Lincrusta was a novelty then and Yandell specialized in its application. Invented around 1877 by the Englishman Frederick Walton, it was also referred to as Lincrusta Walton, and was composed primarily of solidified linseed oil molded in elaborate designs. It had many advantages, not the least of which was that it was washable. No record exists as to when it was replaced by the present paper.

At the end of the Library there is an imposing chimney-breast panelled fireplace in stained wood with pilasters at the corners. The fireplace opening is faced with reddish-yellow marble. The chimney piece is an entablature, the frieze set with paterae. An open book carved in low relief decorates the over-mantel; it is framed with garlands of laurel leaves and cornucopia filled with fruit. On the leaves of the book is a Latin text which reads:

Quod si non hic tantus omnium neque locorum: fructus ostenderetur, et haec studia adulescentiam alunt, senectutum si ex his studiis delectatio sola peteretur, tamen, ut oblectant, secundas res opinor, hanc animi adversionem humanissimmam ac liberalissimam bent, delectant domi, iudicaretis. Nam ceterae non impediunt foris, perneque temporum sunt noctant nobiscum, perneque aetatum egrinantur, rusticantur.

This is part of a speech made on behalf of Archias (*Pro Archia*) by the great Roman orator, politician and philosopher, M.T. Cicero (106-43 B.C.). Archias, a Greek philosopher living in Rome, had been accused by the hardliners of his day. In translation, it reads:

Even if no such reward were forthcoming, and only pleasures sought from these studies, nonetheless, I imagine, you would pronounce this a very humane and liberal relaxation. For other things are neither of all times, nor all ages, nor all places. And these studies nourish Youth, entertain Age, embellish Prosperity, provide refuge and solace in Adversity, give pleasure at home, do not interfere with business, and keep us company—all night, on the road, and in the country.

On the shelf of the fireplace stands a brass Louis XV clock made by Goudin of Paris. Goudin lived in the mid-eighteenth century and it is recorded that in 1744, during the reign of Louis XV, he asked for *logement* in the Louvre. Clockmakers were highly esteemed in those days and many of the famous ones—Martinot, Bidault, and Boule—had lodgings in the Louvre and dined in the palace at the table of the Gentlemen of the Chamber. On both sides of the fire-grating are heavy bronze figures, one a man and the other a woman, formed in the manner of Venetian andirons.

Over the entrance door is a slightly lower, very delicate relief, carved in wood. Atop the bookcases, on the inward curve, are four busts; the likenesses of Dante and Shakespeare are easily recognized and the other ones must belong to the same breed of literary giants.

The imposing ceiling is in harmony with the walls. In its center is a large oblong skylight which originally contained a panel of stained and leaded glass. Surrounding the skylight, in four irregular spaces on a ground the color of lapis lazuli, are groups of two cupids, each pair with an open book. The words, "Scientia, Ars Poesis, Historia and Philosophia" are printed on swags draped around the cupids. They are broadly treated in masses of light and dark and are the work of the American artist, E. E. Simmons. The cove around the ceiling is gold and decorated with rings of laurel wreaths alternating with plaques. The compartments of the ceiling are elaborately framed. The panels at various junctures are joined by cartouches,

The Library in 1895.

flowers and vases in high relief. At one time, there were chandeliers with frosted globes suspended from the ceiling. The whole decorative ensemble is of a very high order.

Edward E. Simmons (1852-1931) studied at the Academie Julien under Gustave C. R. Boulanger and Jules Joseph Lefèvre and painted for many years in Europe. He returned to New York in 1891 and quickly gained an important reputation. Simmons created a highly acclaimed series of murals for the dome of the Manufacturers and Liberal Arts Building at the World's Columbian Exposition of 1893 in Chicago and became a popular choice for decorating the interiors of many public buildings including the Appellate Division Courthouse on Madison Square.

On the north wall of the Library were two large clear-glass windows looking out on the mansion of Elbridge Gerry. But the less appealing bare walls of the Pierre Hotel replaced Ger-

ry's house in 1929; and finally in 1970, stained glass windows were put into the Library. The new windows, designed and signed by Richard Millard of the Millard Studio of New York City, capture the feeling of those over the grand staircase in the Great Hall. They have a silvery-white line augmented with color in the border and yellow flashing in the cartouche. The cartouche enclosing the Club monogram on a blue background is Renaissance in style. The background pattern of the glass reflects the style of the appointments in the Library itself. The ceiling murals of the Library were restored at the same time. They were washed, cleansed and oiled. All windows have gold brocade draperies.

A large table stands in the center of the Library with a display of current publications. Comfortable chairs line the walls.

On the Third Floor are the Main Dining

Room, three private Dining Rooms and the Kitchen. Stepping out of the elevator, one enters the impressive Hall between two Ionic columns twelve feet tall.

The Hall occupies the center of the floor and is twenty-two feet wide and sixty feet long. It is decorated in an eggshell color with gold trim. Each of the two long sides are divided by four pilasters, all with gold trimmings, into five panels. The division is continued across the ceiling by fret bands. Two of the panels have doors, one leading to a private dining room and the other to the kitchen. A third panel is taken up by the stairway coming up from the Second Floor. Here there is a glass case containing many handsome silver cups, wine coolers and goblets which are used in the private dining rooms on special occasions. Much of the silver was donated by the Members of the old Calumet Club when it closed its doors and joined the Metropolitan.

In the other seven panels hang portraits of past and present Presidents of the Club; the first which catches the eye when leaving the elevator is that of Founder-President J. P. Morgan. Next to Morgan's portrait stands a long-case clock, signed by Robert Scholfield, who lived and worked in Manchester, England, during the first half of the eighteenth century.

The most striking feature of the Hall, however, is its Adamesque vaulted ceiling. It is the same color as the walls and is also divided into five panels. The two end panels and the center one have lighting fixtures consisting of clusters of six milk-glass globes. The other two have skylights covered with leaded glass which provide light during the day. The coves, which terminate in winged lions, are decorated with a rhythmic flow of gold arabesque foliage, in a carefully arranged composition of symbols, shields, medallions, lyres, wreaths and cornucopias. The garlands at the top of the vault at either end are very effective. A heavy gilded frieze separates ceiling and walls, underlining the graceful ellipse. The conception, interpreted most eloquently by Robert Adam in the library at Kenwood House in 1768, is freely acknowledged here.

A long table stands in the center of the hall, with a huge flower arrangement on it. Chairs and small tables line the walls. Through an enormous portal flanked by portières, one enters the Main Dining Room.

The Main Dining Room is the most splendid room in the Clubhouse. It is a symphony in gold. It is twenty-two feet nine inches high and in size the same as the West Lounge two floors below, with five windows overlooking Central Park. The opposite wall, however, is not symmetrical as it is in the West Lounge. The wide entrance, framed by red brocade portières, is flanked by only two floor-to-ceiling mirrors. Space was needed for doors leading to the kitchen on the north end and to the former Breakfast Room on the south end. The shorter north and south walls have mirror-topped fireplaces, with two windows on either side. The view from the height of sixty feet over the Park and Grand Army Plaza, with General Sherman's statue and the Plaza Hotel as backdrop, is lovely and captivating in all seasons.

The walls of the Dining Room are gold, cream and egg-shell, except for the dado. The windows have burgundy-red, gold-bordered curtains. The many flat pilasters, with their Corinthian capitals, their flutes partly filled with reedings, their bases resting on the brown dado, establish an enchanting rhythm leading the eye to the sculptured cornice. Their slender properties seem to increase the height of the room. Between the five windows are four panels, each having a shield in its center framed by moldings. The shields are held up by amoretti. Spears, halberds, arrows and other weapons of war and the hunt are grouped around them. On the opposite wall more space is available and the panels are larger. They are framed with festoons hanging from rings in the jaws of lions' heads. All the panels are supported at the bottom corners by masks of satyrs in high relief. The frieze, resting on the pilasters, is a chain of pairs of children's heads, separated by trophies and cartouches. They smile and appear to look down on the diners with approval.

The two fireplaces, identical in design, are the most beautiful in the Clubhouse. The chimney-piece is highly-polished mottled red-and-gray marble, five-and-a-half-feet high. The fireplace opening is lined with iron in the French style. The iron work is figured with a trellis in low relief. The top of the chimney-piece is formed by a high-fluted cyma-reversa block topped by a shelf edged by a wide torus molding. The over-mantel is a rectangular mirror framed by a broad gilded panel the width of the chimney piece. In the upper part of the panel, festoons of fruit and flowers center about a cartouche and hang down on either side. On the shelf, a large Louis XIV clock, signed by Philip Rodel, completes a design of elegance and opulence rarely seen. Viollet-le-Duc, the great restorer and favorite architect of Napoleon III, would have called it: "une grandeur solide, sans faux ornements."

The ceiling has three gigantic paintings against a background of bold panel work in gold. These paintings were executed by Perili in Paris after Cuel's designs.

Here the influence of François Boucher's sensuous side is even more evident than in the ceiling paintings of the West Lounge. All his life, Boucher loved the youthful nude female figure. So he painted them in all forms and postures, clad if at all in diaphanous veils. His models were first his wife, seventeen when he married her, and then sweet young things from the *corps de ballet* of the Paris Opera. And though Leonardo wrote that the female figure in art is only truly beautiful with closed thighs, Boucher painted his in more abandoned poses. They were goddesses and nymphs, amoretti and putti, floating in space. It was rococo at its most

The Dining Room in 1895.

89

appealing.

A circular painting—twenty-one feet in diameter—dominates the room. It shows an *allegoria* with the Goddess of Abundance sitting in a cloud, a cornucopia in one arm. She may be Demeter, the goddess of corn, harvest and fruitfulness. Lightly-clad maidens float on both sides of her, one holding a sheaf of wheat, another a wine goblet and grapes.

This central painting is flanked by two smaller paintings, oblong with semi-circles on the short sides, eighteen by nine feet; they represent the hunt and the sea. On the 60th-Street side is the virgin huntress Diana with a half-moon diadem in her hair, a hunter's bow in one hand, and the hawk her arrow has pierced held victoriously in the other. At her feet are pheasants and other wild birds she has shot. Three nymphs surround her, clad in diaphanous gowns. One blows a hunting horn, another holds a bundle of arrows. In the tableau on the north, Amphitrite, queen of the sea, wife of Poseidon and mother of Triton, is depicted in the middle holding a trident. Three nereids float around her, one holding a net and the others offering fish from a wicker basket; handsome seashells, one a conch, complete the scene.

The cove of the ceiling is the only surface not in gold, but is a darkish-cream color, with relief decoration and panels painted in monochrome. There are two panels on the long side, each nine feet by five feet; four more are in the corners, each three feet by four feet. One sees here scantily-clad female figures surrounded by putti.

Light is provided by five-candle brass brackets on the pilasters, a total of eighteen of them, and by two chandeliers on either side of the center painting. The resplendent chandeliers gracing the ceiling now were not Stanford White's choice. He installed the fixtures fashionable at the time—two clusters of sixteen milk-glass globes hanging close to the ceiling. Many years ago, they were replaced by the nineteenth-century, thirty-two-light, bronze and Baccarat glass chandeliers which hang there now. They can be pronounced a great improvement, enhancing the elegant appearance of the room.

McKim Mead & White were shortly to build another magnificent clubhouse with a most impressive dining room. But here the proportions are not as appealing. The room is too long for its width, like the dining room of the Reform Club in London. It is also too high, like the dining room in George Vanderbilt's Biltmore House. The dark walls, largely of stained oak, give it a somber appearance. But in the Metropolitan Club Dining Room, the team of Stanford White and Gilbert Cuel have created something which stands in a class by itself. The color scheme of gold and egg-shell and cream creates a unique atmosphere of gaiety and elegance and the size of the room is unsurpassed in the grace and happiness of its proportions.

At the time the Club was being planned, the placing of the kitchen on the top floor of fashionable clubs had found favor in Paris, Vienna and St. Petersburg. Much was to be said for this plan because it prevented cooking odors from annoying the members. Of course, domestics then were abundant and inexpensive. Following the fashion and more concerned with esthetics than practicality, Stanford White placed the kitchen of the Metropolitan Club on the top floor. The food was conveyed by dumbwaiters to serving rooms adjoining the Main Dining Room, the Ladies' Restaurant and the Strangers' Dining Room, where it was kept warm until brought to the table. In 1967, the kitchen was finally moved to the third floor adjoining the Main Dining Room (the other two dining rooms had, in the meantime, been discontinued but the dumbwaiters and warming facilities can still be seen); costs were naturally reduced and better service provided. One private dining room fell victim to the need for sufficient kitchen space. These facilities are on the north side of the third floor, looking out on the bleak wall of the Pierre Hotel.

The Dining Room was furnished by Cuel with twenty-five small and four large tables and 150 chairs which were straight-backed and armless with leather seats and backs, the latter decorated with the letter "M" in gold. They were replaced by new, more comfortable, chairs in

1980. There are now about forty-five tables with a seating capacity of one hundred and fifty. It is the only one of the social rooms that remains essentially unchanged from its original form and purpose.

The other rooms on this floor are private dining rooms. Once there were four but today there are only three. The former Breakfast Room right next to the Main Dining Room is now the Levi Parsons Morton room. Next to it is the former Smoking Room, now the Frank K. Sturgis Room. The third, overlooking the Courtyard, is the J. Pierpont Morgan Room. In between the last two is the Nicholas Murray Butler Room where pre-dinner drinks are served. The walls of these rooms are covered with an abundance of gold-leaved bands, lines, garlands and the like, enough to show all variations of the classical decorations, the frets, guilloches, dentils, egg-and-dart and torus bands. The background is a simple egg-shell hue, sometimes a darker cream color.

But the main attractions are the fireplaces in each room. The Morton Room has a very fine corner chimney-piece in the style of William Kent (1685-1748). The mantel frieze is decorated with swags, ribbons and foliage. There is a square over-mantel with a broken pediment on a frieze of laurel bound with ribbons. There are foliage pendants and volutes on either side.

The Sturgis Room has a corner fireplace with a chimney-piece in the style of Sir John Soame (1753-1837) with free-standing columns at the corners and a frieze of delicate scrolls, urns and ribbons, the whole composition gilded.

There is another corner fireplace of ample proportions in the Morgan Room. The opening

A Private Dining Room (now the Frank Knight Sturgis Room)

is surrounded by a broad facing of Siena marble framed with a gilt egg-and-dart molding. The frieze is a cyma reversa set with large acanthus leaves, a plaque in the center.

The fourth floor contains twenty-two bedrooms for Members. They vary in size from twenty feet by thirty feet to twelve feet by sixteen feet and are simply treated with white woodwork and plain wallpapers. Many have fireplaces. Each room has a bath or shower. In the early years, before guests were admitted to the Clubhouse, Members took a room, or several of them, by the year. The most elaborate is the President's Suite on the corner of Fifth Avenue and 60th Street, Rooms 1 and 2. When the Clubhouse was opened in 1894, these rooms were rented for $4 a day, and the smaller mezzanine rooms fetched $2 a day. Henry Rouse took Rooms 5 and 6 for one year for $2,000. The same rooms were later rented by Henry E. Huntington. James Stillman paid $1,000 a year for Room 15. And George C. Taylor was charged $3,000 to reserve Rooms 1 and 2 for a year. These rooms also became very popular as permanent residences of widowed Members. Lee Warren James, one of the outstanding Presidents of the Club, lived there after he lost his wife, and he died there.

Over part of the third floor were private rooms of lesser height; a mezzanine also had bedrooms. Some of these were for Members' use, others for staff use. They have now all been renovated and modernized and are being rented. Together with the bedrooms in the Annex, there are forty-four bedrooms available for Members and guests today.

In the early years, the kitchen, pantry, servants' dining room, laundries, and other facilities were on the roof together with a Roof Garden for the Members.

Before the advent of the automobile, the Roof Garden was used during the summer months for luncheons and dinner and was very fashionable. It was thirty-feet wide and ran the entire length of the building along Fifth Avenue, and it was covered by huge red-and-white awnings. It gave a superb view over the New York skyline then unencumbered with high-rise buildings. The extent of its popularity can be gathered from the orders for flowers for decorations. On June 1, 1895, the Executive Committee gave a contract worth $500 for flowers to George M. Stumpf. In 1896, the Roof was open May 30th to the fall and the cost of the flower arrangements for the season was $650, a lot of money at that time to spend on flowers for two or three months. The equivalent in purchasing power today would be perhaps $15,000 to $20,000. But flowers were more important then than they are now. Those were the days when no young man worthy of his salt ever went to meet a young lady without offering her flowers which he bought made up into a nosegay. Tiny roses with a maidenhair fern background were the most popular.

Roof gardens were very fashionable in those years. New York was on the way to becoming a city of towers, rising higher into the air than men had ever dared to imagine, for the new elevators could whisk people up ten or twenty floors. The first such passenger elevator—named the "vertical railroad"—was installed in 1859 in the legendary Fifth Avenue Hotel which rose eight stories. In that age before air conditioning, the dining rooms and restaurants down below were hot and stuffy and often unbearable in the summer, but the roof garden was open to the stars and usually had a pleasant breeze.

The smartest roof garden in New York around the turn of the century was at the Waldorf. It was the focal point of elegant Manhattan night life. Men sat around the tables, straw hats or panamas on their heads, and the ladies wore the latest creation of their milliners. But there were other roof gardens. There was the New Amsterdam Aerial Roof Garden where George M. Cohan's popular farce *The Governor's Son* had its première. It featured "The Favorite Family of Fun-Makers, the Four Cohans." The most popular was the one on top of Stanford White's most striking early work, the Madison Square Garden building. In its roof theatre on the night of June 25, 1906, a musical entitled *Mamzelle Champagne* had its première, with book by Edgar Allen Wolfe and music by Cassius Freeborn, composer of the music for

The South Lounge — now the Men's Bar — with Régence fireplace.

The Library.

Stained-glass window
by Millard, in the Library.

Entrance Hall on the Third Floor.

Canadian Club lounge in the Annex.

Fireplace in the Main Dining Room.

Main Dining Room.

Rödel clock
on chimney piece
in the Main Dining Room.

Wall panel with trophy
in the center,
Main Dining Room.

A window table
in the Main Dining Room.

Madison Square Roof Garden was one of the most popular roof gardens in New York. Stanford White was shot here, on the roof of the building he had designed.

the memorable hit *The Belle of New York*. Here, on that night, White was shot to death. But roof gardens were doomed, partially because of the pollution of the air by the automobile and partially because of the superior convenience of air conditioning.

The basement of the Club Building was much more important then than it is now. It contained the Board of Governors Room and the Committee Room, a bowling alley underneath what is now the Main Bar, men's dressing rooms with needlebaths, and also the steward's room, engine and boiler rooms, etc. Now it contains the Health Department with a gym, sauna and massage room.

A barber shop is directly above the first floor on the mezzanine story and is reached by the elevator.

At the time of the opening of the Clubhouse, the Ladies' Restaurant was considered one of its most charming rooms. It was situated on the ground floor and had a separate entrance from the Courtyard. Decorated by Cuel in Louis-XV style, the walls had delicate Renaissance designs in white plaster and curtains of a greenish-yellow color. A marble fireplace with a mirror is flanked by pilasters with Corinthian capitals standing on pedestals. Four Corinthian pilasters support the ceiling. Niches in the corners held palms, and illumination was provided by five-candle sconces. Cuel furnished the room with twenty small tables, one large round table and ninety wicker-backed chairs. It measures thirty feet by fifty feet. Service was provided by dumb waiter from the kitchen on the roof. There were private rooms upstairs, consisting of two reception rooms and two large private dining rooms. Now one is used as a conference room and the other as a library. One of these was treated in white and pale pink, the other in white and pale green.

In 1977, when the arrangement was negotiated bringing the Canadian Club in as associated Members, this wing was turned over to them. The lovely dining-room had previously been used as an executive office for the Warner-Lambert Company, which had redecorated it. The walls were painted in false-grain to give the appearance of wood paneling. The side brackets on the pilasters were removed and the lovely carved and decorated ceiling disappeared behind a dropped false ceiling with spotlights in it. The coats-of-arms of the ten Canadian provinces decorate the upper walls with the Canadian government shield above the fireplace. A bar has been installed along the right-hand wall. A portrait of Queen Elizabeth II, painted by Frank Slater, was hung over the fireplace, replacing the mirror which had hung there before. It was unveiled by the Queen Mother on October 27, 1954, while on a visit to New York. The Canadian Club, still in its former premises, gave a large reception for the occasion. In view of the limited space, members who had been officers and governors were invited and, to the extent that space limitations permitted, Members on the basis of seniority of Membership.

In 1912 under Frank Sturgis' Consulship when the property adjoining the Club on 60th Street was purchased from John McGowan for $165,000, the Board commissioned the fashionable architect and designer Ogden Codman Jr. to remodel the exterior and the interior of the building. His work included the removal of a stoop and doorway on 60th Street, the building of a new doorway in the Courtyard, the alterations of the fenestration and the transformation of the facade in keeping with the Italianate Renaissance spirit of the Main Building.

Of great beauty are the heavy bronze doors opening into the Courtyard. Massive and decorated in classical design, each of the two wings of the door has three panels. The upper and the lower have heads of a man and a woman and the middle one has the head of a lion holding a ring between its teeth. They were made in Italy, late in the last century.

One floor was added to the Annex, as it came to be called. The ground and first floors have office space, now leased to the Warner-Lambert Company. The remaining floors were converted into apartments or bedrooms for the use of Members. The cost of the remodeling came to $53,486 in 1912.

No better choice could have been made in the selection of the man to do this work. A talented architect, interior decorator and writer, Ogden Codman came closer to White in his refined taste than any other artist of that period. He practiced mostly in Boston, Newport and New York. As a youth, he spent a great deal of time in France and as a result always had a predilection for French architecture and decorative arts. His remarkable collection of notes, photos and drawings of all the known châteaux of France was willed to the French Government. Together with Edith Wharton, he published in 1897 his *Decoration of Houses*. Both authors were astonished by the popularity of the book which became the bible for turn-of-the-century interior decoration in the classical taste.

Codman had done much work for Members. His first sizable commission was given him in 1894 by Charter Member Harold Brown, a member of one of Rhode Island's oldest families, who in 1892 married Founder W. Watts Sherman's daughter Georgette Wetmore Sherman, a distant cousin of Codman. On their wedding trip to France, the young couple collected Napoleonic furniture and objects and Codman designed a series of Empire interiors as an appropriate setting for the collection. One of Codman's largest commissions was to decorate the second and third floors of the Breakers which Cornelius Vanderbilt was building at that time. The relative simplicity and delicate taste of Codman's work was in marked contrast to the overwhelming opulence of the downstairs rooms at the Breakers, which were decorated by Allard et Fils.

Many of New York's finest decorating firms contributed to the Club's interior. The sculp-

The Ladies' Dining Room (now the Canadian Club Lounge) in 1895.

ture firm of Ellin & Kitson of 519 West 21st Street was paid the highest sums—next to Cuel—in the McKim Mead & White account books. They received $50,000 on June 9, 1893, and $5,000 on March 18, 1894. Hunt employed them to carve the elaborate ornamentation on the William K. Vanderbilt house and White used them in the Villard houses. A. H. Davenport, the famous furniture company, received $34,500 for their services. The cost of delivery and setting the interior marble was $77,560. This work was done by Davidson & Sons Marble Co. in cooperation with Ellin & Kitson and Batterson See & Eisele. Three other firms worked on the interior, F. Beck, Herter Bros. and C. R. Yandell & Co. W. & S. Sloane received $13,629.34 for carpets. Duveen supplied furniture, andirons and some of the clocks and was paid $2,675.

But the lion's share of the work went to Gilbert Cuel. His firm did all the cabinet woodwork, plaster work, painting, gilding, covering of the walls and ceilings, fireplaces, hardware and everything necessary for the complete finishing. He also supplied the curtains, portières and a great deal of the furniture, including one porter's chair and one bench for the front vestibule which are still in use there today.

When the Finance and Building Committee discharged itself in April, 1894, they reported that they had spent $1,777,480. In broad classifications this amount breaks down as follows:

| | | |
|---|---:|---:|
| Land | | $480,000 |
| Building, Exterior | | |
|    Excavation | $ 74,500 | |
|    Marble | 270,000 | |
|    Masonry | 190,000 | |
|    Other | 262,000 | |
| Building, Interior | | |
|    Marble | 54,600 | |
|    Gates & Railings | 15,500 | |
|    Int. Decoration | 25,800 | |
|    Cabinet Work | 48,000 | |
| Furnishings | | 156,000 |
| Architect's Fee | | 60,000 |
| Overhead | | 141,000 |
| | | |
| Total | | $1,777,400 |

The largest single item, outside of the cost of the land which was very low, was the cost of the exterior marble work which amounted to over twenty-five percent of the cost of the building.

Costs of similar buildings, with the figures as given by Leland M. Roth in his book *The Architecture of McKim Mead & White*, compare as follows shown below, with the year given in which the building was finished. Roth gives his cost estimates by capitalizing the architect's fee at 5%.

| | | |
|---|---|---|
| Villard Houses | '85 | $737,000 |
| Madison Square Garden | '91 | $1,380,000 |
| Century Association | '91 | 213,000 |
| Metropolitan Club | '94 | 1,200,000 |
| University Club | '00 | 1,108,000 |
| Harmonie Club | '07 | 463,000 |

The cost of reproducing the Club Building today would be forty to fifty times as much; in other words, it would cost in excess of fifty million dollars. But as Leland M. Roth remarked in his book it is now largely impossible to match the uniformly high quality of workmanship and material found in the work of McKim Mead & White.

In November, 1966, the New York Community Trust awarded a plaque to the Metropolitan Club declaring its Building to be a distinguished landmark of the city. The significance of this plaque is only honorary. In 1965, however, legislation was passed creating the Landmark Preservation Commission, a New York City agency dedicated to the preservation of certain buildings which they designate as landmarks. No changes can be made to the exterior of such buildings without the Commission's approval.

On November 7, 1966, the Board of Governors received notice that the Clubhouse was one of the buildings they intended to designate

as a landmark. Such a designation at the time would have made needed financing more difficult. Consequently the legal adviser and long-time Governor, the Honorable John P. McGrath, was able to postpone any decision by presenting a Resolution to the Commission that there was no intention to sell or alter the structure. The matter remained dormant until 1979 when President Hamilton received a letter from the Landmark Preservation Commission informing him that the Metropolitan Club Building had been designated a landmark. The letter read in part:

On the basis of a careful consideration of the history, the architecture and other features of this building, the Landmarks Preservation Commission finds that the Metropolitan Club Building has a special character, special historical and aesthetic interest and value as part of the development, heritage and cultural characteristics of New York City.

The Commission further finds that, among its important qualities, the Metropolitan Club Building is a magnificent example of neo-Italian Renaissance architecture designed by the prestigious firm of McKim Mead and White; that when built in 1892-94 it was the largest and most imposing New York clubhouse of its day; that the design is a remarkable reflection of both the architects' training at the École des Beaux-Arts in Paris and the founding members' knowledge of European architecture; that with its restrained elegance the Metropolitan Club Building is characteristic of an especially American interpretation of European architecture; that among its notable features are the refined stonework and ornamental detail, the imposing cornice, and the graceful colonnade screening the courtyard; that the design of the building was seen as an appropriate symbol of the newly founded Metropolitan Club; that the clubhouse led the vanguard of development north of 59th Street; that it set the style and high standard of design for the surrounding area; that the annex of 1912 was designed by architect Ogden Codman, Jr., to harmonize with the main building; and that it continues to make a strong contribution to the architectural excellence of the neighborhood.

# Chapter 9

# THE PRESIDENCIES OF MORGAN, MORTON AND STURGIS: 1891-1926

J. Pierpont Morgan was President of the Club during the last decade of the nineteenth century, until February 20, 1900. The first third of his term was one of planning and Clubhouse construction; the balance saw the blossoming of the life of the new Club. In this same decade Morgan also laid the foundations of a career that made him the greatest banker of his time and of succeeding generations.

He had formed J.P. Morgan & Co. in 1895, and by 1901 he had taken the lead in organizing the first billion-dollar company in the history of the country. The planning had been done in the privacy of the Club's Library by him and his associate, Illinois lawyer Elbert Gary. Under Morgan's direction, a number of companies were consolidated into the United States Steel Corporation, and one billion in stocks and bonds were issued to the parties in the transaction. To the Morgan underwriting syndicate, stock having a value of $62.5 million was given as a commission for its services. His leadership during the panic of 1907, when his actions halted the runs on banks throughout the country, ultimately made him the dominant figure in American finance. At the time he heard the news of the panic he was in San Francisco attending the Episcopal Church Assembly, ac-

companied by his great and good friend, Mrs. Markoe of Philadelphia. Ordering his private train to hurry him back to New York, he arranged for the importation from Europe of $100 million in gold. He then collected comparable funds from such men as John D. Rockefeller, E. H. Harriman and Henry Clay Frick, thus enabling the banks to meet the runs and regain public confidence instead of having to close their doors in the faces of frantic depositors.

Morgan's life was also filled by his consuming passion to assemble the greatest library possible, including a thousand medieval and Renaissance manuscripts, 2100 incunabula—books printed before 1501—and the most important collection of master drawings from periods before 1800. In 1900, he commissioned McKim to design the marble building for the Morgan Library at 36th Street and Madison Avenue.

To the Club, he gave his prestige and his guidance. He always acted as *Primus inter pares* and not infrequently motions he proposed were voted down by the Board. Throughout this period, his bank acted as depositary and permitted overdrafts when needed or made loans to the Club for special purposes. But the

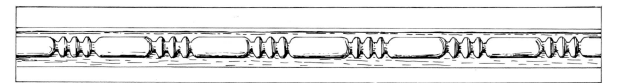

*Bead moulding*

J Pierpont Morgan (1837-1913)
President 1891-1900

actual management from the beginning lay in the hands of W. Watts Sherman. Sherman never wanted to be anything but Secretary, a position he held for twenty years until shortly before his death in 1912. He presided over most of the Board meetings in Morgan's absence, and was responsible for the Membership drive and all organizational problems.

Sidney Webster was Vice President for the first nine years. Webster had studied law at Harvard. When Franklin Pierce became President of the United States in 1852, he took the twenty-four-year-old Sidney along as his secretary. Webster served in Washington until 1857 and met many of the leading men of his time, including Hamilton Fish whose daughter he married in 1860. The post of Club Treasurer was held for the first five years by George Bowdoin, one of Morgan's partners; thereafter by Adrian Iselin.

Management of the daily affairs of the Club was delegated to the Executive Committee, consisting of five members who met at least once a week. Their duties were to regulate prices, order supplies, appoint and dismiss employees, and generally run the Club.

The first meeting of record took place on April 28, 1893, at 1 West 25th Street, the temporary office until the Clubhouse was finished.

Chairman was Henry A. C. Taylor; other Members present were G. C. Haven, W. C. Whitney, D. Ogden Mills and Robert Goelet. Their initial task was to assemble a staff, but there were innumerable other details to arrange, including the design of a Club flag. They chose a flag with the initials M.C. in red and blue on a white background. By December, they had hired a chief bookkeeper at a monthly wage of $100, a second clerk at $75 a month and two assistant clerks at $60 each. The livery for the two door porters had been ordered—"straight coat with yellow cord facings." The elevator boys were to wear "Norfolk jackets, tight in neck, no vest, and trousers to match." Most crucial was the choice of a cook, and after much deliberation, they engaged Albert Winsbach at a salary of $200 a month, but only on a trial basis. This was a higher salary than anyone except the superintendent received, but nowhere near as high as the $10,000 a year salary that the Waldorf Astoria paid its chef, Xavier Kuesmeier, a sum so startling "for merely running a kitchen" that it evoked passionate editorials in both the American and foreign press.

The vitally important duties of selecting wines and "segars" for the gentlemen were entrusted to special committees. Room rents were fixed at $4 a day for main floor rooms and $2 a day for rooms on the mezzanine floor. There was always a great demand for the rooms and a number of them were taken at once on a long-term basis. Rooms 5 and 6, for instance, were taken by Henry Rouse for one year for $2000. A few years later, those same rooms were rented by Henry E. Huntington and served as his headquarters when he assembled his magnificent book and art collection now at the Huntington Art Museum at San Marino outside Pasadena, California. Rooms 1 and 2 brought in as much as $3000 in annual rental.

There were many other details to be arranged. A Club horse-drawn omnibus service was established to take those Members slaving downtown to the Elevated Station at Sixth Avenue and 53rd Street between the hours of nine and ten in the morning and three-thirty and six in the afternoon; the fare was ten cents one way. The Clubhouse was conveniently located

106

as far as transportation facilities were concerned. Buses went up and down Fifth Avenue and Madison Avenue regularly, but the lumbering vehicles were usually crowded and always slow. Anyone in a hurry and able to afford the price would take the shining new hansom cabs that lined up near the hotels and clubs. Riding in a hansom was expensive—they could carry only two passengers, the driver being mounted on an elevated seat behind with the reins running over the roof—but one made quick time. And since these novel two-wheeled vehicles were equipped with rubber tires, the jars and jolts of the ride were greatly reduced. On February 22, 1894, the Executive Committee authorized an arrangement with a Mr. Dacey to furnish night cab service and when he could not furnish enough cabs, an additional arrangement was entered into with the New York Cab Company.

A revolutionary invention of that period was the telephone. When first demonstrated by Alexander Graham Bell in 1876 at the Philadelphia Centennial Exhibition, most people considered it nothing more than an ingenious mechanical toy. By 1878, however, there were 778 telephones in operation in this country and by 1898 there were one million. In Manhattan, when the Club opened its doors, there were 12,000 subscribers. About a dozen central offices, or "exchanges," were able to establish connections in about forty seconds. The Club, of course, had telephones even while it was under construction, but to have one in one's home was still considered a luxury. A telephone then was a wooden box affixed to the wall, with the mouthpiece on a protruding metal neck. A crank on the box had to be turned several times, then one lifted the earpiece from the metal cradle on the side of the box. An agreeable young woman at "Central" responded and soon made the connection. Long distance calls could only be made by special subscription and on April 9, 1894, the Executive Committee decided to install long-distance telephone service for Members who wanted to make calls to Washington, Boston or even to Chicago.

Many rules had to be established. "All car-riages entering the Courtyard must be driven and kept to the right; dung must be swept up as soon as it is dropped." A special policeman was put on duty from 2 p.m. to 2 a.m. at a salary of $50 a month. There was a small lawn and hedge in front of the Building on Fifth Avenue at that time. The firm of Seibrecht & Wadley was engaged to keep this neatly trimmed during the summer for a payment of a lump sum of $50.

The reading of newspapers and periodicals was a very important pastime at the Club. In addition to all the local papers, the *Boston Herald,* the *Washington Post,* the *Cincinnati Enquirer,* the *Chicago Tribune* and the *Philadelphia Ledger* were also available. In the Library, such frivolous foreign periodicals could be found as *La Vie Parisienne,* the *Figaro Illustré,* the *Strand Magazine* and *Die Fliegenden Blätter.* Soon the orders for the daily papers had to be increased from forty-five to sixty copies.

On January 18, 1894, the Executive Committee met for the first time in the new Building in the Stranger's Dining Room. By 1895 the Membership had increased to 1,030, of whom 884 were Regular Members. The 1894 roster included six Harrimans, six Morgans, six Roosevelts, six Cuttings, five Vanderbilts, four Havemeyers, three Duponts, three Auchinclosses, three Frelinghuysens, two Astors and two Rockefellers. Many other men of importance in industry, finance and politics, such as Elbert Gary, Charles Schwab, Andrew Carnegie, Henry Clay Frick, Henry Phipps, and Sir Henry Bessemer were familiar to the Club—although not all were Members. Coal baron Ned Berwind's castle was a few blocks uptown. The story has been told many times of how the merger of many smaller steel companies into the giant U.S. Steel was conceived in the Library. These men found the Club a natural place to meet, hidden from publicity in perfect privacy. No wonder that the *Encyclopedia Britannica* stated that the Club was founded chiefly as a "club for big businessmen."

Members often gave large dinners. Satterlee in his biography of Morgan tells how, on June 25, 1895, after the successful conclusion of an important deal, the banker wanted to take twenty business friends to his yacht, the *Cor-*

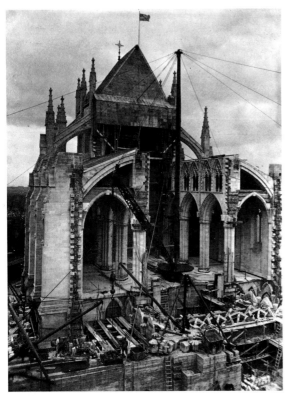

By April of 1925, construction of the National Cathedral in Washington was well underway.

*sair*, for dinner. When bad weather prevented them from boarding the yacht, Morgan took them to the Metropolitan Club. In early September, 1905, during the Peace Conference called by President Theodore Roosevelt in Portsmouth, New Hampshire, to end the Russo-Japanese War, Morgan and Colonel George Harvey gave a dinner at the Club for Special Ambassador Witte, head of the Russian Peace Commission and Baron Rosen, the Russian Ambassador.

But not only business or political matters were discussed in the Club rooms. Although there was at least one Jewish Charter Member, Adolf Ladenburg, and several Catholics, practically the entire Membership at that time was Episcopalian of English and Dutch descent, the "Episcocrats" of the book by Kit and Frederica Konolige, *The Power of their Glory, America's Ruling Class: The Episcopalians.* At the time of the founding of the Metropolitan Club, the main interest of the leaders of the Episcopal establishment was the building of a National

Cathedral in Washington, D.C. The outstanding lay figure in the church was, of course, J. Pierpont Morgan, although he had not been at the initial planning of the project at the home of Charles Carroll Glover on December 8, 1891.. The Konoliges report that Glover frequently discussed the project over lunch and dinner at the Metropolitan Club.

They are probably referring to the Metropolitan Club of Washington, but undoubtedly the same matter was often discussed in the New York Metropolitan Club; many of the men who started and financed the impressive National Cathedral were Club members. Among the Incorporators of the Cathedral in January, 1893, were Members Levi P. Morton, Marshall Field and William C. Whitney. The original money to buy the land on Mount St. Alban, the incomparable site of the Cathedral, was furnished by seven people, four of whom were Members or wives of Members: Mrs. Percy R. Pyne, and Messrs. J. Pierpont Morgan, Cornelius Vanderbilt and William K. Vanderbilt. The ceremonial laying of the cornerstone finally took place at Mount St. Alban on September 29, 1907, in the presence of one of the greatest crowds Washington had ever seen, including Morgan and most of the Episcocrats. In 1927, Club Member Andrew W. Mellon became Treasurer when a major fund-raising campaign was started under the chairmanship of General John J. Pershing.

Unfortunately, no photographs have been found of any of the major social events at the Club during this period. The Executive Committee was adamant on two rules: no reporters and no photographers. On February 15th, 1897, the Minutes read: "Resolved that no reporters be admitted to the Club under no [sic] circumstances." On February 22, 1899, they read: "No portraits or photographs either of Members or of the interior of the Club [may] be given out for publication under any circumstances." And on January 29, 1902, a request from the *Herald Tribune* was turned down with the statement that it was against the rules to photograph the interior.

The judgment of *Town Topics* at the time of the opening of the Clubhouse in 1894 that the

Club would be expensive to run proved correct.

When the Finance and Building Committee discharged itself in April, 1894, they reported that $122,000 were left after all costs for the building had been settled. That seemed like an enormous amount of money but it did not last long. Half of it was lost in the first two years of operation. The deficit for 1895 was $31,605, and for 1896 it was $38,388. Moreover, this loss was before depreciation and before interest on the Income Bonds of $35,000 a year, but payable only if earned.

The financial situation was discussed at length at a Board meeting on January 11, 1897. The Board was reluctant to vote an assessment fearing it might "cause many desirable gentlemen to hesitate in joining the Club." In the hope that the Club would become self-sustaining in the next few years, they voted:

Resolved, that each Governor subscribe a sum not exceeding one thousand dollars annually for three years, payable when called for by the Treasurer, to make up any deficiency that may occur, and prevent the possibility of any assessment on the Members.

This was an unusual and generous measure. The financial statement for the year 1897 showed an income of $22,000, as "subscriptions from twenty-two Governors." The following year, the sum came to $24,000. No such item appeared in 1899; they apparently gave up hope that the Club could be self-sustaining at the current rate of dues.

In 1897, the Union Club was still looking for a site to erect a new building, and a merger of the two clubs was considered. Committees were appointed by both clubs but nothing came of the idea. In 1899, an assessment of $50 per Member had to be voted and a "Committee of Thirteen" appointed to study the finances of the Club. Expenses had been too high in the beginning and it was essential to reduce them.

In 1900, Morgan decided not to stand for re-election as President, but he did remain a Governor until his death in Rome in 1913. While he could not give the Club as much time as

before—he attended only four or five Board Meetings between 1900 and 1910—his interest and concern continued, for, in December, 1911, when the Board decided to purchase the property which is now the Annex for $165,000, J.P. Morgan & Co. lent this amount to the Club at once without collateral. He was not, however, as liberal with the Metropolitan Club as he had been with the New York Yacht Club. In 1898 the latter considered buying two sites on West 44th Street with a frontage of fifty feet for a new clubhouse. At the Board meeting, Morgan, who was Commodore of the Yacht Club from 1897 to 1899, unexpectedly offered to purchase the sites personally as a gift to the Club, with the stipulation that the frontage be seventy-five feet.

If the Club was fortunate to have had an outstanding leader at its helm during the first difficult nine years, it was equally fortunate to have another extraordinary man as its President during the next eleven years, from 1900 to 1911. Born in Vermont in 1824, Levi Parsons Morton was a direct descendant of George Morton, who was the financial agent of the Mayflower Puritans in London and who came over on the ship *Anne* in 1623 with his wife Juliana Carpenter Morton and his five children. Levi's father was the Reverend Daniel Oliver Morton; his mother was Lucretia Parsons, a descendant of Cornet Joseph Parsons, the father of the first child born at Northampton, Massachusetts, on May 2, 1655.

Levi Morton entered business at an early age in Hanover, New Hampshire, and then in Boston, after which he became a partner in a dry-goods store in New York. In 1863 he founded the banking firm of L.P. Morton & Co., with a London branch of which Sir John Rose was the principal member. The American firm assisted in funding the national debt at the time of the resumption of specie payments. The London branch was the fiscal agent of the United States Government from 1873 to 1884, and as such received the $15.5 million awarded by the General Arbitration Board in settlement of the Alabama Claims against Great Britain.

Later Levi Morton entered politics and was elected in 1878 and again in 1881 to the House of Representatives as a Republican. On his retirement from Congress he was appointed United States Minister to France, a post he filled from 1881 to 1885. There in July, 1884, he accepted, on behalf of his Government, Bartholdi's colossal statue, *Liberty Enlightening the World,* now standing in New York Harbor. He was elected Vice President of the United States under President Benjamin Harrison and in 1895 was elected Governor of the State of New York.

His first wife died childless. He then married Anne Livingston Street in 1873 by whom he had five children. One of them, Alice, married Winthrop Rutherfurd, mentioned above as the man whom Consuelo Vanderbilt would have preferred to marry. Another daughter, Helen, married the Duc de Valençay et Sagan at Newport in 1901. One of Winthrop's sons, John P. Rutherfurd, is a Member of the Club today.

The custom of having portraits of past Presidents on the walls of club buildings, the White House, city halls, and similar institutions is well-established. In the Metropolitan Club, the tradition started at the meeting of March 17, 1908, when the Board requested that J.Pierpont Morgan and Levi P. Morton each "furnish a portrait in oil of himself." They obliged promptly, and on May 18, 1908, Morton pre-sented his portrait to the Club; Morgan did the same on June 15th of that year.

Morgan's portrait, hanging in the third-floor foyer leading to the Main Dining Room, was painted five years earlier by the German artist Fedor Encke. Born in 1851 in Berlin, Encke studied painting in Berlin and Weimar, lived in Paris from 1879 to 1883, and visited New York frequently. He painted Theodore Roosevelt, and his portrait of General J.B. Woodward done in 1899 hangs in the Brooklyn Institute.

According to photographer Edward Steichen, when Encke was commissioned to paint the portrait of J.P., the painter found the sittings all too brief and the sitter all too restive. The portrait made slow progress. Encke asked Alfred Stieglitz to recommend a photographer to help him by making a photograph of Morgan. Stieglitz recommended Steichen who describes his meeting with Morgan:

As a result, Encke commissioned me for the job with the inducement that, if I made a photograph of Morgan in the pose Encke was painting that I would be recompensed with orders from Morgan and his family. On the day set for the photographing I had the janitor of the studio building take Morgan's place in a chair arranged as in the unfinished Encke painting, so that I might compose the picture on the ground glass in advance.

Morgan arrived with Encke, took off his large hat, laid a foot-long cigar on the edge of a table, sat in the chair previously occupied by the janitor, and took his habitual Encke portrait pose. After a hasty look at the ground glass I said, "Still," and made the two or three-second exposure required. Then, I took over the making of a negative for myself. I suggested a different position of the hands and a movement of the head. He took the head position, but said, in an irritated tone, that it was uncomfortable, so I suggested he move his head to a position that felt natural. He moved his head several times and ended exactly where it had been "uncomfortable" before, except that this time he took the pose of his own volition. But his expression had sharpened and his body posture became tense, possibly a reflex of his irritation at the suggestion I had made. I saw that a dynamic self-assertion had taken place, whatever its cause, and I quickly made the second exposure, saying, "Thank you, Mr. Morgan," as I took the plate holder out of the camera.

Levi P. Morton (1824-1920)    President 1900-1911

He said, "Is that all?"

"Yes, sir," I answered.

He snorted a reply, "I like you, young man. I think we'll get along first-rate together." Then he clapped his large hat on his massive head, took up his big cigar, and stormed out of the room. Total time, three minutes.

After Encke had escorted Morgan to the elevator, he came back beaming and said that, when Mr. Morgan was about to step into the elevator, he stopped, took out a wad of bills, peeled off five $100 bills and said, "Give this to that young man." *

Steichen went on to tell about Morgan's huge deformed nose and the adventures he had retouching it. This photograph is now displayed in the East Room of the Morgan Library at 36th Street and Madison Avenue.

Levi P. Morton's portrait hanging now in the room named after him was painted by Ellen G. Emmet Rand (Mrs. William Blanchard). Born in San Francisco in 1876, Rand studied in New York and Paris. She became very fashionable in New York, and her portraits of Augustus Saint Gaudens (the great sculptor and friend of Stanford White) and of Benjamin Altman are part of the collection of the Metropolitan Museum of Art. Her portraits of Members Henry A. Du Pont and Henry F. Du Pont hang in the Winterthur Museum.

In May, 1911, at the age of eighty seven, Morton resigned as President of the Club and moved to Washington permanently. His extraordinary life of ninety-six years ended peacefully at his country home, Ellerslie, at Rhinebeck-on-Hudson on May 20, 1920. At his death, the Board of Governors passed the following eulogy to be sent to the family:

The record of Mr. Morton's life may be said to form a very important page in the history of this country since the middle of the nineteenth century.

It is given to few men to attain such varied successes and the scope of his honors, responsibilities and activities comprehended the life of a merchant, banker, statesman and diplomat.

Mr. Morton's abilities were of a high order but perhaps his most useful, if not his very greatest gift, was his ability to meet emergencies and by so moulding his surroundings as to accomplish much

without losing or weakening his hold upon his friends or his influence upon public conditions.

Mr. Morton gave largely and wisely and the memory of his benefactions, his honorable and consistent nature and character is written deeply on the hearts of his surviving friends.

During the twenty years of the Presidencies of Morgan and Morton the Membership remained stable at between 1200 and 1300, of whom about 1000 were Resident Members. The operating deficit proved chronic and was covered by annual assessments of $25 to $40 a member. The Board wanted to increase annual dues to $150 in October, 1906, but met with resistance. Finally, in January, 1907, dues were increased to $125 for Resident and $75 for Non-Resident Members. Taxes on the building had increased from $14,181 in 1895 to $24,000 in 1903.

In 1905, John E. McGowan offered to sell his property at 11 East 60th Street for $200,000; the Board made a counter offer of $140,000, which was not accepted.

In November, 1911, the Board elected one of the Founders and long-time Vice-President of the Club, Frank Knight Sturgis, to the Presidency. His tenancy was the longest of any President so far—fifteen years. Once more, the Club was fortunate to have an outstanding personality at the helm. His life-size portrait, hanging now in the room bearing his name on the Third Floor, describes better than words the superior sort of man he was.

Frank Knight Sturgis was one of the two Founders who lived long enough to see the market collapse of 1929 and the Great Depression. Born in 1851 in New York of an old New England family, he spent his career in the financial field as partner in the brokerage firm of Strong, Sturgis & Co., and was President of the New York Stock Exchange from 1892·to 1894. Active in many fields of sport, he was an accomplished four-in-hand coachman and a member of the Coaching Club from 1882, becoming its President in 1916.

A devotee of racing, he specialized in breeding the "Strawberry Roan" and filled the posi-

Frank K. Sturgis (1851-1932)   President 1911-1926

tion of Chairman of the Board of Stewards of the Jockey Club. He was fond of yachting and kept his yacht *Palmer* at his home in Newport, where he was a Governor of the Newport Casino. He was a gentleman of the old school, meticulous in his dress, and a leader of fashion—the Beau Brummel of his day. At the age of eighty, he was literally carried to his last meeting at the Casino's Governors Room, supported on one side by his nurse and on the other by his valet. He died on June 15, 1932.

The first act of Sturgis' Presidency was to purchase 11 East 60th Street from John McGowan for $165,000, well below the $200,000 asked some years earlier. J. P. Morgan & Co. advanced the funds needed. The building was then remodeled by Ogden Codman at a cost of $53,486.

The purchase price was refinanced the next year when Adrian Iselin offered the Club a long-term loan of $225,000 at 4.5% to pay off J.P. Morgan and Co. Also in 1912, the subway beneath 60th Street was being planned and the Club gave certain consents and easements.

The war in Europe started in 1914, and, in 1917, America entered it. The Board passed a resolution that Members in the service of the United States be exempted from their 1918 dues. A letter from Katherine Woods, of the staff of *The New York Times,* questioning the enthusiasm of the Members in support of the war effort, elicited the reply that in May, 1918, 125 members were in the services of whom three had died, and it further stated that almost 90% of the Club Members were over thirty years of age. Six Members were war casualties and their names, listed on the plaque on the main floor, were:

Captain Riversdale N. Grenfell
Trooper Robert L. Cuthbert
Captain Nicholas L. Tilney
Lieutenant Kenneth S. Goodman
Major Willard Straight
Major James A. Roosevelt

Willard Straight was the husband of Dorothy Whitney, daughter of Founding Father William C. Whitney; Straight had become a Member on May 20, 1913. James A. Roosevelt had joined the Club on December 15, 1914; he was the son of Founder James A. Roosevelt of the Oyster Bay Branch of the family.

As far as finances were concerned, the Club survived World War I without problems. Membership remained constant: in January, 1914, there were 1,371 members of whom 1,114 were Resident Members; at the end of 1919 there were 1,370, of whom 1,102 were Resident Members. The world, however, was changing fundamentally. When the Club was conceived in 1891, wages of factory workers were about twenty cents an hour, but they were slowly edging up, and powerful social forces were at work.

The Guns of August heralded the end of a period of security such as the world has not seen since. They inaugurated a time of war, of inflation, of destruction, of revolution, of the Revolt of the Masses.

By 1920, hourly wage rates had more than tripled. The Wholesale Price Index was 56.2 in 1900; in 1920, it was 154. Then came the post-war commodity and stock exchange collapse of 1921-1923. The effect on the Club was to bring about much higher running costs. In 1919, an assessment of $50 per Member was voted, and in November of that year, the Board voted to increase annual dues to $200 for Resident and

$125 for Non-Resident Members. Eighty-two Members signed a petition objecting to the increase. Federal income taxes had been inaugurated in 1913, and things were not what they used to be. The increase was postponed.

In October, 1921, a $100-per-Member assessment was voted. A year later, the financial position had become so stringent that the Board voted to increase annual dues to $300 for Resident and $135 for Non-Resident Members. Again much objection ensued, and the proposed schedule was never put into effect. In December, 1922, the Board appointed a "Committee of Seven" to make recommendations, one of which was to give consideration to a merger with the Union Club. Committees were appointed by both clubs but in April, 1923, a letter was received from the Union Club stating that "they found a strong sentiment among its membership opposed to a combination of the two clubs."

On December 18, 1917, Congress passed the Volstead Act which, when ratified by thirty-six states, would become the Eighteenth Amendment to the Constitution. It prohibited the manufacture, sale and transportation of intoxicating liquors throughout the country. This disastrous legislation had been imposed on a nation at war by the well-organized militant "drys" mostly centered in the Bible belt of the Midwest. Women were in the forefront of the fight for Prohibition. This Amendment revealed a flaw in the American mentality: the belief that human nature can be changed by legislation. Almost no one in the East and particularly in a city such as New York, including the Members of the Metropolitan Club, had any intention of obeying this law.

None of the men's clubs in the country were

Returning American troops march up Fifth Avenue in a Victory parade in 1919.

very much pleased at the approach of Prohibition. Almost all were having perennial financial problems. A decline in attendance and the loss of revenue from the profitable sales of wines and liquors could prove critical. Since most clubmen belonged to half a dozen or so similar clubs, they consulted each other as to what action to take to meet the new challenge. The problem was on the agenda at every meeting of the boards and committees of the various clubs. At the Metropolitan Club Executive Committee meeting of December 23, 1918, Henry R. Taylor was appointed "a Committee of one with power" to confer with other clubs on the liquor question. A few weeks later Nebraska became the thirty-sixth state to ratify the Amendment.

Most of the spokesmen for the clubs felt that the only way to cope with the problem was to sell the supplies of wine and liquor held by each club to its respective members since the new law did not make it illegal for individuals to own or consume alcoholic beverages. The Metropolitan Club followed this course and the Executive ·Committee at its January 27, 1919, meeting decided that the Club would "sell, in moderate amounts, to Members of the Club certain wines and liquors as Members may request." Faithful past users of the Club's facilities were not to be forgotten. For instance, on March 31st, the Committee authorized the sale of ten cases of champagne, four cases of Bordeaux and one case each of Scotch and rye to the New York Farmers in view of the fact that for twenty years they had held their dinners at the Metropolitan Club. And Henry Taylor's Bridge Dinner Club bought five cases of champagne, one case of Scotch and one case of rye.

As the supplies of wines and liquors moved into private hands, the Club's function was reduced to furnishing set-ups. On September 25th, the minutes read:

RESOLVED, that on and after September 27th, 1919, a service charge of ten cents per glass be made for the serving of drinks from members' bottles and of twenty-five cents corkage on all wines served in the Club.

A question arose concerning the legality of liquor in possession of Club Members but stored on Club premises. The secretary of the Knickerbocker Club addressed a letter to Daniel C. Maper, Commissioner of Internal Revenue, asking whether indeed it had been ruled that private stocks of liquor could be kept in clubs, as reported by a story from Washington. He received no reply. As a result, most clubs, including the Metropolitan Club, fitted a room with lockers which any interested Member was allowed to rent for his own use as he desired. It worked. All clubs kept strictly aloof from any connection with alcoholic beverages in any form, leaving the onus on the individual member. The clubs lost a profitable source of revenue but many a headwaiter was known to have prospered greatly. The country, however, lost much more; it lost respect for the law.

Prohibition drove America's drinking population underground. Speakeasies became popular and men took their friends, wives or girlfriends to these illegal establishments, where cocktails, beer and wine were available and were served with a meal. The cocktail party at home became popular. It was the safest place to drink, and of course the ladies were free to participate. The ladies could not have liked it better.

The decline in the Club's income caused by Prohibition was considerable. In 1914, the profit from the sales of wines and liquors was the largest of any of the services, $8,517, followed by a profit of $6,770 on the sales of cigars. The restaurant showed a loss of $2,515. By 1922, the sales of wine and liquors had shrunk to nothing and the Bar Department showed a loss of $1,895.

In the meantime, membership declined. In January, 1923, it was down to 1,199. In May, the "Committee of Seven" submitted its report to the Board:

The Metropolitan Club has certainly a most admirable location. The Building itself is an architectural monument. It has strength, grace and dignity. The interior is spacious, beautiful, noble. The governing body and the character of the Members are not unworthy of the building, and they should remain so.

The Club must be progressive. When it ceases to progress it will begin to retrograde in obedience to the law that nothing remains stationary, except those things that are dead.

The Club is confronted with a deficit this year, in round figures $120,000. It is probable, or at least possible, that various economies may be instituted that will reduce this deficit without impairing the service of the Members, or in anyway interfering with their comfort. It is certain that the Club dues cannot remain stationary and everything else advance. That some other clubs do not show deficit is only because they have advanced their dues. It seems inevitable that if the dues are not advanced a special assessment of $100 per Member cannot be avoided.

The Club can very easily care for a much larger Membership. It would be unusual and undignified for the Club as a body to attempt to increase the Membership. It is proper for the Members themselves to invite those whom they would like to have in the Club, and whom they think would be desirable members, to permit their names to go before the Membership Committee—they should be encouraged to do this.

We are advised that there are less than a half-dozen Members under thirty years of age. Your Committee, recognizing the importance of inducing young men to join, suggests that a new class of Membership is created and that one hundred members be received between the ages of twenty one and thirty, upon the basis of an initiation fee of $100 and annual dues of $100, such $100 dues to continue for a maximum period of five years after election, and thereafter the regular dues.

They also recommended the creation of a new class of "Foreign Members" with entrance fees of $100 and annual dues of $50. They suggested installing a small gymnasium, equipping it along the lines of those on "the best

One speakeasy is padlocked but scores more continued to flourish as Americans struggled uneasily with Prohibition.

trans-Atlantic liners," increasing the number of bedrooms; appointing an entertainment Committee; restoring the squash court, and permitting smoking in the Dining Room.

In retrospect, the advice that "the Club must be progressive," seems to have heralded a fundamental shift in the composition of the Club which has continued to the present. The Club ceased to be composed almost exclusively of well-born, rich men of Anglo-Saxon or Dutch descent and of middle or advanced age. The push for younger men and the creation of the classification of Foreign Members would soon lead to the admission of Women Members, at first only widows, but later other non-related women. The Club became a much broader-based, but still exclusive, social club. Nevertheless, the financial problems continued to be very serious because of the large and expensive Clubhouse.

Finally, a special Membership Meeting was called for December 12, 1923, and the Board succeeded in securing enough votes to put through an increase in annual dues to $225 for Resident and $150 for Non-Resident Members. Even this increase was not nearly enough to put the Club on a really sound financial basis, but it enabled operations to show a surplus of $7,625 for 1924. It also laid the basis for the restructuring of the cumbersome debt, which was accomplished in 1925, when a five-year 5% first-mortgage loan for $1.5 million was obtained from the Mutual Life Insurance Company of New York and, with the proceeds, all existing debts were paid off. With the future of the Club secure, the Membership increased again and, under the stimulus of the stock market boom, reached a new high of 1,436 in 1929.

The problems of the Club having been solved, Sturgis decided to relinquish the leadership. At the Annual Meeting in February, 1926, he said he had been either Vice President or President for twenty-six years and that should be enough for any man. The time had come to elect a new President.

# Chapter 10

# A LA RECHERCHE DU TEMPS PERDU

Reflecting now on the two decades following the opening of the Club to its Members in 1894, one recognizes a period in which a charming old world died and a new, brash one took its place. The railroads had already been born; they had their beginnings a few years after the Battle of Waterloo. The Baltimore and Ohio Railroad was incorporated in 1827. By 1840, 2800 miles of track had been laid, and on the eve of the War between the States, this had increased to 30,000 miles. In 1869, the first transcontinental route was completed, and the decade from 1880 to 1890 saw feverish activity—70,000 miles of track were laid. The much greater speed and convenience of the railways quickly drove the stagecoach, which had pioneered the opening of the West, into retirement.

Except for inter-city traffic, the universal means of transportation was still horse-drawn conveyances of all kinds. When Morgan wished to have dinner at the Club in 1895, he was driven from his house at 219 Madison Avenue in his landau or his brougham drawn by two horses. The public carriage for hire was a brougham equipped with a meter, known as a hack. The French called it a coupé. The name "landau" came from the city in western Ger-

many where it originated and the "brougham" was named after its inventor, Lord Brougham. A smaller, more agile cab was the "hansom," named after Joseph Hansom (1803-1882) of Leicestershire, England. This was a two-wheeled carriage, highly maneuverable, which could accommodate two passengers. The driver sat on a high seat at the back and usually wore a black felt top hat and light-colored box coat. These cabs lined the sidewalks in front of all hotels and clubs waiting for passengers.

Many other varieties of horse-drawn vehicles were available for different purposes—formal, informal, sporting or utilitarian. Hay wagons competed with beer trucks drawn by enormous Percherons. In the country, the *vis-à-vis* was popular in the summer, and so was the Stanhope gig. For going to the station, taking children to school, for the opera and theater, there was the Private Omnibus or Opera Bus which could accommodate eight or ten people. Although today this world seems far away, it certainly is not: many men or women of seventy-five and over can remember it clearly.

Those years before the internal combustion engine and the income tax were also the last years of the great social extravaganzas. Society spent lavishly on balls and parties, on country

*Ribbons*

117

estates and on travel. A favorite sport of the rich was yachting. Morgan was probably the leader in this sport and his several yachts, all named appropriately enough *Corsair,* were the talk of the world. Many of the early Members owned magnificent yachts. Jack Astor had his *Nourmahal* (the Light of the Harem), Ogden Goelet had his *Mayflower* (he died on board), and Alfred Vanderbilt his *Wayfarer.*

The smartest diversion of society from 1875 to the coming of the automobile was four-in-hand coaching. Colonel William Jay had brought back to friends at the Knickerbocker Club stories of his drives with the Duke of Beaufort, who had sought amusement in reviving the pageantry and exhilaration of the stage-coaches of the pre-railroad age. With the purpose of establishing four-in-hand driving in the United States, the Coaching Club was started in 1875, and six of the nine founding members later became Members of the Metropolitan Club. In order to qualify for membership, a candidate had to be able to drive four horses and own a drag, or at least a one-fourth interest in a drag. Two types of vehicles could appropriately be used—the Road Coach and the Park Drag. The Four-in-Hand Park Drag, as the name indicated, was strictly for driving around the Park and avenues.

It was an expensive sport. The coach line run in 1903 by James Hazen Hyde, the millionaire New York financier, between New York and Lakewood, New Jersey needed ten relays of horses and the services of twenty-five men to make the changes each of which took less than two minutes of time. The fifty-two horses involved an outlay of between $20,000 and $25,000. Coaching became a craze. Even the ladies had their Ladies Four-in-Hand Club. Mrs. Thomas Hastings was its president; she was an outstanding coachwoman and drove in all kinds of weather. Only gentlemen or ladies, of course, could understand the lure and the challenge of coaching. The press could not and one reporter wrote:

The craze for novelty must be overpowering when it will induce a sane man to ride nine hours in a coach when he can make the same trip in less than two hours in a comfortable railroad car.

The Brunswick Hotel on Madison Square was a favorite starting place and gaily adorned four-in-hand coaches lined up in front of it, dashed up Fifth Avenue into Central Park, and headed north to the Westchester Country Club where they arrived about an hour and three quarters later. Operated by James R. Roosevelt

Coaching enthusiasts salute each other in Central Park in May, 1910. Coaching etiquette required that hats be tipped on the first meeting, but a nod would suffice on a second encounter. If two coaches met a third time, they could pass each other without acknowledgement.

and C. Oliver Iselin, both Members, the fare was $2.50 one-way with a box seat fifty cents extra, and the journey required one change of horses. A few years later, the Coaching Club decided to put the coach *Pioneer* on the road from the Holland House to the Ardsley Club at Ardsley-on-Hudson and appointed George Read, Frederic Bronson (both Members) and Reginald Rives to operate it. They ran daily except Sundays, leaving Holland House at 10:15 a.m. and arriving at the club at 12:50. The return trip started at 3:25 p.m. Fare was $3 one-way, $5 round trip with a box seat $1 extra each way. They ran this route from 1898 to 1906. When Frederic Bronson died on a trip to Sicily in 1900, Alfred G. Vanderbilt, who had developed into an excellent whip, took his place. He drove many roads in this country and maintained public coaches in England, one from London to Brighton lasting eight seasons.

Strong arms, endurance and a great deal of skill were required to handle four horses and a coach. An experienced coachman gave this advice to a novice: "Never let your horses know you are driving them, or, like women, they may get restive. Do not pull and haul and stick your arms akimbo, but keep your hands as though you were playing the piano."

The aspect of sport driving, however, which was most familiar to the public was the so-called "carriage parade"—an unorganized form of driving in which members of society drove about city parks and avenues in order to see and be seen by their peers. In New York, every afternoon between the hours of four and seven o'clock, Society took the air in a wide assortment of vehicles, much to the enjoyment of sidewalk spectators.

The Coaching Club had its own, more formal, version of the parade. Its first public parade was held in April, 1876, led by its President, Colonel Jay, in bottle-green coat, with gilt buttons, silk topper, yellow-striped waistcoat, and nosegay. Club Members were sticklers for form. The driver's apron had to be folded, when not in use, outside out, and *de rigueur* were the artificial flowers affixed to the throat-latch of each horse. The third President of the Metropolitan Club, Frank K. Sturgis, was the

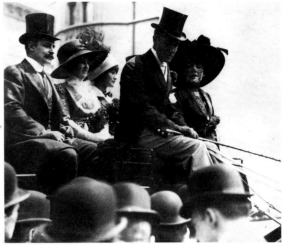

Elegantly and correctly dressed for coaching are (left to right) C. De L. Oelrichs, Miss Howland, Virginia Alexander, John Alexander, Jr., and Mrs. C. De L. Oelrichs.

most celebrated amateur whip, but Robert Livingston Gerry, F. Augustus Schermerhorn, Alfred G. Vanderbilt, C. Oliver Iselin and Theodore Havemeyer were close rivals.

After the opening of the Metropolitan Club Building in its superb location on Central Park, the activities of the Coaching Club shifted more and more to the Club. For a number of years, the Spring Meet started before its doors. On Saturday afternoon, May 4, 1901, to quote *The Coaching Club*, published privately by Reginald W. Rives in 1935:

The twenty-first Parade made as pretty a scene as ever was seen by frequenters of Central Park. Ideal weather favored the occasion and the members of the club and their equipages and the ladies who rode furnished a picture that delighted the throngs lining the route.

The meet was at the Metropolitan Club corner, in Fifth Avenue, at 60th Street. Members of the Coaching Club entertained their parties at luncheon in the Metropolitan Club at two o'clock. The coaches, as fast as they arrived, were drawn up in line on the west side of the Avenue in readiness for the start.

There were seven drags, one less than when the first parade took place in New York twenty-five years ago, and each was pronounced to be perfection in all the details of equipment, which have such an absorbing interest for coaching enthusiasts.

Fifth Avenue, and all the open space about the entrance to the park, were densely packed by the enthusiastic crowd that congregated to see the start. Shortly after four o'clock the whips and their guests came out from their luncheon, and, crossing the avenue under an escort of blue coats, were soon on the coaches.

When Colonel Jay, at the head of the line, set his spicy team going, there was a rattling of bars and the parade was in motion. Turning into the park the line moved briskly away and out of sight.

The route was up the East Drive to the Mall, thence along the West Drive to the circle near 106th Street, where the coaches were reviewed by Colonel Jay.

Then followed an exact description of the occupants of each drag and details of the ladies' dresses. It was reported that Mrs. Jay wore a very stylish costume of silver-gray embroidered crepe over white silk and a crowned black-straw hat dressed with black-and-white feathers. She also wore a black feather boa and a huge bunch of yellow jonquils as a corsage.

There were many excursions over the years. A famous trip took place on June 6, 1894, as a result of a challenge to the Coaching Club by Dr. W. Seward Webb who had become a member in 1887. Twenty teams made the 318-mile trip from New York to Webb's estate in Shelbourne, Vermont, in four days. Of the twelve gentlemen coachmen, eight were Members of the Metropolitan, including Webb's brother-in-law W. K. Vanderbilt, Frank Sturgis, Perry Belmont and W. C. Whitney. As the sun sank over Lake Champlain on June 9th, they arrived at Shelbourne Farms where they relaxed over the weekend as Webb's guests and

Robert L. Gerry turns his coach into Central Park just opposite the Metropolitan Club, with Mrs. Edmund L. Baylies beside him on the box. Seated behind are Miss Theresa Iselin, Miss Babcock, Mr. William P. Burden and Mr. Bradish G. Johnson. The photograph was probably taken in 1902.

returned to New York *via* railroad.

In May, 1903, one excursion started from the Metropolitan Club at 10:15 a.m., thence proceeded to Tarrytown, across the Hudson by ferry, on to lunch at the St. George Hotel at Nyack, then to Tuxedo, and back to the Metropolitan Club the next day.

This outing required five changes of horses.

Popular also were excursions to the Claremont Inn on Riverside Drive, such as the one which took place on May 7, 1910. Luncheon was "served at small tables, which were placed on the west veranda overlooking the Hudson River." Among the participants on that trip were the Misses Irene and Mildred Sherman and Miss Catherine L. Hamersley.

One trip was especially memorable. It took place on Friday, October 7, 1910, on a dreary afternoon. People walking along the north side of 60th Street held umbrellas to protect themselves from the drizzle. As they came to the Metropolitan Club Building, they stopped to watch a coach drawn by four horses with a group of men on top emerge from the Courtyard. What they saw was the last coach-and-four ever to pass through the portals of the Club.

That rainy afternoon Mr. Reginald W. Rives, the leading coachman of his day, was seated on the box of the famous road coach *Pioneer*. Built in 1898 for the Coaching Club by Brewster & Company of New York City, the *Pioneer* was a reproduction, except for its brakes, of the coaches used in England for almost fifty years prior to the advent of the steam railroads. From the standpoint of proportion, engineering and craftsmanship, it was considered the finest coach ever built, a magnificent example of the coach-builder's art. It was licensed by the City of New York as Hack 3044 and the hack license is still in place below the near lamp. In 1929 and 1931 it won First Prize, Plate and Ribbon at the National Horse Shows, and has found an honored and permanent resting place in the New-York Historical Society's Carriage Collection at Central Park West and 76th Street.

Behind Mr. Rives on that rainy October day were seated seven other members of the Coaching Club. They were Club Members Jennings, Haven and Fahnestock, and also Messrs. Browning, Searle Barclay, W. G. Loew, and Captain Duncan Elliott. Alfred G. Vanderbilt had intended to take part in the drive but he had to be at Brockton, Massachusetts, exhibiting his horses. Their destination was Southampton, Long Island, one-hundred-and-four miles away, where they were the guests of Mr. Henry E. Coe.

Starting from the Courtyard of the Metropolitan Club, the *Pioneer* ran by way of Elmhurst and Queens to Hempstead where the last stage of the day ended at the Meadow Brook Club. The gentlemen spent the night there, having dined with Mr. W. Goadby Loew. They resumed the drive on Saturday morning, leaving at twenty minutes before nine, and reached Southampton at half-past five o'clock. The day's run was by way of Massapequa, Babylon, Islip, Sayville, Bayport, Center Moriches, Westhampton and Good Ground.

The gentlemen returned to New York on Sunday, some by train and some on board Alfred Vanderbilt's steam yacht, *Wayfarer*. Some years later, Mr. Rives, reminisced nostalgically about some of his coaching feats in the Courtyard of the Club and that last departure in the *Pioneer*:

Looking now, as I pass, at the closed gates of the Metropolitan Club, I am reminded that I am the only coachman who has driven a coach-and-four in and out of that courtyard, at Fifth Avenue and 60th Street. This I did on three separate occasions, the first as a result of bets. At a dinner of the Coaching Club, I casually remarked that it would be a nice thing if the members could drive into the courtyard and pick up their parties for the annual drive through Central Park after luncheon at the club. To this, Fairman Rogers, a civil engineer, replied:

"It's a mechanical impossibility to drive a coach-and-four in and out of this court. What a mistake not to have enlarged it by several feet and made it practical!"

I challenged this statement and offered to prove that it could be done. I made two bets; one for a dinner for the nine persons present, with Mr. F. K. Sturgis, and the other for $50, with Mr. G. G. Haven. I stipulated that I should make the attempt with my own park drag and four horses. An inter-

Reginald W. Rives was the coachman on this, the last trip leaving the Courtyard of the Club, on October 7, 1910, on his way to Southampton.

The Claremont Inn on Riverside Drive near 125th Street was a popular destination for coaching parties. On May 25, 1895, Charles F. Havemeyer arrives with his coach and guests.

esting feature of the accomplishment was that my drag had just been painted and varnished; I drove in and out at a trot, and the front wheels did not even touch the mud guards. On two later occasions, I drove the road coach *Pioneer* in and out. This was somewhat more difficult, as the body of a road coach is slightly wider than that of a park drag. The last time was the start of the drive to Mr. Henry Coe's country seat at Southampton, Long Island. Feeling that I would never again drive a coach in the streets of New York, I had photographs taken, showing the coach in and coming out of the courtyard.

One of the photographs taken by Haab on that afternoon of October 7, 1910, has graced the cover of the Club's menus for many years.

One of the men riding on top of the *Pioneer* that day continued the coaching tradition for another fifteen years against all odds. Member Harris Fahnestock had been a member of the Coaching Club since 1908 and took part in the last formal parade on May 7, 1910. That parade went from the Clubhouse to the Claremont Inn and at one point "was cut in two by an automobile bus." Mr. Fahnestock maintained his preference for a gentlemen's carriage and continued to drive daily through the streets of New York and Central Park in one of his colorful coaches-and-four with high-stepping chestnut horses, a silk-hatted driver and a pair of uniformed footmen. He drove his guests from his house at 15 East 66th Street to the opera or the theater in his six-passenger horse-drawn opera bus. When his wife died in 1930 he discontinued coaching in New York, the last member of the Coaching Club to do so. After that he confined his coaching to the country near his summer house in Lenox, Massachusetts. But when his coachman Edward Capp, who had served him for forty-five years, died, he gave up coaching altogether and presented his collection of coaches and carriages, one of the finest extant, to the New-York Historical Society.

The time of coaching was drawing to an end. In 1907, the Coaching Club decided to abandon public coaching "because the rapid introduction of the automobile both for pleasure and commercial purposes forced the issue, it being evident there was no room for both on the road, and the excessive speed of the automobile far outdid the coach-and-four." The parades of the drags, so enthusiastically watched by the people of New York, ceased after 1911.

It was a colorful period and those few fortunates who belonged to that era and who still survive may say nostalgically with Talleyrand: "Qui n'a pas connu l'Ancien Régime, n'a pas connu la douceur de vivre."

New Yorkers were passionate cyclists in the 1890s, and Riverside Drive was often crowded with them.

Just when the new Club was being planned in 1891, a new craze struck New York seemingly overnight and that was the bicycle craze. One reason for the choice of the site bought from the Duchess of Marlborough was its proximity to the park and the convenience it offered for riding, driving and bicycling. The bicycle itself was not new. Its ancestor in Europe was the "dandy horse" used as far back as 1790 in Paris. Its two wheels supported the rider who propelled himself forward with his feet on the ground. Then a paddle was affixed on the front wheel. Since the larger the wheel, the greater the speed, it was only the length of the legs that limited the size of the front wheel. The largest wheel was sixty-four inches in diameter. McLaughlin's invention of the treadle and chain in 1839 created the modern bicycle. It was the invention of the pneumatic tire by John Dunlop in 1888, however, that gave the bicycle its wide appeal, not only to men but to the ladies as well.

Soon the whole city was pursuing happiness on wheels. The church increased the popularity of the sport by condemning it from the pulpit. "You cannot serve God and skylark on a bicycle," said the Reverend Asa D. Blackburn, pastor of the Church of the Stranger. But the young, smart set took to the sport enthusiastically. They organized the Michaux Club on Broadway near 53rd Street, where professional racers gave them lessons riding single and tandem wheels. On fine weekday mornings, feminine cyclists thronged the drives of Central Park. Lillian Russell and her friend, Marie Dressler, took up cycling in order to "slenderize" their figures.

Miss Russell became the talk of the town. In a white-serge cycling costume with stylish leg-of-mutton sleeves, she pedaled through the

124

park, making two circuits of the reservoir before stopping to rest. Her bicycle was a national sensation. Entirely gold-plated, its mother-of-pearl handlebars bore her monogram in diamonds and emeralds. The hubs and spokes of the wheels were set with many jewels that sparkled in the sun. Knowing New Yorkers asserted that it was a gift from her great and good friend, "Diamond Jim" Brady.

New Yorkers never wearied of wheeling. Young people made up parties, properly chaperoned, to ride through the park and along Riverside Drive to Grant's Tomb, to lunch or dine at the Claremont Inn and return in the afternoon or evening. At the Claremont, in spring and summer, people dined out of doors, in a garden strung with gay Japanese lanterns, and after dark Riverside Drive seemed alive with fireflies, so numerous were the varicolored bicycle lamps flashing under the trees.

Although the craze was pretty well established when the Metropolitan Clubhouse was being designed, the architect failed to make any

Lillian Russell displays a neatly-turned ankle and her custom-made bicycle in this studio photograph.

provision for stabling the wheels of Members. In the summer of 1894, requests were made to the Board of Governors to provide space for that purpose, but the manager thought it was not possible. Upon urging, he decided in November, 1894, to rebuild the West Wine Room to provide stabling for twenty-five wheels. A monthly rent of $4 for each bike was charged.

In April, 1895, a Committee composed of H. T. Carey and B. K. Stevens was formed to take care of the Bicycle Department. The North Alley was fitted for stalls and the whole alley and the side were covered with a temporary floor and with frames to hold fifty bikes. The next month the Committee was enlarged to five members and an attendant was hired. By January, 1896, they had employed an expert mechanic to make the needed repairs to bikes. He was to be paid $60 a month or $18 a week less $3 a week for board.

Nevertheless, all these preparations seemed insufficient, and the Bicycle Committee cast its eyes on another space—the Bowling Alley Room. Bowling had not proved very popular or profitable, so $2500 was voted to convert the Bowling Alley into stands for bicycles. Bathing facilities were built for the tired, dusty men to freshen up after their workout and a direct stairway led to where the Bar is now so that refreshments were close at hand.

These years saw the high point of the bicycle craze. The influence of tens of thousands of cyclists began to be felt. Cobblestones gave way to asphalt where the endless procession could speed with pleasure, only occasionally interrupted by cops, who once arrested the Duke of Marlborough for "scorching." The Duke pretended he was merely relaxing from his labors as suitor for the hand (and fortune) of Consuelo Vanderbilt.

Now that the Club had all the space and facilities for the flourishing traffic on wheels, a new conveyance that would soon throw cycling to the winds made its appearance. On Decoration Day, 1896, New Yorkers saw for the first time the frightening new horseless carriage. Early in the new century, just as the automobile had driven the four-in-hand coaches into retirement, it made life more and more hazardous and unpleasant for the bicyclists. In 1904 the bowling alleys were rebuilt, and this time they were converted into Squash Tennis Courts at a cost of $13,420.

In 1896, a few years after the opening of the Clubhouse, the new vehicle, which within a generation would change the world beyond recognition, made its appearance. In 1886, Gottfried Daimler patented his high-speed internal combustion engine. The automobile, the frightening new horseless carriage, was soon the talk of the town.

Most New Yorkers were introduced to the automobile for the first time on Decoration Day in 1896 when the editor of *Cosmopolitan*, John Brisbane Walker, organized a race from City Hall to the Ardsley Country Club in Tar-

rytown and back and offered a prize of $3,000 to the winner. An imported Benz competed against three American automobiles made by the brothers Duryea. One of the Duryea cars took the prize. The Duryea firm shortly thereafter set up a "demonstrator" at a store on Broadway. It was advertised as being noiseless, odorless and absolutely safe! New Yorkers were skeptical: although the firm received orders for thirteen vehicles, none of them was bought by a resident of the city.

Naturally the rich were the first to take up the new fad, among them, naturally, many of the Members of the Metropolitan Club. The Astors were typical, and, as Virginia Cowles relates in her book about the family, their garage at Ferncliffe, the magnificent estate they owned near Rhinebeck-on-the Hudson, was stocked

Drivers outside the Vanderbilt mansion on Fifth Avenue at the start of a tour from New York to St. Louis in 1904.

126

The author with his father in a 1910 Adler, Easter, 1911.

with eighteen cars, ranging from a red runabout for Jack's wife, Ava, to a seventeen-horsepower Bentley racer. During the summer of 1900, Jack Astor, William K. Vanderbilt, Harry Payne Whitney and O.H.P. Belmont (all Members) staged a number of races on the beach at Newport, and several weeks later someone organized an obstacle race in which a dozen cars careened wildly around dummies of horses, dogs, children and policemen.

The Automobile Club of America was organized in 1898, and in the autumn of 1899 crowds turned out to see the latest foolish fancy of the idle rich—an automobile parade winding its way from the Waldorf to the Claremont Inn. They were forced to follow a devious route, for the "devil wagons" were still forbidden to enter Central Park. A few months later, Jack Astor with Ava and their son Vincent rode down Fifth Avenue in a surrey with a steam engine under the seat. Crowds gathered on the sidewalks to wave them on when the seat suddenly became unbearably hot. The engine had caught fire and there was no alternative but the decision to leap ignominiously out of the burning vehicle.

Nevertheless, the future belonged to the automobile and it changed the world. The very first automobile show in America took place from November 3 to 9, 1900, at the old Madison Square Garden and was promptly dubbed the Horseless Horse Show. Society mobbed the show under the leadership of the irrepressible Mrs. Stuyvesant Fish and John Jacob Astor. Soon there were auto-cabs lined up in front of hotels and clubhouses. They charged thirty cents for the first half mile and ten cents for

each additional quarter mile. They were only for the affluent in those days.

More astounding innovations were to come. On December 17, 1903, Orville Wright made the first flight in an airplane at Kitty Hawk, North Carolina. Electricity was replacing gaslight as gaslight had replaced the candle before. The income tax first appeared—modestly—in 1913 and increased until it became almost confiscatory. At the end of this first twenty-year period in the Club's history came the Great War, and in the words of Lord Grey, "the lamps [went out] all over Europe" and over the rest of the Western world.

Club records give the names of Members, the level of fees and dues, the revenues and expenses. They tell us little of how often the Members used the Club, what they did or said, how they dressed, or what they ate or drank or smoked. In English clubs, certainly during the last century, members wore hats inside the clubhouse. A history of the Reform Club in London relates that when George Macauley Booth was elected a member in 1899, his cousin and seconder, Rupert Potter, a member since 1854, invited him to his first luncheon. When, after a drink, they rose to go into the Coffee Room (as the Dining Room is called), the older man headed for the cloak room. "Where are you going?" asked Booth. "To get my hat," was the reply. "Your hat? What do you want with your hat?" "Everyone wears hats at luncheon." "My father never does." "Yes, I know, George, but Charles was always a bit of a Bohemian."

Today it is difficult to determine what the custom was at the Metropolitan when it first opened its doors in 1894. *Harper's Weekly* published an illustrated article on the new Clubhouse in its March 10, 1894, issue, a few weeks after the opening. One picture shows the Grand Stairway with two gentlemen walking down the stairs, one with a top hat. A picture of the Main Dining Room shows two diners without hats. But a view of the Lounging Room has two gentlemen, one seated and one standing, both with top hats. Furthermore there is a story, of uncertain origin, that it was the fashion for Members to sit in the Great Hall for drinks, hats on and facing the bar, which then was situated underneath the Great Staircase.

In England, this custom was dying out around 1900, although in political clubs like the Reform, it was prolonged by the presence of many M.Ps.: hats were worn regularly in the House of Commons until World War I. The custom probably died out somewhat earlier in New York. To modern eyes it seems a strange custom, and inconvenient to boot. But to Rupert Potter it was a tradition, a self-inflicted discipline over formlessness, a standard to maintain. And, as Cleveland Amory's curmudgeon would say, a standard, however obscure, is better than what exists today—no standard at all. One has only to look out of the Club windows on Fifth Avenue on any summer's day to see hordes of people walking almost nude, clad merely in a pair of trunks: a return to the primitive, to barbarism.

If the blackballing of a well-known applicant for membership to a well-known club was of great interest to everyone and to the gossip press, the expulsion of a member was even more interesting. The constitution of every club contained a provision permitting the board of governors to expel, suspend or censure a member for ungentlemanly behavior. Probably the most famous single story in the history of American clubdom was that of the expulsion from and later re-instatement to the Union Club of the French Count Loubat.

On the evening of November 28, 1881, Joseph Florimond, Duc de Loubat, joined some friends at the Union Club of which he was a life member. Count Loubat, as he was generally known, was distinguished by family background and accomplishment, although not a wealthy man. That night, he fell into conversation with a man named Henry Turnbull and the name of a woman came up. Turnbull later claimed that the Count used language detrimental to the reputation of the woman. This the Count denied. The exact language was never established in the subsequent proceedings.

Turnbull must have been a narrow-minded and headstrong man. In retrospect, his insistence over an incident as minor as this produced a *cause célèbre* which dragged on for years. Even though the Count went so far as to tender his apologies to the woman involved, the quarrel continued with increasing acrimony until the case, whether one of virginity or veracity, became a national scandal. Finally, on May 15, 1882, six months after the event, the governing committee of the Union Club expelled the Count.

The Count immediately started a court action, which lasted for many years and became generally known as "the Union Suit." His counsel was the celebrated Joseph H. Choate, later a Member of the Metropolitan Club. Choate lost the case in the first instance, but appealed. Two years later, in 1886, at the General Term of the Supreme Court, he obtained a verdict in favor of Count Loubat. Although reinstated, the Count never set foot inside the Union Club again.

Obviously, this infamous affair alerted club governors to the perils of lightly considered expulsions. Loubat's main defense, next to alleged bias, was "whether or not the governing committee, which had not had a full attendance at the time of the vote to expel, had any right to do so." When the Founding Fathers drafted the Constitution of the Metropolitan Club, they benefitted from the costly experience of the Union Club and determined that only the Board of Governors could have such power and then only if fifteen of the twenty-five governors voted affirmatively, that is to say, sixty percent. Subsequently, this was changed to a majority. In addition, the conduct of the accused Member had to be found "to have endangered the welfare, interest or character of the Club." In such a case, a Member "shall forfeit his Membership," or he may be censured or suspended for a suitable period. This rule was laid down in Article XVIII, Section 6, of the Original Constitution, now Article III, Section 12, of the present Constitution, the adherence to which every new Member has pledged by signing the Constitution Book.

In its history, the Board of the Metropolitan Club has exercised its disciplinary powers many times right up to the present. Just a few days after the Clubhouse was opened to Members, Arthur B. Twombly apparently had a little too much to drink and made a nuisance of himself. On March 5, 1894, he received a letter: "The Executive Committee regrets to inform you that your conduct in the Card Room of the Club on Saturday, March 3rd, was very offensive to several Members and to notify you that any repetition of such conduct will be reported to the Board of Governors for their action under Article XVIII, Section 6, of the Constitution." On March 12th, a letter of apology was received from Mr. Twombly and the matter was dropped.

Another incident occurred in March, 1896. George W. Smalley took another gentleman into the Ladies' Dining Room, and, even worse, took three women through the main entrance to show them the Clubhouse, despite the fact that the doorkeeper respectfully informed him that this was against the rules. He was ordered to appear before the Executive Committee to offer an explanation and when he did not keep the appointment, the matter was referred to the full Board for action. He talked himself out of being expelled.

Most of the infractions of Club rules involved nonpayment of debts or passing rubber checks. In 1912, one Member received a jail sentence in England for some "crime or misdemeanor" and was promptly expelled from the Club. One case, however, excited a great deal of comment at the time and was taken very seriously. It happened as follows, according to the minutes of the proceedings before the Board of Governors on February 20, 1906:

Specification:

That on the morning of Wednesday, January 17th, the said John J. Jones [not actual name], in one of the public rooms of the Club, to wit, the West Lounging Room, addressing Mr. A. Newbold Morris, a member of the Board of Governors, assailed the management of the Club, the Board of Governors, and the several Members of said Board using the ungentlemanly, coarse and abusive epithets following, that is to say: "The Governors of the Club are a d——d lot of S—————, and a d——d lot of thieves every one of them. They go down on their knees to beg men to join the Club, and when a good man comes before them, they turn him down." Repeating said epithets several times. That at the time of the occurrence there were present in the room besides Mr. Jones and Mr. Morris one or more Members of the Club.

When he was ordered to appear before the Board, Jones stated that his language was inaccurately quoted but he admitted having made intemperate remarks, claimed to have apologized to Mr. Morris and the Executive Committee, expressed sorrow for the remarks he did make and prayed for consideration.

Of the twenty-five Members of the Board, sixteen were present at the meeting of February 20, 1906. They were asked to vote separately on four motions and were polled individually: first, whether the charge had been fully established; second, whether the excuse presented was sufficient; third, whether Jones's conduct was such as to endanger the welfare, interest and character of the Club; and fourth, whether Jones should be declared to have forfeited his Membership and his name be stricken from the roll of Members. Fifteen Members voted affirmatively on each motion, Mr. Morris abstaining. . . .

Smoking a hundred years ago was as much a subject of heated pros and cons as it is at present. Smoking then usually meant either a pipe or a cigar. The cigarette addiction was practically unknown until World War I. The gentlemen of the period might smoke a cigarette occasionally, for it became fashionable to light a Russian cigarette between the roast and the joint at the enormous dinners of the time "in order to clear the palate." But the desire to smoke became an irrepressible craving to the soldiers of both sides under the tension of trench warfare and has been growing ever since.

Smoking has had its champions. Winston Churchill rationed himself to fifteen cigars a day. He once wrote, "How can I tell that my temper would have been as sweet or my companionship as agreeable if I had abjured from my youth the Goddess of Nicotine." Fortunately, he did not become a visitor to the Metropolitan Club and an Honorable Life Guest until after the prohibition on smoking in the Clubhouse had been lifted.

As a matter of fact, smoking was regarded as an offensive habit at the time the Club was formed, and the Founding Fathers, following English club custom, provided for a special Smoking Room to which the addicts were confined. The original plans show it to be on the third floor, in what is now the Frank K. Sturgis Room, next to the Breakfast Room and near the Main Dining Room. Those who wanted to enjoy their cigar after lunch or dinner could go there. No records or pictures survive to show how the Smoking Room looked, but one may imagine comfortable, upholstered chairs with well-dressed men in them enjoying large Belinda Belindas while talking to their friends, reading the *Wall Street Journal* or just staring into the distance.

In 1907, the Board relaxed the regulations a little, and smoking was permitted in the Main Dining Room after nine p.m. By 1925, smoking, now largely of cigarettes, had become widespread and the only room off-limits to smokers was the Ladies' Restaurant. By then women had begun to smoke more and more, and soon that last prohibition disappeared. As the habit of smoking of expensive cigars declined, the Club lost a very important source of income. In 1914, for instance, the restaurant sales amounted to $79,630 and the sale of wines and liquors to $42,741. But the sales of cigars reached $47,152, on which a profit of $6,770 was made, almost as much as the $8,517 earned on wines. The restaurant lost money. As late as 1948, the dinner menu devoted the whole back page to a list of some thirty different brands of cigar available to Members. The most expensive was a Romeo-Julieta Churchill which cost $1 each.

Fashionable men's clubs in the nineteenth century discouraged their members from bringing guests into the club buildings. London's Carlton Club allowed no guests at all until quite recently. Others had a rather complicated system of admitting "strangers," as guests were called in England, to the clubhouse, but only to specific rooms and under many restrictions.

Many of the eighteenth-century mansions of the British aristocracy had a strangers' wing alongside the family wing. Webster defines a stranger as "A foreigner; one of another place; one unknown or at least nor familiar;" but also as "A guest; a visitor." To modern American ears, the first definitions are more familiar.

When the Reform Club built its *palazzo*-like clubhouse in Pall Mall in 1836, there was a special Strangers' Room where members could entertain guests, provided they were Reformers. The Metropolitan Club followed a similar pattern. It had a special wing for strangers on the mezzanine to the left of the main entrance door. The little room downstairs, now the telephone room, was then the Strangers' Waiting Room. A stairway leads one flight up to what was called the Strangers' Reception Room in the original architect's plans. It was a lovely room with a large fireplace in one corner. Adjoining it was a smaller Strangers' Dining Room. Food was delivered from the main kitchen on the roof by dumbwaiter. In the Club's Constitution a Stranger was defined as a person not residing within fifty miles of New York and not having an office there. He could be given the right to use the Clubhouse for a period of one week and was to use the Strangers' wing. Residents of New York could be invited for lunch or dinner in the Strangers' Dining Room, but not more often than once in seven days.

In 1899 an amendment to the By-laws permitted Members to invite guests to the regular Clubhouse provided they were not residents of the city. The same man could not be invited more than once a month. The word "Stranger" was used in the By-Laws until 1970, when it was replaced by the word "guest." Certain restrictions do remain: "A Member may invite ladies and gentlemen, not Members of the Club, to the Main and Private Dining Rooms and the Great Marble Hall," state the most recent By-laws.

The experiment of transplanting this English custom to American soil was not a successful one. For many years now, the entire Strangers' Wing has been the Manager's office.

Finally, a long-contested struggle took place

over whether and on what terms women might be given more than occasional admittance. Needless to say, the no-women-allowed rule was one of the earliest to be challenged. The modern Women's Movement began in 1890, when the National American Woman Suffrage Association was formed under the leadership of Carrie Chapman Catt. Women had decided that they were tired of being dictated to by men and by the millions became stenographers and private secretaries. Out of sheer curiosity and jealousy if nothing else, women wanted to have access to their husbands' hideaways. Curiously, it was the conventional men's clubs—that is, the non-artistic—which first relaxed their rules. Boston's Somerset Club from its early days had a ladies' dining room, which had proved a successful addition. The Metropolitan Club's original instructions to Stanford White were to include a separate wing for the accommodation of the ladies of a Member's family. Enough space was available for White to design a luxurious Ladies' Dining Room with a separate entrance from the Court, and with two Private Dining Rooms on the second floor. Members were not allowed to eat there unless in the company of a lady.

The Founding Fathers carefully stipulated who was entitled to use the Ladies' Restaurant. The By-Laws, Paragraph XII, Section 1, specify:

Ladies, temporarily or permanently of the family of a Member of the Club, and while residing with him, shall, whether or not attended by such Member be permitted to use the Restaurant for Ladies and be accompanied by other ladies.

This meant that if a women left a Member's "bed and board," she also lost her privileges to the Ladies' Restaurant. Furthermore, she could not bring any male companions with her, and one wonders whether she might have been permitted to bring her brother or Uncle John from Philadelphia. One also wonders whether any young lady "temporarily residing" with a Member could use the Restaurant.

A complication soon arose. What was to be done with the widow of a Member? After many years and much deliberation, in 1935 widows were given the privilege of using the Ladies' Restaurant against payment of annual dues of $50. Of course, it would have been awful to call them "Lady Members" or "Widow Members," so they were labelled "Subscribers Ladies' Annex." They were first listed in the Annual Membership Book in 1941 when there were thirty-six of them.

In the beginning, women were rarely admitted to the Main Clubhouse. With the exception of special dinners or receptions, they could only use the Ladies' Restaurant. After several attempts, the By-laws were finally amended in 1898 so that Members could bring their families to the Main Dining Room on Sunday nights. The private dining room known as the Yellow Room was set aside on those nights as a powder room for the women, with a maid in attendance. But the women were required to use the elevator and were not permitted to walk down the stairway. For those Members wishing to dine without being disturbed by the presence of the fair sex, dinner was served in the South Breakfast Room, now the Levi P. Morton Room. When use of the facilities of the Main Building declined, the Ladies' Restaurant was closed. It was left vacant for years. By 1944, members could bring women as their guests to the Great Hall and the Main and Private Dining Rooms whenever they chose. Then Members and their wives were permitted to use the bedrooms; at first only those in the Annex, but in recent years, those in the Main Building as well. The story—probably apocryphal—is told that during those years a Member asked the front desk whether he could bring any lady to one of the bedrooms. "Certainly, sir," was the answer, "provided she is the wife of a Member." Finally, women were permitted to occupy the bedrooms alone. Soon thereafter, wives were able to come to the Club alone or with friends (male or female) and sign their husbands' names.

As far as Membership for women was concerned, it was restricted to widows (unless they remarried). In 1970 a new classification was created, Annual Lady Guests, because the privilege was granted for one year only. It could be extended for an additional year upon being reviewed by the Admissions Committee. In other words, it was made dependent upon good behavior, so to speak. Finally in 1974, the barriers were broken down completely. The Board of Governors eliminated the categories of Widow Members and Annual Lady Guests and permitted the election of unmarried women to Membership in the Club. They are now called "Women Members." Only Regular Members, however, can propose or second a candidate for Woman Membership. Except for special occasions, women are still excluded from the Men's Bar, the West Lounge and the Second Floor. Their annual dues are fixed at $500. Except for widows of Members, a newly-admitted Woman Member has also to pay an initiation fee of $250.

The Episcocrats comprising the Membership of the Metropolitan Club in its early years knew how to live well. A few of them were very rich, others just rich; most of them were well-educated, traveled and cultured. All were influenced by British customs and habits. After all, their ancestors had come from the British Isles; they still had relatives there perhaps, or daughters who had married into the British aristocracy. W. Watts Sherman's daughter, Mildred, married Lord Camoys, whose family has owned Stonor Park, forty miles from London since 1156. Members frequently travelled to England; Colonel William Jay brought back the passion for four-in-hand coaching as a result of a stay with the Duke of Beaufort.

At the time of the formation of the Club, Britain was at the height of her world power, which reached its apogee just before the Boer War. Understandably, English customs set the pattern for New York's fashionable society.

During the latter part of Queen Victoria's long reign, the upper-class Englishman—as did his American counterpart—had a breakfast in the morning, often of heroic proportions, consisting of boiled eggs, fried eggs and bacon, mutton kidneys, broiled fish and breads of vari-

The spate of arranged marriages between impoverished European aristocrats and the daughters of New American millionaires attracted the caustic pen of a *Life* cartoonist in 1902.

ous kinds and shapes. Then came coffee, tea and cocoa. A writer at the time comments favorably on American as opposed to English coffee, a criticism that still appears justified.

The noon-day meal, in those days called either a *déjeuner à la fourchette* or luncheon, consisted mainly of cold meats, fish, and pudding or sweets. Then came dinner and a late supper. In the 1890s, dining was similar to the modern form, except that people ate much more than they do today. A typical dinner among the upper classes of society might begin with caviar, followed by oysters, soup and a fish dish. Courses of game or roast and then fowl were followed by salad, dessert, cheese and coffee.

As dinner time gradually moved to a later hour, from half-past six to half-past seven, this led to the disappearance of a late supper. Sandwiches, however, were served between ten and eleven o'clock in the evening for any guests who, already having consumed four meals during the day, might still feel themselves in danger of starvation.

In those early years, the Executive Committee entrusted with the duty of running the Club regarded the choosing of wines for the palates of the Members as one of their most precious and treasured duties, a task not to be delegated to anyone else. They appointed a special committee of oenologists to advise them on this important function. Their choice fell on Robert Goelet and Ogden Mills. Another committee was formed at the same time for the selection of "segars," and Robert Goelet and George S. Bowdoin were chosen.

The Minutes of the Executive Committee meetings at that time recorded all orders for wines and liquors. There were orders for whiskeys, vermouth, sherry, rum and gin. Cocktails were just becoming popular, and when aperitifs were taken before dinner, they were usually French or Italian vermouth, sherry or Dubonnet. The Minutes show an order in May, 1896, for ten-dozen bottles of sherry at $24 a dozen. In October, an order was placed for a keg of Glen Avit Whisky from Park & Tilford and for four cases of Antigua rum 1847 at $36 a case. The favorite Scotch for a time was Park & Tilford's Scottish club whiskey. But the choice

of clarets and champagne was what really interested the Committee and it spent a great deal of time over this task.

The Age of Queen Victoria has been called the "classic age of claret." The English preference for the wines of Bordeaux goes back to 1152 when Eleanor of Aquitaine married Henry Plantagenet, Duke of Normandy and Count of Anjou, who in 1154 became King of England. For the next three centuries, Bordeaux was under English rule. The English at that time were avid wine bibbers and they dubbed the red wine from Bordeaux "claret." It was a profitable time for the Bordelais and the popularity of their wines has continued to the present. The wine trade between Bordeaux and England and the northern countries constituted the largest portion of all ocean traffic between those lands during the Middle Ages.

During Victoria's reign the quality of Bordeaux wines steadily improved, largely as a result of the system of quality listing established for the Exposition Universelle in Paris which remained accepted for the next one-hundred years. It included the five Royalties of Bordeaux: Château Lafite and Château Latour, both of Pauillac; Château Margaux of Margaux; Château Haut-Brion of Graves; and Château d'Yquem of Sauternes. Château Mouton-Rothschild of Pauillac was added later by universal acclaim.

The Minutes of the Executive Committee first mentioned the placement of an order for wines on February 4, 1895; four cases of Latour Monopole 1874 and five cases of Château Lafite 1878, along with some others. In April, they ordered four cases of Clos d'Estournel at $35 a case and eight cases of Château Latour at $40 a case. The enormous price indicates that these two must also have been 1870s vintages. But the order placed in January, 1896, really demonstrates the taste of the gentlemen. This was for:

Four cases of Château Lafite 1878 at $40
Five cases of Château Margaux 1877 at $36
Five cases of Château Lafite 1887 at $16.50
Twenty-five cases of Château Mouton-Rothschild at $12.50

Prices of $35 to $40 for a case of wine in 1895 are comparable to $700 to $800 today. As a matter of fact, the 1870s produced some outstanding wines. Only two years in that decade, 1873 and 1876, produced indifferent wines and two, 1872 and 1879, yielded medium wines. As if aware of impending disaster, the vineyards yielded wines of superb quality before devastation set in. Already in 1879 the vintage was scarred by the spreading ravages of the *Phylloxera vastatrix*. Accidentally brought to Europe from the United States, this insect first appeared in France in 1863 and destroyed two-and-a-half million acres of vineyards during the following decade. It was finally conquered when some genius discovered that the only means of saving Europe's vines was to graft them on American roots which are resistant to the insect. A dispute raged for a long time as to whether "pre-*phylloxera*" wines were better than those produced subsequently. It seems difficult, however, to imagine finer wines than those which the great growths offer today.

In November, 1896, orders were placed for seven cases of Château Rauzon 1875 at $31.50 a case, four cases of Château Palmer 1875 at $24.50, seven cases of Léoville-Las-Cases 1878 at $23 and fifteen cases of Mouton-Rothschild.

In December, 1896, Charles Lanier and Frank Sturgis assumed the task of purchasing wines and they asked for proposals on fifty cases each of Latour and Léoville-Las-Cases 1890, a total of 1200 bottles. They were bought the following January from Oswald Jackson Bros. They were less pleased with some California wine they had purchased from Wm. H. Fearing, a dealer with whom they had done a lot of business in the past. So they sent the following letter to him:

The Executive Committee of the Metropolitan Club purchased from you some time since five cases of Krug wine Brut 1880.

While the Committee have been able to dispose of a considerable portion of the wine and while they have no intention of asking you to receive back the unsold portion, yet they desire to express most distinctly their surprise that you should have offered to them a wine of this nature and to state that they consider it detrimental to have been obliged to offer such a wine to the members of the Club.

The Charles Krug Winery was established in 1861 in the Napa Valley and is considered one of the great names in California wine history.

Favorites among the champagnes, were Moët et Chandon, which at the time cost about $35 to $40 a case, and also Veuve Clicquot. In January, 1898, they imported jointly with the Union Club three-dozen cases of Demisny 1884 Brut Champagne.

Looking over these and many other purchases of wines as they are listed in the Executive Committee Minutes, one message comes through loud and clear; these gentlemen of good taste preferred the wines of the Haut-Médoc almost to the exclusion of all others. The wines of Château Latour, Château Margaux and Château Lafite are Haut-Médoc, Premiers Crus; Mouton-Rothschild, Léoville-Las-Cases, Rauzan and Clos-d'Estournel are Seconds Crus, and Château Palmer is Troisième Cru, but experts feel that the wine would be revised one rank higher if the classification of 1855 were brought up to date.

It would be hard to find any better wines. Lichine declares that the Médoc district is rated by many experts as the greatest in the world for fine red wines:

A Médoc is a typical claret, possessed of a subtle bouquet in age which suggests the scent of rose and violet, or an indefinable smell of woods in springtime and clean earthiness. The wines are feminine and delicate. They have often been described as the "queens" of the world's red wines.

The half century from 1875 to 1925 was also the great period of mansion building in American history. Great fortunes were being amassed from new industries, and labor was cheap and abundant. The income tax was not introduced until 1913. The rich were really rich, and when they decided that their wealth and position demanded a mansion in the city and a château in the country, the architect and decorator were under little financial restraint. While some of these rich men and women were uncouth and crude, many were cultured, scholarly and widely traveled, amateur architects and

The Vanderbilt summer "cottage", the Breakers, in Newport.

collectors of books and art.

In 1963, Merrill Folsom published a book entitled *Great American Mansions*. Of the nearly fifty fabulous houses he describes, almost one-quarter were built by and for Members of the Metropolitan Club. The most impressive mansions of the day were built by Richard Morris Hunt who was without equal in this field. Twenty-five years older than Stanford White, he was at the peak of his career in the 1890s. Those great builders, the Vanderbilts, were Hunt's loyal clients; he built The Breakers in Newport for Cornelius in 1892. For George W. he created the fabulous French-Renaissance Château of 250 rooms, Biltmore House, in the Blue Ridge Mountains, surrounded by 130,000 acres of forests and farms. For William K., he built the Marble House in Newport, a temple of white marble with pilasters and capitals modeled after the Temple of the Sun at Baalbek. William K.'s sincere interest in architecture is revealed in the long letter he wrote from Paris in 1892 to Stanford White outlining his own plans for the new Clubhouse.

When the Metropolitan Clubhouse went up, it was the only building on the block. The Club's example, however, caught on, and the land facing Central Park was bought up very quickly. Soon a number of magnificent palaces were built on and adjacent to Fifth Avenue. Next door to the Club on Fifth Avenue, a French castle was designed by Hunt for that well-known figure in New York society, Charter Member Elbridge T. Gerry, founder of the Society for the Prevention of Cruelty to Children, known as the Gerry Society. Commodore Gerry wore a sealskin cap on all occasions and his peculiarities are described in Edith Wharton's book, *The Age of Innocence.*

Sad was the story—told by James T. Maher in *The Twilight of Splendor*—of the mansions designed by the famous Philadelphia architect Horace Trumbauer for two Members of the Metropolitan Club. The first was the stately Palladian palace, Whitemarsh Hall, outside Philadelphia built in 1916 by Edward T. Stotesbury ('94) for his beautiful wife Eva, the widow of Oliver Cromwell ('92) and the mother of Jimmy Cromwell ('50). The cost was upwards of three million dollars. After Stotesbury's death in 1938, the mansion was soon abandoned and eventually ransacked. An almost unbelievable instance of "too little and too late" is the story of Shadow Lane, the mansion Trumbauer built for Hubert Templeton Parsons, or rather Maysie Adelaide Parsons, in West Long Branch, New Jersey. Parsons ('24) had become president of F. W. Woolworth in 1919 and received a huge salary but only owned 50,000 shares of Woolworth stock. He started building the fabulous mansion patterned after the Petit Trianon in Versailles in 1927, after the old house on the property he owned had burned down. It was to cost him $10,000,000. Before it was finished the stock market crash of 1929 and the Great Depression changed the rules of the game. Parsons went bankrupt. The year before he died in 1940, Shadow Lane was sold at auction by the sheriff of Monmouth County. The price: One hundred dollars.

For many Members of the Metropolitan Club, however, Stanford White and his firm were the most popular architects. White made his first contact with a future Member in 1874 while he was working in the Brookline, Massachusetts, office of Henry Hobson Richardson, one of the established architects of that period.

There he was given a large measure of responsibility for redesigning W. Watts Sherman's house in Newport, Rhode Island. White's work on the house produced "an architectural monument of great qualilty." Later, after he became a partner of McKim and Mead, he was responsible for a number of buildings in Newport. In 1879, he designed the Newport Casino for Charter Member James Gordon Bennett, Jr. (editor of the *New York Herald* and founder of the *New York Evening Telegram*). According to tradition, Bennett decided to build his own club when his membership in the Newport Reading Room was canceled, and he hired White to draw up the design. The Casino was built in 1880-81 and cost $125,000. For years it was the center of Newport social life and is today the National Lawn Tennis Hall of Fame.

White undertook many commissions for Bennett, both small and large, including in 1882 the interior of his yacht *Polyana*, and three years later, the interior of his yacht *Namouna*. In 1892, as owner-editor of the *New York Herald*, Bennett commissioned White to design the New York Herald Building at Broadway and 35th Street. Built in 1892-95 at a cost of $559,-815, it was inspired by the Palazzo del Consiglio in Verona.

White designed several other mansions in

Rosecliff in Newport was the summer residence of Mr. and Mrs. Herman Oelrichs.

Newport for Members. The most fabulous was Rosecliff on Bellevue Avenue, the residence of Charter Member Herman Oelrichs and his wife, Theresa Alice Fair. The design was inspired by the Grand Trianon, the palace of Louis XIV at Versailles. It was built from 1899 to 1902 at a cost of $298,000 and is now open to the public. More than any other of the Newport cottages, Rosecliff demonstrates White's good taste, elegance and superior genius. By comparison, the Breakers or Wetmore's Château-sur-Mer or especially Belcourt Castle are overloaded, heavy and sometimes depressing.

Another Newport mansion that White designed for Charter Member Henry A. C. Taylor was built in 1885-86. The design was part of the Adamesque colonial revival that continued through the Second World War. In 1894, White designed the fabulous Taylor residence at 3 East 71st Street, built in imitation of the Palazzo Bartolini-Salebeni in Florence.

White also designed Taylor's mausoleum at Woodlawn Cemetery in 1900 at the enormous cost of $137,000.

The magnificent residence of Charter Member John Inness Kane at 972 Fifth Avenue, built in 1904 at a cost of $511,473, was a McKim Mead & White project. Its inspiration was the Palazzo Massimi alle Colonne, Rome (1535). It was demolished in 1930, before the founding of the Landmark Commission which might have protected it. In its general outline, it resembled the Metropolitan Club Building.

Other White buildings include the residence of Thomas Newbold built in 1891 at 13 East 79th Street, the Casino built for John Jacob Astor in 1902 at Rhinebeck-on-Hudson, and the residence of Thomas B. Clarke at 22 East 35th Street. Clarke was a well-known art collector and intimate friend of White and the interior of his house is one of White's finest accomplishments.

Harbor Hill at Roslyn, Long Island, was designed for Member Clarence H. Mackay in 1902. It was influenced by the Château Maisons-Lafitte outside Paris, built in 1642-46 by François Mansart. White also designed houses for Members Cyrus H. McCormick (Richfield Springs, New York City, 1882); Phillips and Lloyd Phoenix (New York City, 1882); Percy R. Pyne (680 Park Avenue, New York City, 1906); Payne Whitney (975 Fifth Avenue, New York City, 1902, now owned by the French government); and Charles A. Whittier (Boston, 1882).

For the Vanderbilts, McKim Mead & White performed two important tasks. For Mrs. William K. Vanderbilt, Jr., White designed the residence at 666 Fifth Avenue and, for Frederick W. Vanderbilt, the mansion at Hyde Park, New York, now the Vanderbilt Mansion National Historical Site.

A group of outstanding McKim Mead & White buildings are the Henry Villard Houses, a U-shaped group of brownstones at 451-457 Madison Avenue. The structure containing six houses was commissioned by Villard, the railroad magnate who emigrated from Germany after the 1848-49 uprisings.

The cost was $750,000, of which $587,000 was for the Villard House alone—its interior was incomparably magnificent. Based on details from the Cancelleria in Rome, the structure was designed in 1882 and built in 1883-85. During the ceremony for the opening of the Northern Pacific Railroad, Villard heard of the Stock Market manipulations of Jay Gould. He suffered a nervous breakdown and went to Germany to recuperate. Near bankruptcy, he sold the magnificent mansion in which he had lived only briefly to Charter Member Whitelaw Reid in 1886; nevertheless, the complex is known to this day as the Villard Houses. Reid employed Stanford White to supervise various renovations. Two of the other five houses in the complex were also owned by Charter Members. 455 Madison Avenue was owned by Edward D. Adams and 457 by Harris C. Fahnestock who also owned the house at 22 East 51st Street and gave it to his son, William. In recent years, the building was the office of the Catholic Archdiocese of New York, until Harry Helmsley leased it in 1977 in connection with the building of the new Palace Hotel. Protected by the Landmark Commission, the exterior of the original house has been preserved and some of the interior has been restored.

All told, McKim Mead & White numbered

San Marino, built by Henry E. Huntington and left by him to the public after his death.

over twenty Members of the Club as clients. The last major project White received prior to his premature death was the design of J. Pierpont Morgan's library. He was inspired in this assignment by the Nymphaeum in the Villa Papa Giulia in Rome. The exterior is of carefully-laid marble blocks with no mortar, in the classic Greek· manner. Today it is open to the public, another building adding to the embellishment of New York City.

Two more of the many great mansions built for Club Members deserve mention. Henry and Arabella Huntington built San Marino near Pasadena, "the most truly magnificent residence in the whole of California," now open to the public. It is more fully described in Chapter Seventeen. The other is the Frick Mansion still standing on Fifth Avenue between 70th and 71st Streets. It was designed in 1913 by Carrère & Hastings, another of the great architectural firms of the period, as the residence of Henry Clay Frick. Frick joined the Club in 1899 and was an active Member until his death in 1919, and made one of the exclusive and intimate

Bridge Dinner Club circle. His son, Childs Frick, became a Member in 1905. In his business life in the steel industry, Frick was known as a ruthless operator, and only the bad marksmanship of Russian assassin, Alexander Berkman, saved his life in 1892. After the turn of the century, however, he devoted more and more of his energies to establishing his art collection which he did "with love and understanding throughout a long period of years." To house his priceless treasures, he built his mansion reminiscent of a French townhouse of the eighteenth century. It is now a museum open to the public and is one of the greatest art treasures of New York City.

The super rich of America's Gilded Age did not spend their money only on mansions in town and châteaux in the country, on yachts, travels and mistresses. They—or rather their wives—also gave parties to rival those of the courts of France in splendor and lavishness. Hippolyte Adolphe Taine recounts that Marie Antoinette—the personification of extravagance—often spent 400,000 lires (about one million dollars in present-day currency) for one "fairy evening" at Versailles. Our dollar princes, or rather princesses, were not to be outdone. Appropriately enough, Versailles was often the inspiration for the setting of these spectacles.

Observing the events of that time, Thorstein Veblen coined the phrase "conspicuous consumption." The public and the press loved it and millionaire watching then was as popular as following the antics of film stars, boxers, golf or tennis champions today. The press gave much space to descriptions of the balls, coming-out parties, opera nights or dinners of the rich. Unbelievable amounts of money were spent on them. Who would spend $200,000 on a party, even today when the dollar is worth only a small fraction of what it was in 1909? George Jay Gould spent that amount in 1909 on the coming-out party of his daughter Marjory, later Mrs. Drexel. The bill for flowers alone included the cost of 5500 lilies of the valley, 1500 orchids, 15,000 white roses and "every American-beauty rose in the East." The Goulds, however, were not considered "clubba-

ble" at that time. Being avid yatchtsmen, they belonged only to the American Yacht Club started by their father.

Some of the early Members of the Metropolitan Club also contributed their full share of extravagant party giving. Most of the half-dozen or so specially newsworthy extravaganzas which the well-known historians of that era—Cleveland Amory, Dixon Wecter and Kate Simon and others—mention in their books were given by Club Members, or, usually, by their wives. Two of these affairs caused such savage criticism by pulpit, press and public as to induce the hosts to leave the country.

The Bradley-Martin Ball was inspired by the best intentions. The country was suffering a severe depression in 1896 and 1897, and Mrs. Martin was deeply depressed by the widespread unemployment and the suffering of the people. She wanted to do something as "an impetus to trade" and decided to give a fancy dress ball. The Martins had come from Troy, New York, with sacks of money, and by the 1890s had been nouveau-riche long enough to be accepted. Even Mrs. Astor eventually decided to disregard their lineage and invited them to her ball. When the Club was being organized in February, 1891, Bradley Martin and his brother Frederick Townsend Martin were on the list and they became Charter Members. Soon they became the "Bradley-Martins" and married their sixteen-year old daughter to Lord Craven. On January 19, 1897, their eldest son, Bradley Jr., became a Club Member.

Early that same month, Mrs. Bradley-Martin sent out 1200 invitations to a ball to take place at the old Waldorf on February 10th. The theme of the ball was the court of Louis XV and the background, the palace of Versailles. Mrs. Martin presided as a Queen, the wrong Queen—she appeared as Mary Stuart. The Astors were there and Jack won the title "King of the Ball." The affair cost a quarter of a million dollars, equivalent to $6 million today. The guests probably spent the same amount of money on gowns and bijoux. The public and the press, however, had not yet been educated by John Maynard Keynes on the blessings of a consumer society, and they attacked the

A group of the guests at the famous Hyde Ball at Sherry's in 1905. Seated are Sydney Smith and Mrs. Stuyvesant Fish. Standing from left to right are: Mrs. Sydney Smith, Philip A. Clark, Mrs. James A. Burden, Stanford White, James Henry Smith, and J. Norman de R. Whitehouse.

Bradley-Martins mercilessly. Adding injury to insult, New York doubled Bradley-Martin's tax assessment and the family decided to join the voluntary expatriate colony in a more understanding Europe.

James Hazen Hyde had become a Member on October 25, 1898. At twenty-eight, he had inherited control of the Equitable Life Assurance Society from his father. Different from the nouveau-riche Bradley-Martins, Hyde was a cultured man, an intimate of Henry James and his circle and a passionate Francophile. In 1905 he decided to give a fancy party at Sherry's in honor of his niece's coming-out with the inevitable Versailles as background.

The entertainment opened with a gavotte danced by the outstanding debutantes of the season. A comedy, *Entre Deux Portes,* written for the occasion, was acted by the great French actress Madame Réjane. Trumpets summoned the guests to supper in the dining room on the floor below, a creation of Stanford White, who was one of Hyde's guests that evening. The huge room had been transformed into a beautiful Versailles Garden. A rose bush in full bloom decorated each of the sixty tables. After supper Madame Réjane recited a poem by A. A. de Caillavet entitled "A-*propos* in Praise of Franco-American Friendship." After dancing in the Ballroom, a second supper was served in a tent supposedly on the palace lawn while several orchestras, one that of the Metropolitan Opera, played for the guests until a seven-o'clock breakfast was served. It was the first such affair to be photographed. When Hyde admitted that the tab was $200,000, stockholders became suspicious. An inquiry followed and Hyde decided to sell his insurance company and to take up permanent residence in his beloved France.

One custom of the time was to present all guests at such parties with favors. When Mrs. Bradley-Martin was preparing for her big party, she found this a very difficult task. Almost every imaginable article of jewelry or ornament had been used as favors at other balls. After a long search she finally selected small silver figures of appropriate design for gentlemen and ladies. To these two sets a third favor was added—a staff crowned by plumes and other ornaments, such as was carried by heralds and courtiers in the days of the magnificent courts of Versailles and Madrid. They were too heavy to be carried about by the guests and were intended chiefly as souvenirs of the ball.

When the wife of Club Member George Westinghouse (November 18, '02) gave a dinner in this same period in Washington for one hundred guests, she eliminated this time-consuming task. Each guest found a one hundred dollar bill tucked into his or her napkin.

For most women of the period the ultimate achievement was to secure a title for their daughters. The towering purchase price was not difficult to get out of daddy. What did it matter if the object of this desire was feeble-minded, dissolute, debt-ridden or homosexual, as long as his name stood high in the *Almanach de Gotha* or *Debrett's*. Historians estimate that there had been five hundred such marriages by 1909. The Membership of the Metropolitan Club contributed its full complement of heiresses to this game.

A memorable parody on this craze was a party given by that *enfant terrible* of the Four Hundred, Mame Fish, the wife of Charter Member Stuyvesant Fish, known as the famous "Monkey Dinner." The guest of honor was the Prince del Drago—a monkey attired in full dress.

Another outlandish dinner that has gone down in the social annals of the period was the "Horseback Dinner," given by Cornelius K. G. Billings who had migrated to Manhattan from Chicago where his thoughtful father had left him control of a gas company. He joined

C.K.G. Billings' famous "horseback dinner" at Sherry's on March 28, 1903. Billings' own horses were too highly-strung and nervous for such an occasion so he rented thirty-six more tranquil steeds from local riding academies. They were served oats in individual feeding troughs towards the end of dinner.

the Metropolitan Club on February 21, 1899. Known as the "American Horse King," he celebrated the opening of his new quarter-million-dollar stable by inviting thirty-six horse lovers to a "Horseback Dinner" at Sherry's. His racers were too skittish to be relied on, so rented mounts were carried by elevator up to the fourth-floor ballroom, which had been disguised as a woodland garden with a harvest moon overhead and real songbirds in the shrubs. The waiters were dressed as grooms. The mounted guests ate their dinner from tables securely fastened to the flanks of the horses. Champagne was in ice buckets in the saddlebags hanging on the horses.

No description of the period could be complete without mention of *Town Topics*, which chronicled many of the events related here. *Town Topics* was a witty gossip weekly, owned by Colonel William d'Alton Mann, a kindly-looking gentleman with a long white beard. He had informers in many key places, and as a result gained knowledge and evidence which he used for his own financial gain. In other words, he was a blackmailer. Sooner or later he was destined to get into trouble, and this happened in 1905 when he made derogatory remarks about the father of Robert Collier, the owner of *Collier's Weekly*. In the ensuing law suit, Colonel Mann testified, at first with reluctance and finally with a touch of pride, that he had "borrowed" a total of $184,500 from various wealthy men. Among them were five members of the Metropolitan Club, led by William K. Vanderbilt, who had lent $25,000 to the Colonel. Other contributors were Dr. W. Seward Webb with $14,000, William C. Whitney with $10,000, then—believe it or not—J. Pierpont Morgan with $2,500, and, finally George S. Scott with $1,000. Another famous figure of the day, Arabella, wife of Member Henry E. Huntington, was also on the list of Colonel Mann's benefactors. The Colonel must have had a lot of accurate information.

# Chapter 11

# ADMIRAL DEWEY, PRINCE HENRY AND THE PRINCE OF WALES

According to custom in those early years, the courtesies of the Club might be extended to a specific group for a limited period of time, usually three months. Such arrangements were made several times with other clubs to help them over the difficulties of moving or redecorating their clubhouses. In 1895 the Metropolitan Club offered the use of its facilities to the members of the Knickerbocker when they wanted to renovate their quarters at 34th and Fifth Avenue. The fact that Founding Father Frank Sturgis was also Chairman of the Executive Committee of the Knickerbocker at the time did help, of course. In 1899, when the University Club moved to its beautiful new premises at Fifth Avenue and 54th Street, its members were given the privileges of the Metropolitan Clubhouse from May 1st to July 1st. Similar courtesies were extended to the Union Club when it moved to new quarters at Fifth Avenue and 51st Street in January, 1903, and again in 1930 when it moved farther uptown to a new building at Park Avenue and 69th Street.

Of a somewhat different nature were the three-month invitation cards sent on September 30, 1895, to the ministers of Belgium and Turkey. The Ottoman Empire, ruled by Sultan Abdul-Hamid III, was a great power then.

Three times during the first decades of the Club's life, the courtesy of the Clubhouse was extended to the entire officer corps of a naval vessel. On June 27, 1899, an invitation was sent to the officers of the USS *Olympia* commanded by Admiral George Dewey (1837-1917), offering them the freedom of the Clubhouse for a period of three months. On January 21, 1902, a similar invitation was sent to the entourage of Prince Henry of Prussia (1862-1929), arriving aboard the Royal Yacht *Hohenzollern* for the purpose of christening a new Royal Yacht, the *Meteor*. And on November 18, 1919, invitations were extended to the Prince of Wales (1894-1972) a nephew of Prince Henry, and the officers of HMS *Renown*.

Until the turn of the century, American foreign policy was conducted along the lines prescribed in Washington's Farewell Address and the Monroe Doctrine, and rested on the proposition that the fundamental interest of the American people should be concentrated on its continental opportunities. In the early twentieth century, however, strong advocates demanded that America should abandon its insularity and actively intervene in the affairs of

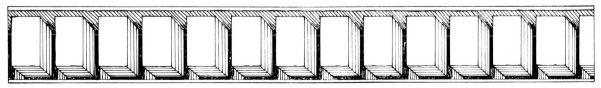

*Dentils*

Asia and Europe, transforming itself into a Great World Power. Prominent among those who advocated such a policy were Theodore Roosevelt, Henry Cabot Lodge and Captain Alfred Thayer Mahan, a naval officer and historian. Many others, most of them Republicans led by President McKinley, joined this group. Josiah Strong, a militant Protestant missionary, wrote that the Anglo-Saxon race was chosen by God to civilize the world.

Those opposed to this philosophy found strong leaders in William Jennings Bryan, William Graham Sumner, Mark Twain and Andrew Carnegie. Sumner published an article attacking the new imperialism which, he contended, would result in bigger armies and navies, bigger debts, a contempt for the Constitution and more wars whenever the politicians decided the country needed them. But the doctrine of Manifest Destiny came out the winner. In 1898, the Hawaiian Islands were annexed. The Spanish-American War broke out in April, 1898, and the *de facto* annexations of Cuba, Puerto Rico, Guam and the Philippines followed. American history and foreign policy had reached a major turning point.

This policy brought the United States into conflict with the other world powers including that other late-comer in the field, Germany. In 1888, the kind and wise Frederick III died prematurely and his son, Wilhelm II, became Emperor. Wilhelm wanted to imitate his cousins across the Channel by building a big navy and acquiring colonies at a time when wiser men had already pronounced the period as the twilight of Colonialism. In 1890, he dismissed Bismarck, the only man who could have prevented the coming collision policy. Soon there were altercations between Germany and the United States over Samoa. Germany yielded the field. Another touchy situation developed when the German Admiral von Diederichs attempted to defy Commodore Dewey's blockade of Manila. Only the intervention of a British

Admiral George Dewey and his dog Bob on the deck of his flagship, *Olympia*.

naval squadron under the command of Captain Sir Edward Chichester prevented a clash between the Americans and Germans. But an insignificant incident which occurred shortly before the battle of Manila Bay excited the public and the press and created a feeling of animosity between the American and German peoples.

Both the Far East squadron of the United States under Commodore Dewey and that of Germany under Prince Henry were in Hong Kong when Prince Henry decided to give a banquet to the representatives of all the fleets in port. As related in the history of the University Club, written by its president, James W. Alexander (who was also a Charter Member of the Metropolitan), the Prince, in proposing the national toasts, omitted the United States in the regulated order of precedence. Dewey, regarding the omission as intentional, left the banquet. The next morning, Prince Henry sent an aide to explain, but Dewey informed him "that the incident required a written or personal apology." The Prince called in person, and Dewey accepted his assurances with prompt good will.

War with Spain came in April, 1898, and Commodore Dewey, then in Hong Kong, received orders "to capture or destroy the Spanish fleet" in the Philippine waters. On May 1st, his quiet order "You may fire when ready, Gridley," destroyed the Spanish squadron without the loss of a single American life. Spanish losses were 1,200 killed or wounded. America had entered the ranks of the Great Powers.

Congress appointed Dewey Admiral of the Navy, a grateful nation presented him, through popular subscriptions, with a house in Washington, and New York gave him the biggest parade the city or the nation has seen before or since. The Metropolitan Club extended the courtesies of its Clubhouse to Dewey and the officers of the *Olympia*.

Admiral Dewey arrived on his flagship *Olympia* on Tuesday, September 26, 1899, two days earlier than expected. His ship anchored in the Hudson off 110th Street, surrounded by some fifteen other warships. The parade started Saturday, September 30th, at 11 o'clock. Thirty thousand men marched down Riverside Drive and along 72nd Street to Central Park West, then to the Plaza at 59th Street and Fifth Avenue. The Plaza and the other hotels, as well as the Metropolitan Clubhouse, were decorated with thousands of feet of colorful bunting, hundreds of flags and endless streams of ribbons. The Executive Committee had voted the funds for lavish decorations of the Clubhouse, and the windows of the Clubhouse were crowded with Members and their wives. The procession moved down Fifth Avenue to Madison Square where a gleaming white Triumphal Arch and Colonnade had been erected. Under this imperial splendor, Dewey stood for four hours reviewing the parade. A total of two-million spectators lined the streets, avenues and plazas to watch the triumphal procession. The occasion was conceived in the style of Titus and Constantine in ancient Rome, and it was the most spectacular of the many parades on Fifth Avenue in those years long gone.

In 1900, Kaiser Wilhelm II ordered a schooner yacht to be built for him in America. The famous ship designer, A. Cary Smith, was commissioned to design it and the Townsend-Downey Shipbuilding Company, whose yards were on Shooter Island just off Staten Island, were to build the ship. The German Foreign Office saw this as an opportunity to improve the German image in America, and early in January, 1902, the Kaiser sent a request to President Theodore Roosevelt that the President's daughter Alice, later Mrs. Nicholas Longworth, should christen the Imperial Yacht, to be named *Meteor III*. The request was promptly granted, and the Emperor sent his eldest brother, Prince Henry of Prussia, to represent him. The Prince had a winning personality and spoke English fluently, since it was literally his mother-tongue—his mother, Princess Victoria, was the daughter of Queen Victoria. The Emperor's Yacht, the *Hohenzollern*, was sent over, but the royal party did not want to brave the Atlantic in February and sailed instead on the North German Lloyd Liner *Kronprinz Wilhelm*. After a stormy crossing, the Prince arrived in

Prince Henry and Alice Roosevelt on their way to the launching of Kaiser Wilhelm's new yacht, *Meteor*, on Staten Island.

New York on February 23rd. The christening was scheduled to take place on the 25th. Prominent among his entourage were Captain von Müller, later Chief of the Naval Cabinet, General von Plessen, Adjutant General of the Kaiser, and Vice Admiral Alfred von Tirpitz who during the First World War was the advocate of unrestricted submarine warfare to destroy Allied commerce.

On January 21, 1902, the Executive Committee of the Metropolitan Club, then headed by George G. Haven, wrote a letter to the German Consul General requesting "a list of the distinguished visitors to arrive with the Prince on the Royal Yacht" in order to issue invitations extending the privileges of the Club to such visitors. On January 29th they wrote a letter to New York's Mayor Seth Low (a Member since November, 1893) offering the Main Dining Room of the Clubhouse "which will comfortably seat over one hundred guests" for the purpose of entertaining H.R.H. Prince Henry on February 25th. They also informed His Honor that no reporters would be allowed on the premises. The demand for invitations was so great that the Mayor later asked for the entire third floor for that evening, but this request was refused.

The visit of the Prince unleashed a whirl of social events. Mrs. Cornelius Vanderbilt, Jr., gave a dinner for fifty-two guests to meet the Prince at her house, which was beautifully decorated for the occasion. They had entertained his brother Wilhelm II on their yacht and were close friends of his English cousin, Edward VII. Mr. and Mrs. Ogden Mills gave a *déjeuner* in the Prince's honor at their residence, 2 East 69th Street, followed by a musicale, at which the principal artists of the Grau opera group sang. On February 27th, J. Pierpont Morgan (who had graduated from the University of Göttingen and spoke German well) gave a lunch at Sherry's for over a hundred leaders of finance, commerce and industry to meet the Prince. The *Times* called it "one of the most notable incidents in the history of New York." The University Club also went out of its way, and gave a dinner for the Prince on March 7th at its new clubhouse, which was attended by one hundred of the most outstanding members of this club, and followed by a reception for about one thousand people. Two days later they gave a farewell luncheon to the visitors.

On the sunny morning of February 25, 1902, the *Meteor III* slid into the water at Shooter Island in what the *Times* called "the presence of the most distinguished gathering ever assembled to witness the naming of a vessel in American waters." The President of the United States, Theodore Roosevelt, watched as "Princess" Alice cut the holding cord with a silver hatchet. The crowd cheered, cannons boomed and drums rattled. That evening, Mayor Low gave his dinner for the visitors at the Metropolitan Club. Among the one hundred guests were all the leaders of banking and industry, including John Jacob Astor and J. Pierpont Morgan, and such German-Americans as Hermann Ridder, Henry O. Havemeyer, James Speyer, Jacob H. Schiff and Isaac N. Seligman. Despite the ban on reporters *The New York Times* had a full report the next day, printing a list of all those present as well as the full menu, at that time an item of general interest. From the account in the paper, the Clubhouse appears to have been elaborately decorated. Eight-thousand American-beauty roses were used on the table display alone, and there were other features that made the banquet one of the most notable ever given in the City of New York.

Mayor Low had arranged for each guest of honor in the Prince's suite to have a personal escort. The hour set for the banquet was half-past six o'clock and' promptly on the minute Captain de Bevoise of Troop E of Brooklyn, which was acting as escort to Prince Henry, halted his command in the courtyard of the Clubhouse where Mayor Low received the Prince and escorted him to a private sitting room. The sky was cloudy and it started to drizzle.

After the usual dress preparations, Mayor Low and Prince Henry took their stand in the foyer of the Club near the entrance to the Din-ing Room. The guests were then introduced personally to Prince Henry who, recognizing many of their names, talked to them about their interests and industries. Prince Henry threw aside all the formalities of royalty and walked about the Clubhouse chatting in an informal manner to many guests. He was surprised at the elaborate décor of the Clubhouse and asked to be shown through. This inspection occupied about ten minutes. The diners then filed into the Dining Room following the order arranged by Mayor Low.

No attempt was made at special decorations except for a profusion of plants and palms, and on the wall the draping of the American and German flags. The table settings were magnificent, with silver and cut-glass set in front of each plate, and a placecard enscribed in gold with the name of the guest. The cover of the

*Meteor* at the Cowes regatta before World War I. *Meteor* was still in service with the German Navy during World War II.

souvenir menu showed the American and German flags crossed and the German Imperial Crown raised in gilded lines. There were engravings of the Capitol in Washington, the Stars and Stripes and New York's City Hall.

While waiting for the banquet to begin, Prince Henry expressed concern for the cavalry escort. He said to Rear Admiral Evans: "It's a shame to keep those men and horses standing out there in the rain. Don't you think they might dismiss them and be satisfied with the police escort to the opera house?" Admiral Evans sent this message to Inspector Thompson to be delivered to Captain de Bevoise, but the captain declined to believe that the order was genuine and held his men until after the dinner was over.

The dinner was served at a crescent-shaped table. Mayor Low sat with Prince Henry on his right and the German Ambassador on his left. The menu is reproduced below:

> Canapé Metropolitan
> Huitres, Buzzard Bay
>   Montrachet 1884
> Crème de volaille à la Princesse
>   Tortue verte claire
>   Amontillado portado
> Mousse de Jambon a l'admiral
>   Alose sur planche en bordure
> Tomates farcie Metropolitan
>   Krug and Co. Brut 1889
> Rôti d'Agneau de printemps, sauce menthe
>   Pointes d'asperges, pommes souflées
> Terrapine á la Baltimore
>   Pâté de Strasbourg
> Canard canvasback, samp bouille
>   Salade Royale
> Château Mouton Rothschild 1871
>   Fromage de Gruyère et Camembert
> Glâce Hohenzollern, Petits Fours
>   Fruits, dessert
> Café
>   Cognac 1803

There were no speeches and only three toasts were proposed: the first to The President of the United States, the second, to The Emperor of Germany and the last to His Royal Highness Prince Henry of Prussia. It was nearly nine thirty before the coffee was served.

At about ten o'clock the Prince and his party arrived for a Gala Performance at the Opera, which Stanford White had set ablaze with the glitter of thousands of tiny electric lights. The names of the occupants of the boxes read like the Membership roster of the Metropolitan Club. Acts or scenes from *Lohengrin, Carmen, Aida, Tannhauser* and *La Traviata* were performed. A minor disturbance occurred when Madame Sembrich refused to sing the part of Violetta because the Prince had left the house just before an act from *La Traviata* was to begin. Understandably, for he had had a full day.

Among the notable people introduced to Prince Henry that winter were Harry Payne Whitney and his wife Gertrude Vanderbilt. They met him again a few years later when in 1911 they took their sailing yacht *Bibelot* over to Kiel for Kaiser Wilhelm's annual regatta week, the Kieler Woche. This event had become second only to Cowes among yachting events, and was European royalty's prime June entertainment. Warships from half-a-dozen countries lined the course. As Edwin P. Hoyt relates in his book about the Whitneys, Harry and Gertrude were invited aboard the Emperor's Yacht *Hohenzollern* for an informal dance, where they met Prince Henry again. On June 27th, the race from Kiel to Eckernförde was to be staged. As was his custom, the Emperor entered his finest and favorite sailing vessel, the Staten-Island-built *Meteor III*. Also entered was the yacht *Germania* owned by Lieutenant zur See Krupp von Bohlen and Halbach. They and the English boat *Waterwitch* were the major competitors. In a gusty, difficult sea, with uncertain winds, the Krupp boat beat the Emperor's *Meteor III*. But the next day, the *Meteor* had her revenge—she defeated everyone in sight.

The biggest event was the Sonderklasse competition, in which Whitney's yacht, *Bibelot*, was entered. There were two other American entries, the *Beaver* and the *Cima*, and three German vessels, the *Tilly XIV*, the *Wannsee* and the *Seehund III*. They had already sailed four days running. *Bibelot* won two races; *Beaver* and *Cima* one each. The contest was to win three. Just before the finish line *Bibelot* caught *Beaver* and passed her, winning the Emperor Wilhelm Cup, the most honored prize of the regatta.

The next day, Wilhelm and Prince Henry appeared at the Yacht Club to award the prizes. Wilhelm was geniality itself, staying far into the evening, and the Whitneys were presented to His Majesty and spent some time with him. Little did Wilhelm or Harry or Gertrude realize in those warm and friendly surroundings that only three years later war between England and Germany would break out, and that Gertrude would lead a whole unit of the American Ambulance Hospital to help the Allied cause against Wilhelm.

During those pre-war years, the Kiel Annual regatta had become very fashionable. The last one opened on June 26, 1914, and was a special event because for the first time a British squadron, with Admiral Sir George Warrender in command, was attending. The Emperor was getting along much better with his English cousin George V than he had with "Uncle Bertie," King Edward VII, who had died in 1910.

The Kiel week opened in an atmosphere of great festivity which was to be short lived. That Sunday afternoon the Emperor put to sea in his favorite yacht, the Staten-Island-built *Meteor III,* to participate in the races. Suddenly a motor launch approached the yacht. In it was the Chief of the Naval Cabinet, Admiral von Müller, the same officer who as captain had been in Prince Henry's entourage in New York twelve years before. He waved a slip of paper. The Emperor leaned over the stern of the *Meteor,* and Müller called out that he was "the bearer of grave news" and would throw the communications aboard. But the Emperor insisted on hearing immediately what was going on. Müller then shouted out his message, that three hours earlier the Archduke Franz Ferdinand, heir to the Austrian throne, and his wife had been killed by the bullets of Serbian assassins at Sarajevo.

Seventeen years would go by before another invitation to the officer complement of a ship would be extended by the Board of the Metropolitan Club, years of World War, of thirty-million casualties, the toppling of centuries-old dynasties and the rise of sinister new dictatorial

powers. In 1919, the victorious British monarchy saw the need to bolster its hold over the far flung empire. It chose the young heir to the throne, Edward Albert Christian George Andrew Patrick David, known to his family as David and to the world at large as Edward, Prince of Wales. He was a kinsman of Prince Henry of Prussia, who was himself a grandson of Queen Victoria. David was a great-grandson. Since he had become immensely popular with the people during the Great War, the British Government decided to send him on tours of the Commonwealth. His first stop was Canada; he landed at the port of St. John in September, 1919. A luxurious train, a hotel deluxe on wheels, carried him across the continent to Vancouver. Towards the end of this tour, President Wilson invited him to the United States, and he traveled to Washington arriving on November 11, Armistice Day. On November 18th he took the train to New York.

As soon as the Prince's schedule became known, the Metropolitan Club Board extended the courtesies of the Club for a period of thirty days to the Prince, his entourage and to the thirty-six officers of HMS *Renown* and HMS *Constance.* The suite of the Prince included Sir Godfrey Thomas, who remained his secretary for seventeen years until, as Edward VIII, he abdicated in 1936. The most important of his equerries was Rear Admiral Sir Lionel Halsey who had been Lord Jellicoe's Captain of the Fleet at the battle of Jutland.

In this same year, 1919, a girl named Wallis Warfield still lived in obscurity in Washington. She was recently divorced from her second husband of only two years, Lt. Earl Winfield Simpson—"Win" to his wife—a brilliant Navy pilot but a drunkard and sadist who used to lock Wallis in the bathroom to keep her from going out. Some eighteen years would pass before she was be catapulted to notoriety as the woman for whom Edward VIII gave up his throne.

Because the official welcome was to take place in the harbor, the Prince's train was sent to Jersey City, where he boarded an Admiral's barge and sailed across New York bay to Pier A, the Battery, while scores of vessels blew their whistles in welcome. As he stepped from the

Edward, Prince of Wales, arrives in New York in 1919.

barge, his hand at the salute, the guard of honor slowly dipped the colors to a roll of drums, while guns boomed and the crowd cheered. From the Battery he drove to City Hall, where he was welcomed by the Secretary of State and the Mayor of New York, and was given the Freedom of the City. On his route he drove in an open motor-car, and, as he passed beneath the offices of the stockbrokerage community, he was greeted by streams of ticker tape floating down from the windows. In response, he rose from his sitting position in the car, bowing and smiling. That night he went to a gala at the Metropolitan Opera House, where Caruso and Rosa Ponselle sang.

During the next four days the Prince reviewed the troops and cadets at West Point, decorated American soldiers, dined with the Pilgrims of the U.S.A., attended a ball at Mrs. Whitelaw Reid's house and went to a luncheon party at the Piping Rock Club. The Canadian Club, joining with other Canadian and British organizations in New York, entertained the Prince at the Hotel Biltmore on November 19th. On Friday afternoon, November 21, he gave a tea party on the *Renown* for a thousand New York school boys and girls, and on Saturday morning he held an investiture. He stood in naval uniform between two members of his suite in the full dress uniform of the Guards with bearskins. Behind him the officers of the *Renown* were drawn up in a semicircle. After distributing over one-hundred decorations, he then moved aft and began a farewell oration to hundreds of people. Later he went over the side and stepped onto a barge to review five-thousand Boy Scouts drawn up on the river bank, returning to his own ship for a farewell luncheon party. That afternoon the *Renown* sailed for home.

# Chapter 12

# A CLUB
# WITHIN A CLUB

The exclusive men's clubs at the turn of the century usually had between 500 and 1200 members. They were essentially a homogeneous group of men, with similar backgrounds and education. Still, it was only natural that cliques should form, small groups of men who found each other's company especially congenial. They might simply lunch or dine together more or less regularly. Such meetings might develop into a more or less organized circle meeting regularly, a group of "good fellows" often with an appreciation of gourmet dinners. Some of these groups eventually established their own by-laws, dues, club songs and club flags.

Records exist of a number of these satellite organizations. One of the first about which there is any information was the Zodiacs who, formed in 1868 and, domiciled within the walls of the Union Club in New York, kept records of their meetings.

The Union also produced the Kittens, which started around 1890 with twelve members and grew to have twenty. At their dinners the table was decorated with a cat and her kittens and the presiding member was addressed as the Tomcat. At the Knickerbocker, the most famous club-within-a-club was the Roundabout, which began as a result of a bachelor dinner given to Columbus O'Donnell Iselin by his friends in April, 1876, on the eve of his wedding. The evening proved so enjoyable that the participants slowly formed a regular organization. Amos Tuck French was an enthusiastic member of the Roundabout and in 1913 compiled a privately-printed book which included a thumbnail sketch of the organization and a listing of all of its first 225 dinners. Other satellites of the Knickerbocker were the Beefsteak, the Happy Family and the Growlers. They also claim the Coaching Club as a satellite because it was organized within the Knickerbocker's walls in 1875. There is still a Coaching Club Room there today. Boston's Algonquin had the Beacon Society and the Philadelphia Club had the Decanter and the Pee Wee clubs.

Cleveland Amory wrote a fascinating book recently about such a club-within-a-club. Its title: *The Trouble With Nowadays: A Curmudgeon Strikes Back.* Amory's club was called the Fortnightly. It was not easy to become a member. First, naturally, you had to be a member of the parent club. Then it helped if you were Class of '29, or close to it. Then you were put on a seven-year waiting list. And finally, you might be blackballed. Understandably, the waiting list was long.

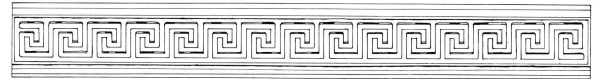

*Greek fret*

The Fortnightly invited speakers to its dinners, frequently from Washington. But when the speaker was finished, the members did not put questions to him. He was expected to ask them questions so that he could have the benefit of their opinions when he returned to Washington or wherever he came from. One member of the Fortnightly formed his own Society-to-Put-Things-Back-the-Way-They-Were. The members were broad-minded, most of them without prejudices, being, of course, Episcopalian; one of them announced proudly, "Some of my best friends are Unitarians."

The Metropolitan Club had its share of clubs-within-a-club. The latest of record—or rather no record—called itself the Busybody Associates. They had a president, usually between twenty-five and thirty members all called vice presidents, and met every two weeks for lunch. Dick West was their last president and when he was called to his ancestors in 1977, the Busybodies died too.

The best-documented club-within-a-club in the Metropolitan named itself The Metropolitan Club Bridge Dinner Club.

Fortunately for posterity, only a few years after it started, the group began to keep records of its activities, which were printed in loose-leaf form from time to time. The first twenty-five years, 1906 to 1931, were later printed and published in a leather-bound volume of 345 pages. The edition was limited to twenty-five copies and contained photographs of many of those active in the group. Records of subsequent years were kept in loose-leaf form. The idea of keeping those records came from E.A.S. Clarke. At the regular dinner in December, 1916, he related that he had seen an interesting book, the above-mentioned records of the Zodiacs. It was promptly decided to keep minutes of all future dinners and outings, and Clarke assumed this task. As a result, all subsequent events are related with a much fuller description of date and place, those present, the menus as well as the wines and cigars served, and a good account of what went on, including songs, speeches, poetry, political and economic discussions, bawdy stories and badinage.

The idea of the Bridge Dinner Club was born

at an all-night bridge game in the Card Room of the Metropolitan Club early in 1906. The next step was a dinner given at the Clubhouse on January 11, 1906, by Henry R. Taylor, son of Founding Member Henry A.C. Taylor, and a Charter Member himself. His guests were Henry R. Beans, Acosta Nichols, Stephen Peabody, Henry Pendleham Rogers, Joseph H. Seaman, John Targee Sill and Oliver C. Townsend. Acosta Nichols gave a second dinner on January 19 at which the same men were present and the idea of forming a permanent dining organization was enthusiastically received. Further dinners followed during the year. In the fall of 1906, John E. Bonne, Henry C. Frick, John P. Grier, J. Horace Harding, Edward H. Harriman, Alvin W. Krech, Dudley Alcott II, John E. Roosevelt and Robert Smith were asked to join. Three dinners were given: on December 6, 1906, and January 31 and March 28, 1907. Joseph K. Choate and Levi C. Weir joined in 1907 and E.A.S. Clarke and W. Watts Sherman in 1908.

As time passed, the loose association became more formal. By-laws were adopted in 1914. They limited the number of members to twenty, and stipulated that an affirmative vote of at least eleven members was necessary to fill a vacancy. Dues were set at $30 a year. There were to be two regular dinners a year, one on the first Thursday in December and the other on the first Thursday following the 15th day of April. Extra dinners could be held, and the custom in time emerged of having such a dinner in January. All regular dinners were held in one of the private dining rooms of the Metropolitan Club. A committee of three was elected each year to arrange these dinners, and they had sole power to invite guests. No dinner could take place unless one of the three presided.

Over the years the number of cups proliferated. The club cup was used at all dinners; it was placed in the center of the table and constituted the principal table decoration. On it were inscribed the names of all past and present members. Preceding each man's name was the year in which he was elected, and following his name the year in which he ceased to be a member. The next most important cup was the

Chase-the-ace Cup, which went into the possession of a three-time winner. Since all members were avid golf players, there were many golf cups, and between six and ten golf outings were arranged each year. Usually they were hosted by members having estates outside New York, in Long Island, Westchester or New Jersey. Often it was a weekend affair. All cups were placed in the center of the table at the regular dinners, and at one dinner the record indicates that there were twenty-one cups on the table.

Of course there had to be a club song as there were many potential, though frustrated, Carusos among the members.

Club Song
written by
John A. Black
Air: "I Don't Care for Violets" from The Arcadians.
We don't want any aces!
Let them go astray
Queens are fair, very rare,
But often are taken away.
Rule one in the art of "chasing"
Of which we all would sing,
If the "persim" you would win,
And you want to begin,
Turn up a King!

The first of the regular dinners about which more detailed information is available was the 22nd dinner given on December 4, 1913, at the Clubhouse. Sixteen men participated. The menu:

Caviar
Lynnhaven Oysters
Green Turtle Soup
Celery — Olives — Radishes — Almonds
Broiled Lake Superior Whitefish
Cucumbers à la Krech
Broiled Fresh Mushrooms
Red Head Duck
Hominy — Samp — Wild Rice
Hearts of Lettuce
Cheese
Coffee

| | |
|---|---|
| Cocktails | Corona Coronas |
| East India Sherry | Villar Gems |
| Moët et Chandon, 1900, Magnums | Club Cigarettes |
| White Port | |
| 1848 Brandy | |
| Chartreuse | J. & B. Scotch—Patterson Bourbon |

The Lake Superior Whitefish was arranged by E.A.S. Clarke, who secured it through the Chicago Club, and had it brought on "special" by the New York Central's Century Limited. Thomas J. Barbour secured the Red Head Ducks through friends in Philadelphia, making the journey over and back himself to get them.

In the early years of the Dinner Club's life, the menu remained essentially the same. It usually started out with caviar, undoubtedly the finest Beluga. Several times, the menu specified "Fresh Caviar," being the best quality with no more than two-percent of salt added. Caviar has been appreciated by connoisseurs for centuries. At today's prices, it has become an epicurean legend.

Caviar was followed by oysters, then soup and a fish dish. Interesting are the "Cucumbers à la Krech." Could member Alvin W. Krech have concocted the dressing? All this was followed by a roast or fowl, salad, cheese and coffee. Duck was a favorite and many times came from the shoot of a fellow member. The choice of libations and cigars was liberal and the dinners became more and more roisterous as time went by.

An opulent dinner at the time was almost unthinkable without duck, and the favorite by far was the canvasback. Like the red head duck, the canvasback is a sea duck which has webbed hind toes and dives under water to feed, in contrast to river ducks like the mallard or black duck. The Earl of Rosebery, former British Prime Minister, on a visit to New York, was given canvasback at dinner five nights in a row. "You Americans," he protested to his host, Member Ward McAllister, "have made a mistake. Your emblematic bird should have been a canvasback, not an eagle." Unfortunately the poor canvasback was in such demand that it was overhunted and has become very rare today. In later years, the problem of getting good duck became so acute that a special Duck Committee was appointed.

There was much singing, speechmaking, telling of jokes and kidding during these dinners. Ribald jokes were told of which the following is a good sample:

Hickory, dickory, dock-ing!
Two mice ran up a girl's stocking.
One stopped at her garter;
The other was smarter,
Hickory, dickory, dock-ing!

As the evening progressed the members started to play bridge or poker. A ritual observed by the Club from the beginning to the present time is the Chase-the-Ace competition. John A. Black donated the Chase-the-Ace Cup which went into the permanent possession of a three-time winner. The terms of this popular competition are reproduced below. A midnight supper might be served and the record of more than one meeting stated that "adjournment was gradual, and some real detective work had to be done the following day, before all the party were located and reached home."

On April 2, 1914, at the Metropolitan Club a memorable dinner was given on the invitation of another group which called itself the Small Association of Dinner Substitutes (S.A.D.S.). The invitations took the form of a legal summons. It turned out to be a very amusing evening and there was much singing "of the usual calibre." Speakers alleged that the initials S.A.D.S. really stood for all kinds of

other titles such as "Sons and Daughters of Sin."

The twenty-fifth regular dinner was held on December 3, 1914, with eighteen men present. The rumble of the Guns of August had not yet penetrated into the rarefied atmosphere of the Club. Two cups were donated that evening by F. H. Eaton for the runners-up of the Chase-the-Ace cup and the Taylor Golf Cup.

On April 6, 1917, America declared war on the Central Powers. The dinners continued unchanged, with the usual caviar menu and bantering. But world events finally penetrated the proceedings and at the thirty-third regular dinner, Krech proposed a toast "To our boys over there, and to those who are going over there," which was drunk standing. From then on, this toast was drunk during every dinner until the war was won. In January, 1919, a new toast was adopted and is still used by the Dinner Club today: "To our Country and its Glorious Flag."

By 1919, the Dinner Club had not only a club song but a club flag. They requested the Metropolitan management to permit this flag to be displayed on the Clubhouse when they held their dinners. This request was granted but only until the formal declaration of peace, at which time it was proposed to take all flags down.

Under the impact of America's new world role, the character of the dinner meetings slowly changed. War heroes were invited and feted. There were thirty-seven members and guests at the dinner given by Norrie Sellar (son-in-law of W. Watts Sherman) at the Clubhouse on February 14, 1919 in honor of Captain Alfred F.B. Carpenter, V.C.,* of the *H.M.S. Vindictive*, the hero of Zeebrügge. He was presented with two $1,000 Liberty Bonds. At the following dinner Lieut. Col D.F. Coffin, Lord Fairfax and Mr. Percy Furber were guests. The last reported on conditions in London which were changing for the worse "due to Bolshevism and especially to women's suffrage."

* When this story appeared in the Monthly Bulletin of May, 1980, Peter C.A. Carpenter ('76), a Foreign Member living in Cadiz, Spain, wrote to the Club as follows:
The Captain A.F.B. Carpenter for whom the Dinner Club Dinner of February 14th, 1919, was given happens to have been my father's cousin. I only met him once when he lectured on the Zeebrügge Raid at Wellington College, but I had some very amusing correspondence with him about 25 years ago as a result of which he left me a very fine water color portrait of my great-great-grandfather James Carpenter who was also a naval officer and fought in the Napoleonic War. This hangs on the wall just above the desk where I am writing this letter. Small world.

Prohibition was first mentioned at the Bridge Dinner Club Dinner on May 18, 1918. At the following December meeting, the question of approaching prohibition was earnestly discussed and resulted in the adoption of the following resolution:

RESOLVED: that the Chairman appoint a committee of three to acquire, if practicable, the amount of wines and liquors necessary during seven years following the beginning of prohibition, for the three regular dinners of the Club, with power to assess the members pro rata, for the cost thereof.

The Chairman appointed the following as such committee: Taylor, Chairman, Franklin and Krech.

Taylor offered, with generous insistence, to contribute the wines for the next dinner, and his offer was promptly and unanimously accepted, with thanks.

Their guess of a seven years' drought fell

short of the actual length—fifteen years—of the Noble Experiment.

The sentiment with which Prohibition was received by these gentlemen becomes evident from the proceedings of the fortieth dinner held December 4, 1919, at the Metropolitan Club and chaired by Krech. Fourteen members and two guests were present. The proceedings, after the usual duck dinner, were reported as follows:

There was the usual enthusiastic response to the first toast "Our Country and Its Glorious Flag," after which the Chairman, in a few words which showed his deep feeling, proposed a toast to the memory of Henry C. Frick, formerly a Member of the Bridge Dinner Club, and often its guest, who died December 2, 1919. The toast was drunk in deep silence.

The Chairman then toasted "The Founders," which brought a return toast to "The Other Members!"

The Chair, calling attention to the fact that all important events have their historian or prophet, asked the members to listen carefully to the words of a song by Judge Morgan O'Brien, which seemed to him most fitting:

I want Booze!
When I choose!
I don't want those lemon-drops you hand me,
I don't want any Huyler's sweet candy,
I want Booze!—when I choose!
I don't want any ice cream sodas,
I want Booze!

The enthusiasm with which this little gem was sung, fully justified the Chairman's action.

The "Club Song" led by Mackay was then sung, and Black's health given in appreciation of his having provided the ducks. Choate supplemented by singing his simple song to Black. Mackay then gave "My Beautiful Irish Maid" in his best style.

The Chair, in graceful words, proposed the health of the guests to which the members drank enthusiastically, Black suggesting that before the guests reply, the Chair advise them of their rights and privileges in the matter of entertaining the Bridge Club. Mr. Samuel Mather, replying for the guests, regretted that the "Pontiac Rule" was not in effect in New York. He explained that this rule, which obtains in Cleveland, his home, and takes its name from first being in effect on the S.S. Pontiac, permits one whose health is being drunk to join in the drinking; and pointed out the wisdom of the rule which ensures against any discrimination as to capacity between toaster and toastee. He then invited Mr. Jackson on the principle of "Better late, than never" to rise and drink with him to "Our Hosts." Jackson, although he had suggested that he would do the drinking to the Bridge Club while Mather did the talking, tried to make a speech, but was finally squelched by the chant "Sit down! Sit down! Sit down! You're rocking the boat!"

Talking and interruptions had by this time become so fast and furious that the Chair announced the rule that those desiring to address the Chair must rise. Franklin was promptly fined $25 for disrespect in persisting in ignoring this rule, but when it transpired that his object was to make a generous offer to the Club, the fine was remitted. As, owing to interruptions and suggestions, there seemed some doubt as to just what Franklin's offer was, the Chair announced his understanding as follows:

Franklin is responsible for two silver cups of substantial proportion, to be played for at Golf in the Spring of 1920 under conditions to be named by Franklin and approved by the Committee.

The understanding of the Chair as expressed was confirmed by unanimous vote.

The Eighteenth Amendment had been ratified by Congress in January, 1919, and the dry period began one year later, on January 16, 1920. At first, the management of the Metropolitan Club expressed doubt whether it could serve the Bridge Club with its own wines after that date, so they decided to crowd in several dinners before the 16th of January in an effort to reduce the wine stock. They were uncertain during the first weeks of the dry period how to handle this problem. So Norrie Sellar invited the group to his residence, Cedarhurst, should there be any trouble, adding that he was the owner of seven magnums of champagne. But at the next meeting in March, Sellar had to withdraw the invitation since his house had been destroyed by fire, including almost his entire stock of wines. He stated, however, that he still had the seven magnums he had mentioned and the question of how to use them was referred to the proper Committee, with power.

Nobody, of course, ever mentioned the idea of giving up drinking. The solution finally decided upon was to present the balance of the

Club stock of wines and liquors to Taylor. He kept it at his residence a few blocks away and brought along enough bottles at each future dinner to satisfy the thirst of those attending. The Club management by that time had overcome its scruples and provided glasses and service.

Prohibition created its own songs. One went like this:

Oh! when I die—don't bury me at all
Just pickle my bones—in alcohol,
Put a bottle of booze—at my head and my feet,
And leave me alone—and I guess I'll keep!

The members joined with enthusiasm, and then followed with "I Want Booze!"

A toast was drunk to the guest, who endeavored to make a speech, but was prevented by loud chanting of "Sit Down! You're rocking the boat!" the members preferring to hear Mackay sing "My Beautiful Irish Maid."

All during the remaining years of Prohibition, this arrangement lasted. When the Club's stock was exhausted, some of the Members managed to get their hands on new supplies. For example, the Forty-fourth Dinner took place at the Clubhouse on January 27, 1921. The record shows that the beverages were contributed by Taylor, Grier and Sellar, with Sellar presenting the Sherry and the St. Marceaux, Taylor the Cordon Rouge, Scotch and rye, and Grier, the Ruinart.

At the Fiftieth regular Dinner, held on January 25, 1923, Nichols and Taylor were the only Founders among the thirteen Members present. The Duck Committee had arranged for the ducks, Taylor had furnished the cocktails and scotch, Peabody and Nichols, the champagne and Benedictine. The menu was as follows:

Caviar
Oysters
Strained Ox-tail Soup
Broiled Shad and Roe
Cucumbers
Ducks
Fried Hominy — Wild Rice
Cheese
Coffee
Cocktails

| | |
|---|---|
| Pommery & Greno, 1914 | Club Cigarettes |
| Scotch | Villar Selectos |
| Benedictine | Villar Grandes |

The club toast, "To Our Country and its Glorious Flag," was given early and drunk standing, as usual, after which the Chairman called for a toast to Peabody, one of the Founding Members, who unfortunately was unable to be present, but who had furnished such good cheer.

The club song was sung, after which Mackay gave his rendition of "My Beautiful Irish Maid" by request. The Secretary referred to the recent items in the press regarding the serious illness of Maggie Cline, the old-time vaudeville star, asking whether anybody knew the chorus of the celebrated song, "Throw 'em Down, McCloskey!" Nichols seemed to be the only one, and gave it with much spirit.

The Chair called attention to the fact that this was the Fiftieth regular Dinner of the association, being the seventeenth consecutive season. He spoke of all the good fellows who had belonged to the club, and particularly named a distinguished list of those who had "gone West," and suggested singing "The Long, Long Trail," which was done in a very reverent spirit, followed by a silent toast to the dead.

John A. Black had decided a biography was in order, and he had composed a facetious short story concerning each of the founders. Of Henry R. Taylor, for instance, he wrote:

Owns a large part of the Farmers Loan and Trust Company and Bloomingdale Asylum, and is a founder of the Dinner Club.

Also has millions of cash and securities and thousands of pints, quarts and magnums.

Is the hero of Olcott's poem, "The Moisture in the Fifth Floor Back"—shakes a cocktail like a professional bartender and is most generous with all kinds of booze. Started the Woodrow Wilson Memorial and spent a large part of his fortune in the support of Volstead and now economizes by sleeping on a private car in Florida during the winter.

He is brief and decisive as an orator. His 1919 address on the League of Nations—"Nothing In It"—will always be the Club Classic for brevity. He originated the Border Line with some profit to himself, and in donating the Taylor Cup started golf activities which have been responsible for much good fellowship and outdoor amusement. He is a most honorary member of the Poker Club, became Chairman of the Duck Committee when Clarke was forcibly retired, and is a good linguist.

Most of the members were avid golfers and each Spring a schedule was prepared of the golf events of the season, with the names of the hosts and the courses. In 1925, for example, they arranged twelve events at clubs around New York such as the Piping Rock, the Links, the Creek, the Rumson, and the National.

As the older fellows dropped out, new faces appeared: Banker Charles Hayden joined in 1924, and Percy R. Payne in 1926. Eugene G. Grace and C. Ledyard Blair of Blairsden, near Peapack, New Jersey, followed shortly.

Charlie Hayden frequently invited the members to the Creek. Gene Grace often talked about the steel business and particularly Bethlehem Steel, the second largest in the country, founded by member Charles Schwab ('01) who was then the head of it. During the Second World War Grace reported frequently on the progress of the arms build-up. Several times he invited the members of the Bridge Dinner Club to his beautiful house in Bethlehem, Pennsylvania. The first such outing took place June 5, 1928, when Grace's private car *Bethlehem* left with the members at 4:07 p.m. from Penn Station running special over the Lehigh tracks. The fellows played bridge en route and arrived at 5:53 p.m. in Bethlehem. Grace, after assigning each one his room, showed them through his magnificent house with its unusual art treasures. After dinner there was more bridge, and the next day golf at the Saucon Valley Golf Club. Grace's private car returned them to Penn Station in the afternoon.

Another regular annual outing was a weekend at Blair's magnificent house near Peapack, New Jersey. Overlooking Blair's Lake, the vista down his Villa d'Este Avenue at sunset was thrilling. The men spent the night and played the Somerset Hills Country Club course the next morning.

The main events, however, remained the regular dinners at the Metropolitan Club. Although long gone, Prohibition had changed drinking habits—less wine was consumed and more hard liquor. The proceedings of the December, 1938, dinner reflect the new spirit:

Cocktails, including Old Fashioneds, which seem to be so popular nowadays, were soon flowing freely amongst the Members, and the caviar on the iced elephant inspired the Secretary to sing Arthur Clark's old song:
Caviar comes from Virgin Sturgeon,
 Virgin Sturgeon, very fine fish,
 Virgin Sturgeon needs no urging,
 That's why caviar is our dish.
It was very cold outside, and the warmth produced by our Wine Committee was most appreciated.

After a little gossip and a few remarks on the dilapidated state of the country, Phil Franklin, whom we all so enjoyed having with us, became hungry and insisted on our moving on to our Private Dining Room.

Everyone admired the table with our galaxy of Cups and the Flags dear old Dutilh Smith gave us so many years ago. A commotion was caused as Acosta missed the flag on the Hole-in-One cup, but it was soon found and restored. There is no name on the cup as yet, but it is hoped that now that we have two new members of such renowned fame in golf, that one of their names will soon be on the cup.

The Metropolitan Club treated us to their usual delicious dinner:
Beulah Beulah Soup
Sole à la meuniére
Breast of Guinea Hen on Czechoslovakia Ham
Fresh Asparagus
Cheese and Crackers

The food of the Metropolitan was as much admired then as it is today. Beulah Beulah soup was a favorite. It was half clear turtle and half pea with a *soupçon* of Sherry, baked in an oven for a few minutes, with cream on top. Ducks remained a favorite but the canvasback became harder to obtain. A specialty of the Club's kitchen was Baked Flanked Boned Shad and Roe, then as now a delicacy every spring.

Metropolitan Club problems were also discussed occasionally and the minutes of the December, 1931, meeting are revealing:

Jennings then brought up the subject of the future of the Metropolitan Club and launched into a brilliant and touching oration on the advantages of opening up the club to both sexes, an idea so new and so startling that it quite took the breath away from the members present. Grier, however, endorsed the new idea with enthusiasm and called for an opinion on so important a question from each one present in succession. Mixed views were expressed and when it came to Tom McCarter, in his usual gruff way, he wished to know whether Jennings' innovation applied to the bedrooms as well. George Roosevelt, as President of the Club, very tactfully refused to give his opinions on the subject, but the consensus of opinion of most of those present was that it would be a noble experiment and a courageous one.

The negotiations with the Calumet Club were discussed at the January, 1934, meeting:

After Nichols in a few delightful words had proposed a silent standing toast to those of our members who had passed on, Jennings asked the waiters to retire and called on Franklin for a report on his negotiations with the Calumet Club. All the members were interested to hear how successful Franklin's Committee had been so far in negotiating a consolidation with the Calumet Club, which all felt might be the salvation of the Metropolitan Club. Jennings, also, strongly advocated the changing of the South room into a grill where drinks might be served, which was strongly seconded by Hurry and Bodman.


At the bridge games the stakes were often heavy but none of them was recorded for obvious reasons: gambling was illegal. One evening in 1944, however, before the Chase-the-Ace, Gene Grace began to reminisce about a game of bridge played years ago, when Alvin Krech challenged Grace and Schwab to two rubbers. Krech started by suggesting they play for ten cents a point, but after some heckling by Krech, Schwab finally agreed to play for one dollar a point. Only three rubbers were played, but Grace received Alvin Krech's check for $3,600. As Tom McCarter would say "Thems were the good old days."

Next to Henry R. Taylor and Acosta Nichols, Krech had been one of the mainstays of the Dinner Club from its inception. Born in 1858 in Hannibal, Missouri, the son of a professor who had left Germany during the 1848 Revolution, Krech came to New York in 1895 and soon was one of the leading bankers in Wall Street. He joined the Metropolitan Club in 1898. He was a dynamic personality and was president of the Equitable Trust Company, member of many corporate boards, a civic leader and active on the Metropolitan Opera Board. In 1919, he had toured war-devastated Europe, visiting fifteen countries, and gave an interesting account of his impressions to the Dinner Club upon his return. He died in 1928.

During its first thirty years, all members of the Bridge Dinner Club were also Members of the Metropolitan Club. At the end of 1933, however, a discussion began about whether this was necessary. The question arose as the result of the resignation of a member from the parent organization. The consensus was that such a member could certainly remain in the Bridge Dinner Club.

Once or twice friction developed concerning the private dining room. On one occasion, the Ninety-first regular Dinner of Thursday, December 4, 1941—three days prior to Pearl Harbor—took place in the Ladies' Annex. This had happened before and was most disturbing as the minutes indicate: "We sacrificed our regular suite for the good of the Club. The Cincinnati Society in which we were not interested but who were paying royally for a dinner at the Club was the cause of our being moved."

The One-hundredth regular Dinner took place on April 18, 1946. The last of the original founders, Acosta Nichols, had died the year before, on February 8, 1945. The menu had by that time become much simpler than in the early years.

Menu
Fresh Russian Caviar
Bluepoint Oyster Cocktail
Baked Beulah Soup
Filet Mignon with Mushrooms
Potatoes au Gratin
New Peas
Asparagus Hollandaise
Ice Cream à la Bombe
Petits Fours
Demi Tasse
Assorted Cocktails
Old Armory Scotch
Perrier Jouet Champagne 1937

# Chapter 13

# THE DEPRESSION AND WAR YEARS: 1926-1950

In 1926, Frank Sturgis had served, first as Vice President, then as President, for a total of twenty-six years. That year at the Membership Meeting he announced that this was long enough and that he would not stand for re-election. His logical successor would have been Henry Richmond Taylor, son of Founding Member Henry A.C. Taylor. He had been Vice President since February, 1923, a Member of Bridge Dinner Club and very active in Club affairs. When he died unexpectedly and prematurely on the morning of December 5, 1925, the Board issued this statement:

Not only did the social world lose a bright and loved member from its circle—but the broader field of finance and public service were deprived of a strong and able supporter. To the Metropolitan Club, he was a warm friend, a loyal officer and to him is due very much of the Club's high standing and character.

Henry R. Taylor was not easily replaced. The Board of Governors took several months to find a new President. Finally, on May 18, 1926, they chose a Member belonging to a family long and intimately connected with the history of New York, Newbold Morris.

The first of his family to come to these shores was Richard Morris, a Captain in Cromwell's Army and a merchant in Barbados, who came to New York in the 1660s. He bought a large plantation north of the Bronx River, part of the property of Joseph Bronck, or Bronx, a Hollander who had acquired the property from the Indians. In 1691, Richard Morris's son Lewis inherited the 1,900-acre estate, and in 1697, Governor Fletcher elevated the lands into a lordship or manor under the name of Morrisania. Born in 1672, Lewis became the first native-born Chief Justice of the State of New York. The second Lewis Morris (1698-1762) was several times a member of the Colonial Assembly. Among his children were General Lewis Morris, a signer of the Declaration of Independence; the Hon. Richard Morris, Judge of the High Court of the Admiralty; and the Hon. Gouverneur Morris, delegate to the Constitutional Convention (1787) and Minister to France in 1792.

Newbold Morris was a descendent of General Lewis Morris of Morrisania. His father, Augustus Newbold Morris, was one of the original twenty-five Founders of the Club. Born in New York in 1868, he was a lawyer and a sol-

*Astragal*

dier. He studied law at Columbia, was admitted to the bar in 1892 and then founded the firm of Emmet and Morris. He resigned from that firm in 1898 to devote himself to military matters. He was a captain during the Spanish-American War and a lieutenant colonel during World War I. In 1896, he married Helen Schermerhorn Kingsland. They had three children. One of them was Newbold Morris, our late and beloved Park Commissioner.

Morris' term as President was, however, a short one. He, too, died unexpectedly, on December 20, 1928, after serving only two-and-a-half years.

The portrait of Newbold Morris hanging in the Library was made in 1899 by John W. Alexander. Born in Allegheny City, Pennsylvania, Alexander studied in Munich, Venice, Florence and Paris. Upon his return to America in 1881, he became a fashionable portraitist in New York. Three of his portraits of women were accepted by the Paris Salon of 1891. He painted the titanic murals in the Carnegie Institute of Pittsburgh, and was president of the National Academy of Design until his death in 1915.

Morris's successor was chosen from another old family whose impact upon American history was second to none—the Roosevelts. George Emlen Roosevelt was born in 1887, son of William Emlen Roosevelt, a Member of the Club since 1894 and nephew of Founding Member James A. Roosevelt. George Emlen was president of Roosevelt & Sons and was on numerous boards of directors and charitable boards. He was a member of many clubs, including the Downtown Association, Union, Links, Piping Rock, Seawanhaka Corinthian, Royal Bermuda Yacht Club and others. His firm came bravely to the financial aid of the Club in 1934 by lending it $168,000 to meet a maturity. He served as President of the Club for five years until January 19, 1934.

Roosevelt was succeeded by Ambrose D. Henry (1883-1939), who served only three-quarters of a year, resigning as President in November 1934 because of ill health. Henry had been a Member since 1909.

The nine-year period of the Morris-Roosevelt-Henry Presidencies from 1926 to 1934 was one of constant financial crises. Real-estate taxes had increased each year since 1895, when they had amounted to $14,181, climbing to $70,980 in 1928.

When in February, 1929, the mansion of Elbridge T. Gerry to the north of the Club building was torn down to make way for the new Pierre Hotel, the Board feared this might result in another serious increase in the valuation of the Club property.

The building of the forty-five floor structure of the new Hotel was the first of the unfortunate developments that eventually surrounded the Clubhouse with high-rise buildings and effectively cut off the sunshine and light which Stanford White had taken for granted to be there forever. When old Commodore Gerry died in 1928, his son and heir, Robert Livingston Gerry, wanted no part of the pink château. A syndicate bought it, among whom were Club Members Finley J. Shepherd (who had married Helen Gould), Edward F. Hutton, Walter P. Chrysler, and Robert L. Gerry himself. Their plan was to establish a hotel and restaurant worthy of one of the famous restaurateurs of the period, Charles Pierre. Born Charles Pierre Caselesco, this ambitious youngster had left his native Corsica to learn the restaurant and hotel business in France and London. There he was discovered by Louis Sherry. After a few years with Sherry's, he started his own restaurant.

It was no consolation to the Clubmembers that the new venture soon went into bankruptcy. 1929 was the wrong year to start any such venture. In 1934 Charles Pierre died and in 1938 J. Paul Getty bought the hotel, which had originally cost $15,000,000, for $2,500,000.

But in the nation and the world even bigger events with far-reaching consequences for the Club were taking place. Owing to the stock-market boom from 1927 to 1929, Membership had grown to an all-time high of 1,436. Then in October of 1929 came the stock-market crash, followed by the devastating depression that shook the nation to its foundations and destroyed the wealth of innumerable families, including, of course, that of many Members of the Club. Resignations were submitted in droves and no new men could be found to re-

William A. Barber (1870-1950)    President 1935-1944

place the lost Members. By the end of 1934 the number of Members had shrunk to 864, a decline of forty percent.

The 1932 operating deficit before depreciation was $49,420, and real-estate taxes had risen steeply to $85,000, more than triple their pre-war level. At a special Board meeting in January, 1933, the effects of the Depression were discussed, and fears were expressed that an assessment of $50 a Member might result in many more resignations. The only solution seemed to be the raising of new funds to cover the operating losses. Consequently, the Board authorized a loan of $200,000 to meet obligations. By June, $50,000 of a three-year 4% note had been subscribed to by the Members, $12,900 by Governors and $37,100 by others. The operating deficit in 1933 was $51,435.

This was the dismal financial situation which William A. Barber inherited when in 1935, upon Henry's resignation, the Board chose him as President. Born in 1870 in South Carolina, he was the son of Captain Osmond Barber, a confederate officer. He studied law at the University of South Carolina and became the At-torney General of South Carolina at an early age. In 1899, he moved to New York and became a member of the law firm Barber, Giddings and Grunden. When his first wife died, he married, in 1920, the beautiful and talented Melanie Gordon of Anisbon, Alabama. Barber died in 1950 in Taconic, Connecticut, where his wife still lives. His portrait by Ellen G. Emmet Rand hangs in the Library.

In 1933, when Franklin D. Roosevelt became President he soon repealed Prohibition. Clubmen had at first hoped that Prohibition would prove a boon to clubs with their secret lockers, but in the end it had hurt attendance—men preferred to stop off at a speakeasy. Repeal was bound to bring the men back, and the Membership generally felt that the new bar should not be replaced in the Main Hall but in a more intimate location. In October, 1933, Members petitioned the Board to convert the South Lounging Room into a bar and this has since become one of the most popular rooms at the Clubhouse. Also in March, 1933, President Roosevelt ordered all banks to be closed. The gold standard was abandoned and the price of gold rose from $23 to over $30 an ounce. In order to bring more people into the Clubhouse, it was decided to open it to women, and on Sunday, December 10, 1933, women were admitted for dinner. That day, the price per plate was $2 and 442 covers were served. But for the rest of the week, women were still restricted to the Ladies' Dining Room in the Annex.

At this time talks began with the Calumet Club, which also had gotten into serious financial difficulties. It had become absolutely imperative to gain new Members. In an attempt to accomplish this, the entrance fee was revoked in 1934 until two-hundred new Resident and fifty Non-Resident Members had been admitted. In January, 1935, widows of Members were given the privilege of using the Annex for dues of $50 a year. Then in May, 1935, under the Consulship of President Barber, eighty-nine members of the Calumet Club were admitted en bloc. As a result of all these measures, Membership rose to 1,120 by the end of 1936. The economy and the financial market were also showing some improvement.

The famous Calumet Club had been organized in 1879 by sons of members of the Union Club who could not join that club because of its long waiting list. Originally, it occupied rented rooms at 21 East 17th Street. Moving uptown three times, it finally settled at 12 West 56th Street in 1910, where it remained until it closed its doors in 1935.

The Calumet had always been a relatively small club with a membership of less than two hundred. A wonderful spirit of intimacy and camaraderie existed which was unique. The large, long pipe, or calumet, of peace which was always placed in a prominent place in the club was more than just a symbol.

The following story, contributed by William V. Logan, highlights the fact that club life was not always stuffy in the '20s and '30s in New York. He relates that in those days such clubs as the Lotus, Manhattan, Knickerbocker, Calumet and Metropolitan customarily vied with each other as to which could serve the best dinner or furnish the best entertainment. One such dinner at the Calumet had as its entertainer a vaudevillian masquerading as a waiter, whose forte was to disturb guests by spilling soup or coffee, or some other form of practical joke— but innocently. That evening he picked on one of the governors of the Calumet and spilled coffee on him. The governor ordered him out of the room, and followed in order to reprimand him and dismiss him. The supposed waiter started to cry and said his wife was sick and his numerous children had nothing to eat, and pleaded to be reinstated—upon which the governor gave him $5 and told him to go back into the dining room. The relenting governor was not told that the waiter was a phony until the next day.

When economics and the great depression caused the Calumet to close its doors in 1935, the members moved over to the Metropolitan. Two members eventually became Presidents of the Metropolitan Club. They were George W. Whitaker, who was elected President in 1951, and Thomas O'Hara, who was elected in 1955. Others who served as Governors were Nelson E. Griffiths, Wiley R. Reynolds, Louis R. In-

Thomas A. O'Hara (1888-1958)
President 1956-1957

graham, Miles R. Johnson, Henry A. Johnston, William V. Logan and Edmund E. Thomas.

Lester P. Deeves deserves a chapter unto himself. He had had such a wonderful time with his cronies at the Calumet and spent so much time there that when its doors closed and all his friends moved to 1 East 60th, his wife put her foot down. "No," she said. He was not going to join the Metropolitan; he would again spend too much time with his pals and not enough with her. He had to work on her for twenty-seven years until she finally relented. He joined the Metropolitan Club in 1962 and was appointed Chairman of the Bridge Committee at once. In 1971, he was elected to the Board of Governors and became very constructive in the direction of the Club. He was active in the negotiations for the merger with the Canadian Club. Deeves died in 1979.

With World War II beginning in Europe in 1939, things were once more becoming difficult for the Club. The number of Members declined, reaching an all-time low of 710 in 1942, of whom 481 were Resident Members. This was less than half of the 1929 high. In addition, any Member called into the military or naval services of the country had his dues remitted. Certain parts of the basement were equipped with beds for servicemen who could find no other accommodations in the city.

During these war years, women—wives, daughters, and guests—began to be admitted into parts of the Clubhouse. The Great Hall was turned into a lounge where women could enjoy an apéritif, and they could dine in the Main Dining Room on the third floor, although the second floor remained off-limits. At this time also, the management encouraged Members to hold debutante parties and similar festivities at the Clubhouse.

The halfway mark to a century in the Club's existence was approaching, and a big Anniversary dinner was arranged. It was to take place on February 20, 1941, the same day on which,

fifty years earlier, W. Watts Sherman had invited twenty-five men to the dinner at the Knickerbocker Club at which the Constitution would be signed. A special Semi-Centennial Committee was put together with Robert A. Grannis as Chairman. It included such notables as George Allen, George Gordon Battle, Pierre S. du Pont, Alfred P. Sloan, Jr., and Samuel Seabury. Since the occasion was of interest and importance to the other men's clubs, invitations were extended to the presidents of the Union Club, the Knickerbocker Club and the Racquet and Tennis Club. Mr. Howard A. Plummer contributed an article, entitled "Historical Reminiscences of the Metropolitan Club," which was included in the elaborate anniversary program. The final paragraph read:

The Club is a living testimonial of constructive endeavour and achievement. Membership therein is

Black Tuesday, October 29, 1929 — the day the stock market crashed.

a valued privilege for, in addition to its beauty and its facilities, there pervades throughout that intangible but cherished spirit of fellowship and friendship. During the fifty years that have passed with their ever changing customs and conditions, this spirit has prevailed. May the flame of this spirit so shine on—undimmed, unmarked and inviolate—and as the expression of this vital force may the Metropolitan Club and its Clubhouse live on through the years to come!

Ironically, only four years later, both Messrs. Grannis and Plummer would advocate and vote for the surrender of the Clubhouse in order to pay the mortgage.

At the dinner, the Reverend Roelif H. Brooks pronounced the invocation. The menu was as elaborate as usual.

At the time, five Charter Members, each admitted on February 20, 1891, were still on the Club's roster:

Eugene Higgins
Arthur Curtis James
Hamilton Fish Kean
Arden M. Robbins
Grenville L. Winthrop

The Metropolitan Club had survived the difficult Depression years, when some other less fortunate clubs were forced to disband, and it had celebrated in royal fashion its Fiftieth Anniversary, but the truth was it was still not out of the red and continued to be faced with increasing financial problems.

# Chapter 14

# A NEAR-RUN THING

The Club continued to conduct its affairs with little imagination on the part of the management and with little realism on the part of the Membership, which refused to pay increases in annual dues which would reflect the rising costs of living. As a result, operating losses soared; they amounted to $265,000 for the three years from 1942 to 1944. In reality they were even higher, for no depreciation was charged. But it was unwise handling of finances by the Board that almost forced the sale of the Clubhouse.

In 1925, at the end of Frank Sturgis' Presidency, Mutual Life Insurance Company of New York lent the Club $1.5 million on a five-year-mortgage. The loan maturity had been extended several times and it was due in 1945. No sinking fund provision had been made; earnings had been so meager during that period that no funds were available in any case. Furthermore, at the end of 1944, the Club was in arrears on the real-estate taxes due the City of New York in the amount of $58,054, and no interest had been paid on the mortgage for some time. Interest arrears since February 1, 1941, amounted to $136,875. Obviously neither were very happy with this situation.

In March, 1944, Barber decided that he would not stand for re-election as President, having filled that office for nine years and being in ill health. The financial problems were becoming overwhelming. A fierce struggle ensued over the election of his successor, one faction pushing for Guernsey Curran, the other for Lee Warren James. Board Member George A. Ellis, a well-known lawyer, had sent out a written appeal to all fellow Board Members on James's behalf. Nevertheless, at the May 16 meeting, Guernsey Curran was elected President, and James, Vice President; James was also elected Chairman of the Realty Committee. Barber was given an Honorary Life Membership and remained on the Board.

Lee Warren James hailed from Dayton, Ohio where he was born in 1889. He had studied law and formed the firm of James and Coolidge with offices in New York and Dayton. He was president of the Day-Fan Electric Company until 1929 when that company was acquired by General Motors. He was Chairman of Trustees of the National Safety Council. He had one son, Robert L. James, and three daughters.

The Mutual was beginning to insist that the problem of the mortgage be dealt with. James

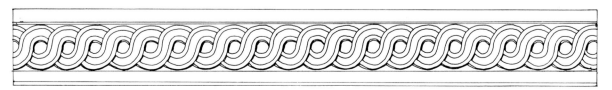

*Guilloche*

167

Lee Warren James (1891-1963)
President 1945-1951, 1957

was handling most of the negotiations and, at the October 17 meeting, he reported that the Mutual was willing to settle for $1 million in cash for the mortgage and accrued interest, which together amounted to over $1.6 million. But James had no suggestions for the raising of such a sum. At the next meeting, on November 8, James reported that the Mutual had an outside offer of $1 million for the building, but would still accept $1 million in settlement from the Club. Curran was pessimistic about reaching any solution.

Frequent Board meetings and discussions with the Mutual took place. At the November 21, 1944, Board meeting, Curran related that

the Mutual felt that they had been very lenient but that they were not a charitable organization and that they had to consider this a business proposition in justice to the policy holders; that in 1928 they had written to the Board suggesting that in view of the substantial income of the Club at that time, some amount should be applied to the reduction of the mortgage, and this was never done.

Mutual wanted $1 million down, which they later reduced to $250,000 plus interest arrears. They had withdrawn an earlier offer to take $1 million cash in full settlement for the mortgage plus interest, since they feared criticism for taking a loss on a mortgage loan on the Millionaires' Club building.

The opposing ranks were now forming, Curran and his followers contending that the only solution was to relinquish the Building for the mortgage and buy a smaller clubhouse. Where the money would come from for a new building they knew not. James and his supporters wanted to raise enough money to make a down payment to the Mutual and pay the tax arrears. At the Board meeting of February 1, 1945, Curran put his cards on the table. He spoke at length, reviewing the negotiations with Mutual over the past few months. "He had become convinced that it was not practical for us to stay here," the Minutes related. He had investigated many other properties, he said, one of which in his opinion was satisfactory and adequate. This was the building at 1 East 67th Street, owned by Countess Laszlo Szechenyi (née Gladys Vanderbilt), which she was willing to sell for $500,000 in cash. He was prepared to place this offer before the Annual Meeting with the support of the Governing Committee. The Board then unanimously voted that to remain in the old building was impractical, and that they would surrender, on certain conditions, the deed to the Mutual Life Insurance Company. An offer of $350,000 was made to Countess Szechenyi for the building at 1 East 67th Street. Luckily she turned it down.

James, while voting for the measure, had quietly been working to find financial support from the Membership. Already at the January 16, 1945, Board meeting, he had reported that he had received substantial financial encouragement from a number of Members who were anxious to maintain the present location. There were two more Board meetings, February 20th and 26th, with Curran and his supporters pushing to relinquish Stanford White's creation for the mortgage. Countess Szechenyi, he reported, had come down to $400,000. At the latter meeting, Curran expressed his doubts that the funds necessary to stay at the old building could be raised. He said that he would subscribe $25,000 to a new home, but not a cent to remain.

No vote was taken, however, because Barber pointed out that only twenty Governors were present and such a question was too important to be acted on by so few. But Curran's group were resolved not to compromise, and they were determined to sell the building and buy a new one.

Finally Curran lost, and he resigned as President and Board Member, and shortly thereafter, as a Member of the Club. He had been a Life Member. Some of his supporters also resigned, including Howard A. Plummer, James L. Ashley, Robert A. Grannis and Samuel R. Fuller, Jr.

The resignations were submitted at a Board meeting called for March 20, 1945, chaired by Lee Warren James as Vice President, and were accepted "with regret." James then outlined his tentative financing plan which was fully submitted on April 17. He had been able to negotiate a plan whereby the Mutual accepted an immediate payment of $100,000 and took $125,000 in payment of all interest arrears. The maturity date of the mortgage was advanced to April, 1953, but a sinking fund of $50,000 a quarter was demanded. This soon turned out to be too heavy a burden. To make these payments and pay tax arrears, James had been able to raise $269,480 from Members on voluntary open-account advances. He also advocated the creation of a $2 million, 25-year 2.5% Refunding Mortgage issue to be offered to Members at 90% of par, somewhat similar to the $700,000 issue subscribed by Members at the time of the founding in 1891. The new issue was to have a "kicker"—holders were to share with the Club in the proceeds of any sale of the Clubhouse at a price exceeding $2 million. By that time, there were several offers from outside buyers willing to pay $2 million for the property.

At the Board Meeting following the Annual Meeting on May 10, 1945, James was elected President which office he held until 1951. The vacancies on the Board left by the resignations of Curran and his supporters were filled by George Washington Hill, president of American Tobacco; Grover A. Whalen, "Mr. New York" of that time; George A. Ellis, W. Winan Freeman and Henry Alan Johnston.

It had been a near-run thing, but again the Club had been saved embarrassment or demise by the devotion of its Members, their attach-

ment to the Club, its Building and its tradition. They followed in the footsteps of J. Pierpont Morgan when he advanced the funds needed to buy the Annex in 1911, of Adrian Iselin when he extended a long-term loan in 1912 and of George Emlen Roosevelt when his firm, Roosevelt and Sons, advanced $168,000 in 1926 to meet a maturity.

James then proceeded with the reorganization plan, satisfied the Mutual, paid arrears and filed a $2 million issue with the Securities and Exchange Commission in Washington to be offered to Members on August 1, 1945, at

Now began the period of reconstruction. At the Annual Meeting of April 25, 1946, James outlined four points high on the agenda for the coming year. These were first, the sale of bonds to meet the financial requirements; second, necessary improvements in the physical property of the Club; third, steps to increase the membership; and, fourth, various activities to restore the Club's prestige. Of utmost importance, he said, was the sale of at least $400,000 of the bonds by the end of the year. This suggests that they were not selling too well, despite the fact that James reported that he had a firm offer of $3.5 million for the property. James also announced that they would give consideration to the restoration of an initiation fee. In October of that year, Annual Dues were increased to $250 and an Initiation Fee of $200 was to be restored if Resident Membership exceeded 750.

Women had already been admitted to the Main Hall on the ground floor and to the Dining Room on the third floor by resolution of the Board on January 18, 1944. At the same time the Ladies' Restaurant in the Annex was closed. This step would eventually change the entire atmosphere of the Club and permit it to develop the activities necessary to maintain the large and expensive building. In November, 1946, a proposition to rent the Annex as a retail store was submitted to the Board and turned down.

James remained President until April, 1951. He had prevented the humiliation and indignity of having the building repossessed for the mortgage, had avoided bankruptcy and turned the fortunes of the Club upwards again. Operations showed a moderate profit every year during his remaining term and a number of overdue improvements were made to the Building, such as the installation of new electric elevators to replace the old hydraulic ones. The fundamental problems continued, however, and would haunt the Club over the next thirty years. When James negotiated the new terms with the Mutual and agreed to a sinking fund of $50,000 quarterly, or $200,000 a year, he probably realized that he could not possibly meet the payments—unless he could sell most of the Second Mortgage bonds. This proved a difficult task. As early as January, 1947, he was unable to meet the Mutual sinking-fund installment and had to renegotiate the terms of the loan.

On May 23, 1950, a grateful Board elected James an Honorary Life Member, and a portrait of him was commissioned and painted by the well-known artist, Howard Chandler Christie. A Testimonial Dinner was given him on November 30, 1950. At the next Membership Meeting, he asked to be released of his duties as President.

James was once more drafted for the Presidency in 1956 when the then-holder of that office, Thomas O'Hara, became seriously ill. He held office less than a year, but became the only man to occupy the Presidency for two unconnected terms. In June, 1959, the Tap Room on the second floor was renamed after him and his portrait by Howard Chandler Christie hangs there now. Christie was a well-known portrait painter who had started his career as an illustrator for *Harper's* and *Scribner's* magazines. Among his best-known works are the portraits of Mrs. William Randolph Hearst and of Secretary of State and Chief Justice Charles Evans Hughes.

On September 12, 1960, a special Luncheon was given for James's eighty-third birthday and, in 1963, the Board presented a plaque to his family. When his wife died in 1963, he moved into one of the rooms of the Clubhouse and he died there shortly afterward.

# Chapter 15

# THE SOCIAL SEASON

The first lavish dinner dance in the Club's history was given on Washington's Birthday, February 22, 1895, which coincided approximately with the anniversary of the Founders' Dinner at the old Knickerbocker Club on February 20, 1891. This became the big social affair of the season and remained so for many years.

At that time, January and February were the height of the social season in New York. Society did not yet pack up after the New Year and migrate *en masse* to Palm Beach or Palm Springs. In that pre-air-conditioning age, the winter with all its snow, ice and subzero temperatures was more bearable than July and August with attendant humidity and heat. During those months the fashionable world was in Newport or Lenox and, socially speaking, New York was dead. The furniture in townhouses and apartments was protected with slip covers and all the curtains and portières were taken down.

The most important event of the season was Mrs. Astor's Ball which always took place either on the first or second Monday in January. During those winter months, party followed party: the Patriarch's Ball, the Family Circle Dancing Class, private balls, opera twice a week, simple dinner parties for forty people

and the like.

On Saturday afternoons the Metropolitan Club was crowded with Members. An orchestra played background music. In January, 1895, the Executive Committee had asked several well-known orchestra leaders for bids. Frank's band of eight to ten pieces wanted $60 for the afternoon, Berger's, $72 and Lander's, $75. They hired Lander, who also provided the dance music for the first George Washington's Birthday Ball. His price for a twelve-piece orchestra was $120 for playing from seven to twelve in the evening. Lander was the most sought-after bandleader at that time—he always played at Mrs. Astor's Ball, his orchestra dressed in Astor-blue uniforms, sitting in a small balcony banked with orchids. All of the great families had their own "house colors" in which the household staff was dressed. The color of the house of Vanderbilt was dark red and that of the Oelrichs was tan trimmed with red.

The Club's George Washington's Birthday Ball was very popular for many years. The price charged for the first dinner was $3 a cover without drinks, plus $2 for the supper, which was served at eleven. In 1897, Members were informed that out of necessity reservations had to

*Vitruvian scroll*

be limited to 250 on a first-come-first-served basis and that the price would be $5 a plate.

Another of the great annual functions in the Club's early life was the Spring Meet of the Coaching Club, which assembled at the Clubhouse and then drove to the Claremont Inn on Riverside Drive for luncheon. Later on, for a period of several years, its annual breakfast was held on a Saturday in May in the Ladies' Annex. It afforded an attractive and colorful spectacle, for the members wore dark-green coats with silver buttons and silk toppers, and the women were dressed in formal afternoon attire, with corsage flowers in the color of the coach upon which they rode. After luncheon, from ten to twenty four-in-hand drags lined up for parade on the west side of Fifth Avenue, facing the Club and heading south, the coachman and footmen in boots and breeches and their respective liveries. The footmen sounded the Yard of Tin, as the long coaching horns were called, and the drags drove into and around the park. After maneuvers, they lined up and the President of the Coaching Club drove by on his coach amid the salutations of the amateur coachmen and the parade disbanded.

Even in the Club's early years, the kitchen had an excellent reputation and the wine cellar was famous for its rare vintages. Innumerable parties were, therefore, given in the private dining rooms. Few records of such dinners have come down to us but the menu of a memorable one is still in the archives of the Fahnestock family. William Fahnestock, who had become a Member in 1894, became engaged to Julia Strong Goetchius a few years later. On November 5, 1898, his brothers, Ernest, Clarence and Harris, gave him a bachelor dinner at the Club. The menu on this occasion still exists, and it is typical of the repasts the Members particularly enjoyed in those years.

The menu reproduced here was printed on heavy embossed paper. On the cover was the picture of a Regency dandy holding a young woman by the arm and swinging a walking stick. Inside are listed the names of all invited guests, friends and relatives, a total of sixteen.

The menu was naturally printed in French.

Dinner began with the customary caviar, then oysters (perhaps twelve?), then clear turtle soup. The next dish was crabmeat in cream sauce with cucumbers, followed by saddle of venison with currant jelly, apple sauce and peas. Then a dish of fresh champignons in butter was served. To settle the digestion, a punch of grapefruit juice à la Metropolitan came next. Finally, the inevitable duck appeared. This time it was ruddy duck, a common sea duck, smaller than the canvasback or redhead. The side dish was truffle salad. *Pour terminer*, there was cheese, Nesselrode pudding (a rum-flavored pudding of fruit and chestnuts), dessert, fruit and cookies, coffee and liqueurs. The wines were equally august. With the oysters came an 1874 sauterne, with the soup an 1851 amontillado, champagne with the venison and red wine, a Château Lafite 1874, with the duck. The 1870s were outstanding vintage years.

Although bicycling and bowling were popular entertainments among the Members, the mainstay activities during the Club's history up to recent years took place on the second floor in the Cardrooms and the Billiard Room. All afternoon and evening, crowds of men congregated there. Waiters were in attendance, and adjoining the large Cardroom was a small kitchen serving simple luncheons, dinners or suppers. Drinks were available until late in the evening. The Members were always expected to be properly dressed—taking off one's coat was very much frowned upon.

The extent of the activity is reflected in the proliferation of the games committees. There was a Billiard Committee which occasionally hired instructors, a Bridge Committee, a Gin Rummy Committee, and a Backgammon Committee. Poker was a very popular game, as the many framed hands of royal flushes with the date and name of the lucky holder testify. The original Constitution tried to provide for some control over gambling in the Clubhouse. It gave the Executive Committee power to regulate the kinds of games and the sums or stakes permitted by posting the regulations on the wall in the Cardroom. Such controls, however, were soon dropped, and many stories circulated that stakes were often very high.

Former President Cornelius Reid recalls how he became a Member in 1946 as result of a poker game. A friend had long urged him to become a Member but Neil felt he belonged to enough clubs to suit him. One night he had dinner at the Club with a friend and was talked into staying on for a game with some other friends. Neil was lucky that night and when settlement time came, the loser promised to send a check for his not-inconsiderable loss the next day. No check came the next day or for some time after. But one day a letter arrived informing him that he had been elected a Member and that the initiation fee and one year's dues had been paid. Enclosed also was a check for the balance due on the gambling debt.

The tasks of the various committees included the organization of tournaments, mostly bridge, gin rummy, backgammon and billiards.

Billiards in those early years was a popular activity; the Billiard Room on the Second Floor held nine billiard tables with strong lights above each table. The Committee arranged several tournaments a year. To increase the proficiency of the Members in this sport, professional instructors were hired. The Executive Committee's minutes record that Mr. McLaughlin was hired at a salary of $100 a month. He remained for several years, until May, 1899, when a Mr. Behrens was hired for the year, except during the months of July and August.

Most of the tournaments at that time were intra-club, because a close relationship existed with many other men's clubs in New York and other cities. Few records remain of such tournaments except that the dates are given in the Minutes of Meetings of the Board of Governors, until in May, 1963, the Monthly Bulletin was started. The announced purpose of the Bulletin was: "The Bulletin will appear monthly and it will endeavor to keep Members *au courant* of what events take place in the Club, as well as in office holdings and also some sidelights on how the Club came into existence." Since that time the Bulletin has been published regularly eleven times a year, and is of great value to any present or future historian.

The creator and editor of the Bulletin until his death was Eustace A. L. Bennett, known to one and all as "Eal." He was born in England in 1884, educated at Charterhouse and New College, Oxford University, and was decorated in both World Wars; he was a veteran of both the British and American Armed Forces. In his salad days, he had travelled widely and gathered around him a host of friends all over the world.

Eal was a prodigious reader of both poetry and prose, an admirer of the classics generally, and of the *Diary of Samuel Pepys* and John Keats's poetry in particular. He was fascinated by American, English and Continental history and he knew the blood lines of the great and the near-great by heart. Eal became a Member in April, 1946, and lived at the Clubhouse for the last ten years of his life. When he met with financial reverses, he was made an Honorary Life Member, Corresponding Secretary, Librarian and a Member of the Liaison Committee. He was in constant demand socially and there was hardly a week right up to the morning of his death when he was not engaged in a round of luncheons, dinners, parties and other events. He died in his sleep the morning of Saturday, September 26, 1964, in his room at the Clubhouse.

The Bulletin still bears the stamp of his personality.

Of special interest were the Interclub Tournaments and the most popular among these were Backgammon Tournaments, which took place twice a year at the Clubhouse over a period of thirty or forty years. The January, 1964, issue of the Monthly Bulletin gives a lengthy description of one of these meetings, which took place on October 9, 1963, and will serve as an example of this favorite event.

On Wednesday, October 9th, the Interclub Backgammon Tournament was held at our Clubhouse. After a dinner in the Warren James Room, attended by over forty entrants, play was started in the Card Room. A very pleasant evening was spent, thoroughly enjoyed by the participants.

There were nine clubs contesting—namely; in order of their respective standing for the first session of the tournament:

Stock Exchange (plus 66); Racquet and Tennis, N.Y. (plus 57); Metropolitan Club (plus 26); Racquet Club, Philadelphia (plus 9); Piping Rock, N.Y. (minus 12); Brook Club (minus 15); St. Nicholas (minus 39); Everglades, Palm Beach (minus 40) and Whist Club (minus 54).

The Metropolitan team was made up of Messrs. Baldwin, Farnell, Barclay and Nadal, with Mr. Arthur Newton of the University Club substituting for Mr. Jesse Livermore, who could not be present.

The highest individual score was made by Mr. J.M. Fox of the Racquet and Tennis Club, and the second highest by Mr. Robert Gill of the Stock Exchange team. Mr. Jack Rainier is President of the Interclub Tournament Committee and Mr. G.W.E. Baldwin is Secretary and Treasurer. The tournament will be continued at a later date.

Actually this is one of the most interesting events of the year staged at the Metropolitan Club. The League was started in 1929, and the member clubs are: The Brook, The Everglades of Palm Beach, the Piping Rock, the Metropolitan, The Racquet and Tennis, the St. Nicholas, The Stock Exchange Club, The Tuxedo, The Union Club, The University and The Whist Club.

The tournament holds two dinners, followed by backgammon, every year in October and November; they always take place at the Metropolitan Club, and are black-tie affairs. Each club has a team of five, and the captain of each team is on the League Board of Directors. Jack Rainier has served as Secretary-Treasurer, Vice President, President and is now Chairman of the Board. G.W.E. (Joe) Baldwin, also of the Metropolitan Club, is the Secretary-Treasurer of the League.

The regular games start after dinner and go on to midnight, or later, but some of the players keep on playing until next morning.

In the 1930s, Sunday afternoon lectures were popular. Member Burton Holmes and his travelogues always drew a large attendance in the West Lounge.

For many years an extremely popular event, strictly stag, was the Grand National Sweepstakes Dinner, given every year on the night preceding the actual event in England. After dinner in the Main Dining Room, a stand was erected in the center of the room and the horses were bid upon by auction. John Daly and George Allen were the favorite auctioneers. Favorites might fetch as much as $2,000. Thirty to forty horses usually ran. A month before, books of tickets on the horses were presold at $2 a ticket or $20 a book. The money from the sale of the tickets plus the auction was put in a pool, and then divided among the holders of the winning horse. A percentage of the pool went to the Policemen's Protective Association as "protection" since the legality of the auction was questionable.

Slowly, however, attendance began to lag and in 1957 Chairman Admiral Bergen of the Special Events Committee suggested that women be invited. That was the end. No man in his right mind would bid $1,000 on a horse with his wife sitting next to him. ("So you have money for that nonsense but when I wanted that $750 mink coat, you said you could not afford it.")

With women taking a greater role in the life of the Club, it was only a matter of time before a Womens' Committee was formed to enlist their aid in stimulating social activities. The formation of such a Committee was first suggested by Ambassador James H. R. Cromwell at the Board Meeting of June, 1963. The Board took up the suggestion and invited a number of women to form such a Committee. An organizational meeting took place on November 12, 1963. Present were Mmes. John Brown, Eugene Hill-Smith, Jean Koree, Rudolph Bernatschke, A. Preston Lewis, Paul Porzelt, Charles Baehler, Chester Dudley, Robert Lea and Countess Annesley. Jim Cromwell attended as an observer.

Between dances in 1977, right to left, President Alger Chapman, Klara Porzelt, and Fred Paton.

The Debutante Ball, 1977.

The Chair at this first meeting was taken by Mrs. Preston Lewis. At the subsequent meeting on November 18, 1963, Mrs. Paul Porzelt was elected Chairman of the Committee, an appointment which she held until her death in March, 1981. Under her energetic and devoted leadership, the social life of the Club has become more active and colorful.

The first new feature introduced and organized by Klara Porzelt were the monthly dinner-dances. They filled a need in the social life of the group, as entertainment of this sort in hotels and nightclubs became less desirable, the ladies being reluctant to wear their sometimes fabulous bijoux in public places. The first of these dances took place on October 24th of that same year. The Great Marble Hall was filled with people drinking cocktails at seven o'clock, and about an hour later they moved up to the Main Dining Room, where a Buffet Dinner was served. A dance floor had been provided in the center of the room by removing

part of the red carpet, and music was supplied by Michel Dunn's orchestra. About 120 people attended. The routine then established has continued to the present day.

These dances increased in popularity. On October 21, 1965, over 175 Members and their guests attended. Many hostesses had taken tables of forty or more to entertain friends. At that time, the charge was $8.00 for dinner and dancing with beverages extra. About eight evenings a year were earmarked for this event. In later years, the January and February dances were canceled since too many of the Members, in particular their wives, preferred to spend New York's colder months in warmer climates.

The traditional Annual Ball always has been the Club's principal social event. After the First World War, its date was moved from the evening of Washington's Birthday to the first week of December. For the occasion, the Great Marble Hall is stripped of its carpet and all furniture. A score of red-coated violinists line the railing of the historic stairway, and the strains of their music greet the Members and their guests as they arrive and pass through the Hall to the West Lounge for drinks. At nine o'clock dinner is announced and the long procession of people take the elevator or walk up the stairs en route to the Main Dining Room on the Third Floor. During dinner, strolling violinists serenade the diners from table to table. Traditional for many years has been Terrapine à la Maryland as the fish course on the menu. At the end of the dinner, everyone descends to the Great Hall for the ball. Champagne is served in the West Lounge and dancing continues into the small hours of the morning.

Another lasting achievement of the Women's Committee has been the Annual Debutante Ball, now given every year between Christmas and New Year's Day. The custom of presenting eligible young women to society is well established, even though wags may refer to it as Society's Fertility Rites. Slightly out of favor during the Vietnam war years, the Annual Debutante Ball is presently regaining its former popularity.

Before 1966, the Metropolitan Club had never held any debutante parties. A group known as the Metropolitan Dancing Class, so-called from a brief season at the Metropolitan Club, had no connection with the Club. It was a group of sixteen sub-debutantes of impeccable family background who later met at the Ritz for dancing and who were in this manner introduced to Old Society.

At one time two to three-hundred debutante balls were held in New York every year. Many were private parties given by rich families to present their daughters to society and lavish amounts of money were spent. When George Gould presented his daughter Marjorie (later Mrs. Drexel) to Society at the Plaza Hotel in 1909, the tab was $200,000 (1909 dollars). For many years, the guardian of the exclusive set was the Metropolitan Junior Assembly. They published a booklet called *The Metropolitan Junior and Senior Index* which contained the names of 1,200 eligible young ladies and desirable escorts. They also gave the names of preferred preparatory schools and colleges and

a Metropolitan Social Calendar. This listed the approved dancing classes for various age groups, 5 to 15, 14 to 16 (juniors) and 16 through 18 (senior). To be presented at the approved Debutante and Presentation Balls, it was necessary to apply four years prior to graduation. Among the approved balls were the Society of Mayflower Descendants Debutante Ball, the Assembly and New Year's Ball, the New York Junior League Debutante Ball, The First and Second Junior Assemblies, the Debutante Cotillion Christmas Ball and about ten others.

Today, the two principal coming-out parties in New York are the Debutante Cotillion Christmas Ball for the New York Infirmary, and the International Debutante Ball for the Soldiers, Sailor's and Airmen's Club, both taking place at the Waldorf. A special feature of the latter are the many young beauties from the Lone Star State making the Texas Bow to the great applause of their admirers. The Junior Assembly is still also very popular.

While as many as seventy-five young women may be presented at the public debutante balls (and the cost is often tax-deductible), the Ball at the Metropolitan Club is more restricted. Only young women who are related to a Member qualify so the number at such an evening usually is from four to eight debutantes.

But none of the other debutante parties has the backdrop provided by the Great Hall of the Metropolitan Club. Members are invited to wear white tie and decorations. The debutantes wear a red sash over their white gowns. After dinner in the Main Dining Room, the guests assemble in the Great Marble Hall on the first floor. At the opening of the Presentation, the Ladies of the Ball Committee, led by Chairman Mrs. Paul Porzelt and accompanied by their husbands or escorts, walk down the stairway, their names announced by the President of the Club as they reach the halfway landing. The Committee Members are then seated in front of the fireplace, with their escorts standing behind their chairs. Then the debutantes descend one by one, each flanked by her father and her escort, their names announced as they reach the

Debutante Anne Bunte Spencer descends the staircase into the Great Hall, escorted by her father John Hutchings Spencer and Brent Baker, December, 1977.

The Debutante Cotillon, December, 1978.

At a costume ball on May 7, 1976, the Club celebrated America's 200th birthday and the Club's own 85th anniversary.

landing. They dance a minuette with their fathers, who then hand them over to their escorts, and the general dancing begins—and lasts well through the night.

At the first Debutante Ball, held on January 12, 1966, a granddaughter of Ambassador Braden, Alina Braden, and five other young women were presented. These affairs have continued each year up to the present and have proven to be one of the high points of the season.

Shortly before her death on March 31, 1981, the Board of Governors bestowed a singular honor upon the Chairman of the Women's Committee, Mrs. Paul Porzelt. It authorized the hanging of a portrait of her by her friend Valerie, wife of Member George T. Delacorte, in the Ladies' Lounge on the First Floor of the Clubhouse. The unveiling took place in the presence of President Harold B. Hamilton, the Hon. Mr. James Cromwell, and many Members, friends and employees of the Club. Her portrait is the only one of a wife of a Member hanging in the Clubhouse.

The social life in the Club has run along a well-established pattern during the last few decades. The luncheon hour is increasingly popular and the Main Dining Room is usually filled to overflowing. The Men's Grill in the Morgan room is for men only. Between September and May, a Sunday Brunch is served. The outstanding buffet, the seafood bar, the salad bar and specially prepared dishes have made it a very popular feature; its fame has spread beyond the Club walls. Attendance often reaches 350 or more.

The year begins with the traditional New Year's Open House from noon to three o'clock. The St. Patrick's Day Parade is watched from the windows of the West Lounge where cocktails and Irish Coffee are served and from the Main Dining Room where a special St. Patrick's Day Buffet is offered from noon on. Theater parties are popular throughout the year. A gourmet dinner at the Club, bus transportation to the theater and return and—*pour terminer*—a nightcap and a snack at the Clubhouse complete the evening. Stag affairs are Sportsmen's

game dinners, at which a good part of the delicacies served are donated by the many hunters among the Members, and several Old Fashioned Beefsteak Dinners. A Golf Championship Tournament is held usually in June.

The monthly Dinner Dances remain popular, although they are no longer scheduled for January, February and March. Too many of the hostesses who like to entertain their friends at those events are in Palm Beach or Palm Springs avoiding the New York winter. In 1980, the first one was held on April 17, and the next, dubbed the Spring Festival Ball, was held on May 22. Dancing is to Eddie Lane's music. Attendance was 185 members and their guests.

After Labor Day, the new season is opened by a President's Reception given jointly by the presidents of the two clubs, the Metropolitan and the Canadian clubs. October, November and December are the busiest time of the year. In 1980, there were Dinner Dances on October 23 and November 20, an "Oktoberfest" on October 15, a Beefsteak Dinner on November 10, a Thanksgiving Day Dinner and then the Annual Ball on December 12. A colorful note was added to the first Sunday Brunch in November when Associate Member John Fairclough brought his four-in-hand coach to the Club's Courtyard and took Members on a nostalgic coachride through the Park interrupted by the serving of champagne at the Tavern-on-the-Green court.

December is perhaps the busiest month, starting with the Annual Ball during the first week. The whole Building is lavishly decorated in the Christmas spirit with a huge tree in the corner of the Great Hall. A Yuletide Luncheon is served December 12th, with roast turkey, chestnuts, and Christmas Carols afterwards in the Great Hall. A children's party has become traditional the week before Christmas with Santa Claus, puppeteers, Christmas carols, gifts and refreshments. The Debutante Ball falls between Christmas and New Year's Day. On New Year's Eve there is a dance, and a buffet is served in the Main Dining Room from 10 p.m. to whenever the spirit fades. On New Year's Day, there is Open House for Members and their families only.

# Chapter 16

# THE FOUNDING FAMILIES

Joining a club at the turn of the century was very much a family affair. Many brothers, brothers-in-law, cousins, sons and grandsons of the Founders and other early members joined the Metropolitan Club sooner or later.

J. Pierpont Morgan's son joined as a matter of course, as did his brother Junius S. Morgan. J. Pierpont, Jr., was a Governor from 1913, when he took his father's seat, to 1932 when he died. Morgan's son-in-law, W. Pierson Hamilton, joined in 1896 and was a Governor from 1915 to 1924. His son, Morgan's grandson, Laurens Morgan Hamilton, became a Life Member in 1939 and was often seen in the Clubhouse until his death in 1979.

Many of Morgan's partners joined the Club over the years, one of the first being Edward T. Stotesbury, who joined in 1894, together with some of his Drexel partners. In January, 1912, he married Eva, the beautiful and charming widow of Member Oliver Eaton Cromwell, a descendant of England's Lord Protector. Their son, James H. R. Cromwell, has been a Member since 1950 and was a Governor from 1961 to 1968. Shortly after Stotesbury married Eva, they decided to build the magnificent mansion, Whitemarsh Hall. Located outside Philadelphia, the stately palace was built by architect

Horace Trumbauer and decorated by the gifted team of Joseph Duveen, Charles Garrick Allom and Lucien Alavoine. James T. Maher, in *The Twilight of Splendor* writes:

The fine country house, a ducal Georgian presence, sober and majestic, rises in stony silence above the Whitemarsh Valley. Once it was common for two hundred, and sometimes as many as six hundred, guests to gather there for tea. Princes and Statesmen visiting the United States as guests of the nation slept in its gilded suites.

Eight Vanderbilts were Members of the Club in those early early years. Cornelius and William K. were particularly interested in seeing the new Club a success because of the black-balling by the Union Club of Dr. William Seward Webb, who had married their sister, Eliza Osgood Vanderbilt. Webb was invited to become a Charter Member and his two brothers, H. Walter and J. Louis Webb, also received invitations. Of the other two Vanderbilt sisters, Florence Adèle married Hamilton McKown Twombly and Emily Thom married William D. Sloane, both of whom became Charter Members. Two other brothers became Charter Members, Frederick Vanderbilt, who built a mansion

*Honeysuckle band*

at Hyde Park, and George Washington Vanderbilt II. The latter was an interesting man, and an example of how few generations it takes to produce a cultured gentleman. A portrait of him shows an elegant, aristocratic-looking man with a slender sensitive face. He took some of the twenty-million dollars he inherited from his father to build the most astonishing house in America, Biltmore House, with 255 rooms, 57 fireplaces and 35 baths, located on 130,000 acres of forest land near Asheville, North Carolina. His gardens were designed by Frederick Law Olmstead, the designer of Central Park, and Hunt built the house in the Vanderbilt Château style. Here, as Kate Simon describes it, George Vanderbilt

carved out a complete life rather like that of Frederick II, the thirteenth-century Hohenstaufen King of the Two Sicilies. Like the Holy Roman Emperor, George learned languages, sciences, literature, art and history from an entourage of learned men. He built houses, schools and a hospital for the citizenry, taught them scientific farming as Frederick did and forestry and established regulations by which they must live. His house contained the largest single room in the United States, immense picture galleries and courts and an imposing banqueting hall. He collected hundreds of thousands of books, Dürer etchings, tapestries woven for the French court and adornments of kings. On his death in 1914 much of Biltmore was sold off, the forests given to the government as national park and the château available to the public for an admission fee. . . .

Biltmore House is now owned by George Vanderbilt's grandson, William A.V. Cecil.

Later joiners of the Club were Cornelius Vanderbilt, Jr. (Oct., '94), Alfred Gwynne Vanderbilt (Jan., '99) who went down on the *Lusitania,* and Reginald C. Vanderbilt (Jan., '02), the father of Gloria, and William K. Vanderbilt, Jr. (Feb., '02).

In 1871, Founding Father W. Watts Sherman married Annie Darby Rogers, daughter of William Shepard Wetmore, with whom he had two daughters. Brother-in-law George Peabody Wetmore became a Charter Member. Sherman's second daughter, Sybil Katherine, married Norrie Sellar who became a Member in 1905 and was active in the Bridge Dinner Club. Their son, Norrie Sherman Sellar, was a third-generation Member of the Metropolitan Club from 1943 until his death in October, 1979. He divided his time between his houses in Newport and St. Croix and was often seen at the Club on his trips to New York.

After the death of his first wife, Sherman married Sophie Augusta Brown in 1885. She was the daughter of John Carter Brown of Providence, Rhode Island, whose father founded the University bearing their name, and her brother was Charter Member John Nicholas Brown. They had two daughters, Mildred Constance and Irene Muriel. Mrs. Sherman was one of the great hostesses of New York during those years, and her name often appeared on the list printed by *Town Topics* of all the private dinner parties given by society women. Cleveland Amory, in *Who Killed Society*, tells of the glamorous ball Mrs. Sherman gave in 1909 at Sherry's for her daughter, Mildred. The crowning glory of the party was a huge swan which floated among the 1,200 guests, then suddenly exploded to shoot some ten-thousand pink roses into the air.

Two years after this party, Mildred Sherman married Baron Camoys of Stonor Park. Located in the Chiltern Hills forty miles from London, Stonor Park has been the home of the Stonors at least since 1156 and probably well before that. Probably no other house in England, Windsor Castle included, has been continuously occupied for so long by one family. In the 1700s, the Stonors married into the Camoys family and since then the head of the family carries the title, Baron Camoys. Mildred had three children of whom the eldest, Sherman Stonor, died in 1978. His son, the present Baron Camoys, moved back to Stonor Park in August, 1979, with his wife and four children. Family folklore relates that when grandmother Mildred came over from America, she brought twenty-one van loads of furniture with her.

The Goelet family also gave the Metropolitan Club its share of Members. In 1879 Founding Father Robert Goelet married Henrietta

Louise, daughter of Charter Member George Henry Warren, Jr. They had two children, Robert Walton Goelet and Beatrice Goelet. Robert Walton became a Member on March 19, 1901, after the death of his father. He perpetuated the oenological predilections of his forebears by marrying Anne-Marie Guestier of the Bordeaux wine dynasty of Barton & Guestier.

In 1877, Founding Father Ogden Goelet married Mary R. Wilson, daughter of Charter Member Richard T. Wilson. They had one daughter, Mary, and one son, Robert Goelet (1880-1941), who in 1901 became a Member after his father's death.

Twice a widower, Founder William C. Whitney, left four children. His two sons became Club members, Harry Payne Whitney in March, 1904, and Payne Whitney in October, 1901.They also married daughters of Club Members: Harry Payne married Gertrude Vanderbilt, daughter of Cornelius, and Payne's bride was Helen Hay, daughter of John Hay. Both women were outstanding in their own right. Gertrude became famous as the First Lady of American Art. Helen Hay Whitney became known as the First Lady of the American Turf. When Payne Whitney died in 1927, he left an estate of $194 million. Harry Payne Whitney's estate in 1930 was valued at only $40 million.

Of William C. Whitney's two daughters, one, Pauline, was married in 1895 to Member Almeric Hugh Paget (Feb. '96), son of Lord Paget, who later became Lord Queensboro. The other daughter, Dorothy, in 1911 married Willard Straight, son of a China missionary, who became a Member on May 20, 1913. During the War, he was attached to the Headquarters of the US First Army with the rank of Major. He died in December, 1918, as a result of injuries and his name is on the Plaque of Members who died in World War I.

In 1854, Founder Darius Ogden Mills married Janet, daughter of James Cunningham. They had one son, Ogden Mills, who became a Charter Member, and a daughter, who married

Charter Member Whitelaw Reid. A grandson, Ogden L. Mills, joined in January, 1913. Son-in-law Whitelaw Reid was a famous Civil-War correspondent, publisher, candidate for Vice President on the Republican ticket, and then Ambassador to Great Britain. In 1886, he and his wife bought the house that Stanford White had designed for Henry Villard, and made it a center of social life in New York.

The Roosevelts contributed more Members to the Metropolitan Club than any other clan. They trace their beginnings in America to Claes Martenszen van Rosenvelt who arrived on these shores in 1638 from Holland. His descendants became famous shopkeepers, soldiers, politicians and bankers. Two branches of the family developed during the eighteenth century: from Johannes (1689-?) came the Oyster Bay Branch and from Jacobus (1692-1776), the Hyde Park Branch. Each branch gave the nation a President. To the Club, they gave one President and a total of thirteen Members. Besides Founder James Alfred Roosevelt (of the Oyster Bay Branch), three other Roosevelts were Charter Members: James Roosevelt (1828-1900) of the Hyde Park Branch, whose son by a first marriage was Charter Member James Roosevelt (Rosy) Roosevelt (1855-1927), and who married Helen Astor. His son by a second marriage to Sara Delano was Franklin Delano Roosevelt. The third Roosevelt Charter Member was William Emlen Roosevelt of the Oyster Bay Branch. He was with the family firm and in 1871 fulfilled its last large contract for the plateglass destroyed by the Chicago fire before the firm entered the banking business.

The son of W. Emlen Roosevelt, who served as Governor from 1912 to his death in 1930, George Emlen Roosevelt, became a member on June 18, 1912, was elected a Governor in 1921, and served as President of the Club from 1929 to 1934. A Harvard graduate and Army captain, he ended the First World War as Chief of Staff of the 82nd Division. At one time head of Roosevelt & Son, he was a distinguished mathematician and the mathematics center at Harvard is named for him. Other Roosevelts who became Members were:

| | |
|---|---|
| Frederick Roosevelt | March, 1892 |
| John E. Roosevelt | March, 1894 |
| Robert B. Roosevelt | March, 1905 |
| Philip James Roosevelt | March, 1912 |
| James A. Roosevelt | December, 1914 |
| John Kean Roosevelt | March, 1916 |
| Theodore Roosevelt, Jr. | Nov., 1916 |
| James Roosevelt | April, 1972 |

James A. Roosevelt, son of the Founder of the same name, died as a result of wounds received in the First World War and his name is inscribed on the plaque on the First Floor. Theodore Roosevelt, Jr., the son of President Theodore Roosevelt, died of a heart attack while fighting in France during the Second World War. The only present Roosevelt Member, James, is the oldest son of President Franklin D. Roosevelt.

Founding Father August Newbold Morris married Eleanor Jones, daughter of General James I. Jones. His son, Newbold Morris, became a Charter Member and was President of the Club from 1926-29. Founding Father Samuel Dennison Babcock's son, Henry D. Babcock, became a Charter Member. Two sons of Founding Father George Peabody Wetmore, Edmund Wetmore and George Peabody Wetmore, became Charter Members and the latter was a Governor from 1915 to 1921. George Sullivan Bowdoin was a friend of J. Pierpont Morgan from boyhood and later became his partner in the Bank. His son, Temple Bowdoin, became a Charter Member. He also became a Member of the Board of Governors but died soon afterwards, in 1914.

The Iselins were another enthusiastic family at the time of the founding and joined *en masse*. The patriarch, Adrian (George) Iselin (1818-1905) became a Charter Member. His son, Adrian (George) Iselin, Jr., was a Founding Father and remained on the Board until his death in 1935. The latter's brothers, Columbus O'Donnel Iselin and William E. Iselin, also became Charter Members, as did his brother-in-law Delancy Astor Kane and his cousin Isaac Iselin. His son Ernest Iselin became a Member on November 19, 1912.

Founding Father Charles Lanier, a school friend and partner of Morgan, married Sarah Egleston and had two sons, Charles G. Lanier and James F. D. Lanier, who became Charter Members. A daughter married Francis C. Lawrance, Jr., a Charter Member.

In 1832, Moses Taylor married Catharine Wilson. One of their daughters, Alberta, married Percy R. Pyne who was a Charter Member as were their sons, Percy R. Pyne, Jr., and Moses Taylor Pyne. Another daughter, Katherine, married Charter Member Robert Winthrop, and their son Robert Dudley Winthrop was also a Charter Member. Moses Taylor's son George C. Taylor was a Charter Member and his second son Moses became a Member in 1894. His youngest son was Founder Henry A.C. Taylor. The latter's son, Henry Richmond Taylor, was a Charter Member and very active in Club affairs. In 1906 he organized the satellite club, the Bridge Dinner Club. Only his premature death in 1926 prevented Henry R. Taylor from becoming President of the Club.

After Founder Griswold Haven's first wife died in 1872, he married in 1880 the widow of Richard Suydam Palmer. Her son, bearing the name of his deceased father, became a Charter Member. Haven's sons by his first wife, Joseph Woodward Haven and George Griswold Haven, Jr., also were Charter Members.

Founder John Mountandevert Waterbury, who married Kate Anthony Furman in 1874, had eight children. One, John R. Waterbury, became a Member in 1895.

Hamilton Fish Webster, son of Founding Member Sidney Webster, was a Charter Member.

The tradition of generations succeeding each other as Members has continued from the days of the Founding Fathers to the present. Perhaps the most interesting case in recent years is the Klein family. E. Stanley Klein became a Member in 1963 and was a Governor from 1969 to 1973. His son E. Stanley Klein, Jr. joined in 1965 as did another son, Arthur M. Klein. Then in 1968, a grandson, Arthur M., applied for Resident Jr. Membership. It was probably the only time in the Club's history that a candidate was proposed by his grandfather and seconded by his father.

# Chapter 17

# THE ARISTOCRACY
# OF ACHIEVEMENT

Social clubs in the Anglo-Saxon world were formed as places where gentlemen of essentially similar background and opinions could gather, meet their friends and make new friends, sit down with them for a drink and a chat, or for a rubber of bridge or backgammon. The clubs were exclusive; that is, they excluded those whom they believed did not share their ideas or manners, even though they might be of similar background. The unwillingness of the Membership of the Metropolitan Club to accept the eminent divine Dr. William S. Rainford because of his liberal views is a case in point. The Club for them was not a place for political, social or religious arguments but a place to relax among their friends and have a good time. Ungentlemanly behaviour, whether non-payment of an obligation or use of insulting language, met with disciplinary action.

When the Metropolitan Club was formed in 1891, it drew upon a relatively narrow base for its Membership, upon the old, established and well-to-do New Yorkers, and some out-of-towners of English and Dutch descent, with a sprinkling of Germans and Irish. The composition of the Membership in those days closely follows the description given by Dixon Wecter in the Chapter "The Gentleman and his Club" in *The Saga of American Society:*

One is likely to meet doctors here and almost certainly surgeons, but never a dentist. There will be many lawyers—barristers, as they style them in Pall Mall, but not solicitors. Bankers and brokers, of course, who come from the best Nordic families, and wholesale merchants rather than retail. Retired military officers, with their excellent horsemanship, their erect carriage, white hair, and fine apoplectic flush, are also in the best Piccadilly tradition. Two or three Episcopal clergymen, preferably deans, lie lightly upon the consciences and the budget of the Club. Artists, musicians, and authors are regarded with suspicion unless their family names and background are quite trustworthy, and set them clear of raffish bohemia. The Union, the Knickerbocker, the Racquet, and the Metropolitan condescend to the Century, where achievement outweighs blood and wealth. A stage player is very seldom seen, though the fashionable architect—as the tradition of Richard Hunt and Stanford White, or even Addison Mizner in Palm Beach, demonstrates—may be quite a swell and amusing fellow. With what Henry James called "a certain light of the fine old gentlemanly prejudice to guide it," the preeminently social club welcomes the serious frivolity of horses, hounds, foxes and books, but not the effeminate frivolity of aestheticism.

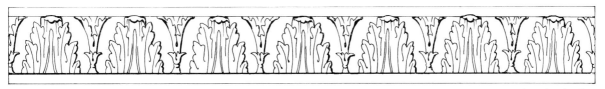

*Acanthus border*

183

This, of course, would change as the composition of American Society and society at large changed under the impact of immigration, war and social revolution. In addition, Wecter was wrong in his assessment that "the Metropolitan condescends to the Century, where achievement outweighs blood and wealth."

Certainly he overlooked one group of achievers which was quite prominent in the Club's early, as well as later, years—the industrialists who built up the colossal economic might of the North American Empire.

Essentially, the new Club appealed more to the newer American aristocracy of achievement than to the Establishment of old families. These were the men who built the petroleum and utility industries, the agricultural-implement and motorcar companies, the coal, iron-and-steel and machinery companies, and the industries based on electronics and computer sciences. All became rich, some very rich, and many used a great part of their wealth to found universities and colleges, to establish museums and libraries.

In an earlier chapter, the Vanderbilts and the Morgans were mentioned among the Founders, as well as the Iselins and Morrises, the Roosevelts and the Whitneys, all men of action. But there were many other well-known people who joined the Club at the beginning, the Charter Members with the magical date of Sherman's dinner at the Knickerbocker, February 20, 1891, after their names in subsequent Membership Lists. Among them were William Rockefeller, John D. Rockefeller's brother; Edward H. Harriman, the railroad magnate; Edward J. Berwind, the coal baron; George F. Baker, founder of the First National Bank of New York; James Gordon Bennett, newspaper man, owner of the *Herald* and the founder of the *New York Evening Telegram*; Chauncey M. Depew, railroad president, politician and famous orator; Hamilton Fish (1849-1936), lawyer, politician and Assistant Treasurer of the United States; Theodore A. Havemeyer, sugar industrialist whose notable art collection was bequeathed to the Metropolitan Museum in 1929; John Hay, author and diplomat, journalist, Lincoln's secretary and later Secretary of

State; Arthur Curtis James, railroad magnate; Augustus D. Juilliard, founder of the Juilliard School of Music; Louis Comfort Tiffany, artist, interior decorator and art patron, mostly remembered as the creator of the Tiffany lamp; Whitelaw Reid, journalist and diplomat, editor of the *New York Tribune*, Ambassador to the Court of St. James from 1905 to his death in 1912; and Elihu Root, lawyer, statesman, Secretary of War under McKinley and Theodore Roosevelt, internationalist and recipient of the 1912 Nobel Peace Prize.

Of course the old Knickerbocker families were represented. There were one Beekman, two van Cortlandts, two Schermerhorns, two Kips, one Rhinelander and one Van Rensselaer among others.

But the industrialists were equally prominent. Two Du Ponts were Charter Members: Henry A. and William Du Pont. They were descended from Pierre Samuel Du Pont de Nemours who left France in 1800 with his sons Eleuthère Irenée and Victor-Marie to found one of the leading industrial dynasties in the world. The Du Pont Company of Wilmington, Delaware, which now employs 132,000 people in more than thirty countries is one of the giants of the world chemical industry. The family played an important role in making General Motors the gigantic enterprise it is today. Now numbering about 1,700, this family dynasty has ruled its empire for 170 years, amassing a fortune calculated at $5 billion.

A total of eight Du Ponts joined the Club over the years. Henry F., Pierre S., T.C. and Alexis I. Second joined in 1902; Lammot in 1919 and Irenée in 1920. When in 1919 the family put up the money to rescue General Motors from financial collapse in exchange for thirty-eight percent of its stock, Pierre S. Du Pont became G.M.'s president. He turned that office over to Alfred P. Sloan, Jr., in 1923.

Sloan joined the Club on February 20, 1923, and became an active Member. Born in New Haven in 1875, he was president of General Motors from 1923 to 1937 when he became Chairman. He and Pierre S. Du Pont established the pattern of professional management techniques which have become the archetype for other companies.

Since there are only some three-hundred people with the name Auchincloss living today, it is reasonable to assume that anybody carrying this unique name is descended from the Scotsman Hugh Auchincloss, who arrived here in 1803. While the family fortune does not total in the billions, they have been, as Louis Auchincloss put it, "respectfully affluent." They have also been prominent in Society for generations and have been called "the most marvelously-connected family in New York." Three of the clan were Charter Members: Edgar S., John W. and Hugh D. Auchincloss. Another Auchincloss, Samuel Sloan, joined the Club in January, 1906. Hugh D. Auchincloss married a daughter of Oliver B. Jennings, a founder of the Standard Oil Co. Their son is "Hughdie," who married Janet Lee Bouvier as his third wife, thus becoming the stepfather of Jacqueline Bouvier Kennedy Onassis.

Louis Auchincloss once commented, "We have always been more a fraternity than a family." They have adopted an unusual family motto: "Obedience to the unenforceable." The motto implies that a man's first duty is to obey that which he cannot be forced to obey; that is to say, the moral or human obligations which cannot be legislated. Their motto conforms to Kant's Categorical Imperative and is the great unwritten law of any worthwhile society.

Before the Clubhouse was completed, two other dynasty founders became Non-Resident Members, both from Chicago—Cyrus Hall McCormick and Marshall Field. Born of a family which had come to America in 1734, Cyrus McCormick was an inventor. He developed the McCormick Reaper, a threshing machine first produced by his father. When he could not sell it in his native Virginia, he took it to Chicago in 1847 and built his own factory. The McCormick Reaper Works became the International Harvester Co., a multi-billion dollar concern. In all of its 148 years, a McCormick has either headed it or has been waiting in the wings to do so. Cyrus brought two brothers with him to Chicago. One of their many descendants, Colonel Robert R. McCormick, made the *Chicago Tribune* newspaper one of the nation's staunchest and loudest voices of conservatism before he died in 1955. A great-granddaughter of Cyrus McCormick bought the *New Republic* magazine, one of the country's best-known liberal journals.

Marshall Field was born in Conway, Massachusetts, in 1834. After clerking in a Pittsfield dry-goods store, he went to Chicago, and, in 1865, in partnership with Levi Leiter bought the fabulous department store founded by Potter Palmer on Lake Street. A score of years later he bought Leiter out. In 1905, the "merchant of merchants" was the largest individual taxpayer in the United States. His son, Marshall Field II, died early. Most of the family later moved to England. Marshall Field III grew up in England but returned in 1914 and served in the U.S. army during the First World War. Later he went into publishing, first as the owner of the short-lived *PM Sun*. Then, in 1947, he bought the *Chicago Times*, and, in 1959, he added the *Chicago Daily News*, succeeding the colonel as first publisher of Chicago.

Three other families who were invited to be Charter Members were very popular socially although they did not belong to Old New York families—the Havemeyers, the Oelrichs and Adolf Ladenburg. The Havemeyers were descendents of two brothers, William Frederick (originally unquestionably Wilhelm Friederich) and Frederick Christian Havemeyer, who came to America from Bückeburg, Germany, around 1800. The brothers made their fortune in the sugar-refining business. Three were invited to become Charter Members, Charles F., Theodore A., and Theodore A., Jr. A fourth, J. Craig Havemeyer, joined in 1899. All three Charter Members were avid sportsmen and were also members of the Coaching Club. The Havemeyer name has a special place in New York's cultural history due to the artistic instincts of Henry Osborne Havemeyer (1842-1907), brother of Theodore A. and grandson of the German immigrants. Henry and his charming and gifted wife Louisine had one of the most cultured houses in New York, at 1 East

66th Street. They used a large part of their wealth to assemble a collection of rare paintings and other art objects. Starting with Oriental art, they also acquired eight Rembrandts, two Franz Hals, and works by Holbein, Bronzini, Cranach and El Greco. Through Louisine's friendship with Mary Cassatt, they learned to know and love the French impressionist masters and, as their greatest achievement, bought many Monets, Manets, Renoirs, Pissarros and Degas. When Louisine died in 1929, the Metropolitan Museum received nearly one hundred and fifty of our age's masterpieces.

Hermann Oelrich and his brother Charles May Oelrich were both Charter Members. Hermann was born in 1850 in Baltimore, the city to which his father had immigrated ten years earlier from his native Germany. He went to school in Baltimore and later in New York after his parents moved there. Completing his education in Germany, he returned to the United States in 1871, and entered the firm of Oelrich & Co., shipping merchants and agents of the North German Lloyd Steamship Company. Hermann was an excellent businessman, a dashing sportsman, good natured, and with a great sense of humor and a remarkable facility for writing verse. On a trip to San Francisco, he met Theresa Alice, one of the two daughters of Senator James G. Fair, one of the discoverers of the Comstock Lode and, by then, fabulously wealthy. When they married in 1890, San Francisco had never seen a bigger wedding. Back East, Tessie bought the Rosecliff estate in Newport in 1891 and had Stanford White build on it the most tasteful and graceful mansion of that famous resort, a palace worthy of Marie Antoinette herself.

Tessie was a vigorous and extravagant social leader and became, with Mrs. Stuyvesant Fish and Mrs. O.H.P. Belmont, one of the three great hostesses of Newport. Her most famous party was the Bal Blanc, given in August, 1904. All the guests wore white costumes and powdered wigs; white flowers festooned the exquisite salons, swans floated in the pools, and a dozen white-hulled ships were anchored off shore. In all weather, she rode out in her carriages with silver fittings, her coachmen dressed

in the Oelrichs colors, tan trimmed with red. Later she drove around Newport in an electric car accompanied by a Maltese terrier named Hercules. Her sister Virginia Graham Fair, Birdie to her friends, married Member William K. Vanderbilt, Jr. ('02), the fun-loving pioneer motorist. They were divorced in 1909.

Also invited to become a Charter Member was Adolf Ladenburg, scion of an old German-Jewish banking family in Frankfurt. Together with Ernst Thalmann, he founded the venerable investment banking house of Ladenburg, Thalmann & Co., one of the few firms in Wall Street never to change its original name. In 1884, he married Emily Louise Stevens, daughter of Charter Member Alexander Henry Stevens. They had one daughter, Eugenia Mary, who later married Preston Davie. Ladenburg died mysteriously—he disappeared from the deck of the liner *Niagara* on the return trip from Nassau on February 20, 1896. He had been in ill health and was traveling with a nurse, who shortly before his disappearance had given him a sedative. His wife was a popular member of New York society and died in 1928.

No history of the Metropolitan Club would be complete without mention of one of the greatest of the American Dynasties. For many years the name Astor has been linked with the Metropolitan; there were two Astors among the Charter Members, John Jacob Astor IV (1864-1912) and William Waldorf Astor, First Viscount Astor (1848-1919). The dynasty was founded by Johann Jakob Astor, who was born in Waldorf near Heidelberg in 1763 and came to America in 1784. He entered the fur trade, prospered greatly, but from the first channeled his profits into New York real estate. His son, who enlarged his holdings, was known as the Landlord of New York. The family name lives on in the landmark Waldorf-Astoria Hotel, in Astor Place, in Astoria, a large section of the borough of Queens, and in a hundred other uses of the name. Shortly after he became a Charter Member, great-grandson William Waldorf Astor deserted America for England, having lost two races for election to Congress in which his wealth was an issue. "America," he declared angrily on his departure, "is not a fit place for a gentleman to live." The English branch of the family has since become the more dynamic one.

The Club was conceived during the reign over Society of The Mrs. Astor, née Caroline Schermerhorn, wife of William Backhouse Astor and mother of Charter Member John Jacob Astor IV. Her rule of New York society was—if not unchallenged—certainly unbroken for a generation. Her ascendancy was soundly based; her parties were more luxurious, more attractive, and better arranged than anyone else's. In 1890, her son John Jacob IV married the beautiful Ava Willing of Philadelphia. The next year, a son William Vincent Astor was born.

With fame and notoriety, however, may sometimes come scandal. The first occurred in 1892 when Caroline Astor's daughter Charlotte Augusta left her husband James Drayton and ran off to Europe with another man. Then, in 1908, "Queen Caroline" died and the second scandal hit the headlines: her son John Jacob Astor IV had secretly divorced Ava. The marriage had never been a good one. Ava, "the Wicked Queen," was a cold and unpleasant woman with a contempt for her awkward husband. Jack understandably had spent most of his time away from his wife on his beloved yacht, Nourmahal, the Light of the Harem, with more congenial companions. Strangely enough, the Nourmahal was accident prone, and the belief spread that she was jinxed, making it difficult to find captains for her. Jack was destined to find a watery grave, although not aboard the Nourmahal.

Not long after his divorce, Jack was seen in the company of the pretty eighteen-year-old Madeleine Force. No one took this seriously because, not only was she considered most unsuitable, but also she was younger than Jack's son Vincent. Before long, however, the two were married and Jack finally found happiness at what was to be end of his life. A year later, returning from a trip to Europe, the newlyweds decided to book passage on the maiden voyage of the most luxurious liner the world had ever seen, the Titanic, the ship that "God himself

Mrs. William Astor — the Mrs. Astor — in a portrait by the French artist Charles Emile Carolus-Duran. Mrs. Astor stood beneath this portrait to receive her guests at her famous balls, dinners and at-homes, and it was draped in black when she died.

Vincent Astor's yacht, *Nourmahal*.

could not sink."

There were four Club Members with their families on the *Titanic* on that fateful night of April 14, 1912. They were Charles M. Hays, John Bradley Cumings, Frederick M. Hoyt and John Jacob Astor. A fifth, Alfred G. Vanderbilt, had intended to sail, but had changed his mind at the last minute, as his relieved mother in New York learned when she received a cable telling her that he was safe in London. He did not escape the sea, however. Three years later he went down with the *Lusitania*, when, it was reported, he gave up his seat in the lifeboat to a woman.

Charles M. Hays joined the Club on March 19, 1901. Born in 1856 in Illinois of an old American family, he had entered the railroad business and at one time had been president of the Wabash. By 1912, he was president of the Grand Trunk Railroad. He married Clara J. Gregg of St. Louis in 1881 and they had four daughters. Margaret, the youngest, accompanied them on that fateful trip. Mrs. Hays' maid was also on the voyage.

When the impact was felt, Hays went on deck and talked to a friend, Major Peuthen. "Why, she is listing!" cried the Major. "She should not do that. The weather is calm and the boat has stopped." "Oh, I don't know," Hays replied placidly, "you cannot sink this boat." Soon the order came to uncover the lifeboats and Hays helped his wife, daughter and their maid into lifeboat No. 3, promising to follow as soon as possible. When young Margaret—or May as she was called—sat down on the bench she realized that she had stepped on something soft. It was a six-month-old baby. She picked it up and, finding no mother to claim it, she held it in her arms until hours later when she was lifted to the deck of the *Carpathia*, the Cunard Liner which had rushed to the rescue. As the night wore on, Clara Hays hailed the boats that came near, searching for her husband. "Charles Hays, are you there?" She called his name over and over, but she never saw him again.

John Bradley Cumings came to New York from Boston in 1902 and became a Club Member on December 15, 1908. He was the senior partner of the Stock Exchange firm of Cumings and Markwald. He also was a director of the Subsurface Torpedo Boat Company and belonged to the Racquet, Riding and Knollwood Country Clubs. He lived at 60 East 64th Street with his wife, Florence B. Thayer, sister of Member Rodney Thayer. When the call came for women and children to get into the lifeboats, he helped his wife into one of them and stayed behind hoping to get into another one. He did not succeed.

Frederick M. Hoyt joined the Club on February 16, 1908. He was one of the best-known yachtsmen on the Massachusetts coast, and he and his wife had a summer house in Marblehead. He was a member of the New York, Corinthian and Eastern Yacht Clubs. Hoyt and his wife waited together on A Deck till near the end. At two o'clock, Captain Smith announced, "You all have done your duty. Now it's every man for himself." Hoyt saw his wife into collapsible D, the last boat to leave. Then he leaped into the twenty-eight-degree-Fahrenheit water and swam to where he thought the boat might pass. He guessed well. In a few minutes, Boat D splashed by and hauled him in. He was one of the thirteen people saved out of many hundreds swimming around, hoping to be picked up by the eighteen lifeboats that hovered around the sinking ship. For the rest of the night he sat, soaked to the skin, rowing hard to keep from freezing to death. Collapsible D had a rough time, and when the *Carpathia* loomed up, it was in bad shape—low in the water and few oars to work. Boat No. 14 took them in tow. Finally, at 4:45 a.m., numb with the cold, the Hoyts were lifted aboard the *Carpathia*. He was the only one of the four Club Members aboard the *Titanic* to survive.

When the White Star Liner struck the iceberg at 11:40 that Sunday night, the Astors were in their cabin. They were traveling with a manservant, a maid and their airedale, Kitty. Mrs. Astor was in bed, and thought there was some mishap in the kitchen. Jack seemed undisturbed by the jar of the collision, yet he went up to investigate. He returned to tell his wife that the ship had struck ice, but that it did not look serious. He was very calm.

At fifteen minutes past midnight Captain Smith gave the order to uncover the lifeboats and muster the passengers. The Astors came up, she in an attractive light dress looking as if she had stepped out of a bandbox. They went to the brightly lighted gym, just off the Boat Deck, and sat side by side on a pair of motionless mechanical horses. They wore their lifebelts and he had an extra one on his lap. When the ship's officers called for women and children to get into lifeboat No. 6, the response was anything but enthusiastic. Why trade the bright decks of the *Titanic* for a few dark hours in a rowboat? Astor ridiculed the idea: "We are safer here than in that little boat." After all, the *Titanic* could not sink.

But by 1:45 a.m. the ship was listing. Officer Lightoller had had trouble with lifeboat No. 4. He had lowered it to A Deck planning to fill it from there through the windows, but they could not be opened. The passengers waiting to board No. 4 were the cream of New York and Philadelphia society—the Astors, Wideners,

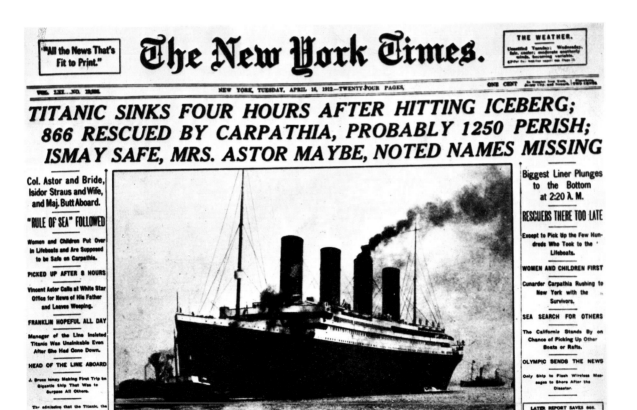

# The New York Times.

VOL. LXI...NO. 19,582.  NEW YORK, TUESDAY, APRIL 16, 1912.—TWENTY-FOUR PAGES.  ONE CENT

## TITANIC SINKS FOUR HOURS AFTER HITTING ICEBERG; 866 RESCUED BY CARPATHIA, PROBABLY 1250 PERISH; ISMAY SAFE, MRS. ASTOR MAYBE, NOTED NAMES MISSING

**Col. Astor and Bride, Isidor Straus and Wife, and Maj. Butt Aboard.**

**"RULE OF SEA" FOLLOWED**

Women and Children Put Over in Lifeboats and Are Supposed to be Safe on Carpathia.

**PICKED UP AFTER 8 HOURS**

Vincent Astor Calls at White Star Office for News of His Father and Leaves Weeping.

**FRANKLIN HOPEFUL ALL DAY**

Manager of the Line Insisted Titanic Was Unsinkable Even After She Had Gone Down.

**HEAD OF THE LINE ABOARD**

J. Bruce Ismay Making First Trip on Gigantic Ship That Was to Surpass All Others.

The admission that the Titanic, the biggest steamship in the world, had been sunk by an iceberg and had gone to the bottom of the Atlantic, probably carrying more than 1,600 of her passengers and crew with her, was made at the White Star Line offices, 9 Broadway, at 8:20 o'clock last night. Then P. A. S. Franklin, Vice President

**Biggest Liner Plunges to the Bottom at 2:20 A. M.**

**RESCUERS THERE TOO LATE**

Except to Pick Up the Few Hundreds Who Took to the Lifeboats.

**WOMEN AND CHILDREN FIRST**

Cunarder Carpathia Rushing to New York with the Survivors.

**SEA SEARCH FOR OTHERS**

The California Stands By on Chance of Picking Up Other Boats or Rafts.

**OLYMPIC SENDS THE NEWS**

Only Ship to Flash Wireless Messages to Shore After the Disaster.

**LATER REPORT SAVES 866.**

BOSTON, April 15.—A wireless message picked up late to-night, relayed from the Olympic, says that the Carpathia is on her way to New York with 866 passengers from the steamer Titanic aboard. They are mostly women and children.

The Lost Titanic Being Towed Out of Belfast Harbor.

Thayers, Carters, and Ryersons. After a time, the windows were smashed and Lightoller loaded the boat with women and children as the men stood by. Jack Astor helped his wife across the frame, then asked if he could join her; she was, as he put it, "in a delicate condition." "No, sir," Lightoller replied, "no men are allowed in these boats until the women are loaded first." Astor then asked which boat it was in order to locate his wife later, and Lightoller said, "Number 4." Lifeboat No. 4 took off about sixty-percent full. Lifeboat No. 5 had taken off with forty people in a boat that could hold sixty-five; No. 6 had only twenty-eight people in it, but had a capacity of sixty-five. No wonder that out of a total of 2,207 people on board and a lifeboat capacity of 1,178, only 651 were saved.

With the lifeboats gone, quiet settled upon the men left behind. It must have been a sad and moving sight, these Edwardian gentlemen, awaiting the inevitable. The men from New York and Philadelphia continued to stick together, John B. Thayer, George and Harry Widener, and Duane Williams forming a little knot. New Yorker Clinch Smith had worked hard helping where he could and now joined them. He had been seated at Stanford White's table on the night in 1906 at Madison Square Garden when Harry K. Thaw shot the architect. Astor remained pretty much alone. Isidore Strauss and his wife sat down on deck chairs. Benjamin Guggenheim and his valet went downstairs to change into their evening clothes. "We have dressed in our best and are prepared to go down like gentlemen," he explained. At 2:15 a.m., Bandmaster Hartley tapped his violin. The ragtime ended and the strains of the Episcopal hymn "Autumn" flowed across the deck and drifted into the still night far out over the water.

At 2:20 a.m. the ship foundered.

When she was launched, the Titanic seemed to be a symbol of the times, of a hundred years of progress and increasing affluence. Her comforts and luxury seemed an appropriate background for the super-rich who, before the advent of movie stars and sports figures, stood in the center of public attention. The names

of many of the 190 families in first class, who were attended by ten personal manservants, twenty-one maids and two nurses, along with hundreds of stewards and stewardesses, were household words. The Titanic's unsinkable construction was a superb technological achievement, a herald of the achievements of generations to come. Since she was unsinkable, there was no need for more than a minimum of lifeboats nor for drills to train the crew to fill those few available. Nor was there need to reduce her speed of 22.5 knots—her highest speed to date—despite the repeated warnings of huge icefields directly in her path.

Two-and-a-half years later, our western world would just as recklessly and arrogantly rush into the bloodiest war in history which would topple centuries-old dynasties, leave behind ten-million dead and twenty-million wounded and inflict Godless dictatorships over much of the world. A curtain was going down over a unique period.

With the women-and-children-first rule of conduct interpreted by ships' officers as women-and-children-only, it took bold action for a man to save himself as Fred Hoyt managed to do. A few others succeeded and, since one of them became a Member a few years later, the last hours of the Titanic were often told over drinks and dinner at the Club. Lieutenant Hokan Bjornstrom Steffanson, a young Swedish military attaché, was on his way to his new assignment in Washington. When the ship struck the iceberg, he was sitting in the Smoking Room with Hugh Woolner, the son of the English sculptor, and had just ordered a hot lemonade. At the next table a bridge game went on undisturbed until a ship's officer appeared at the door: "Men, get on your life belts, there's trouble ahead." Woolner and Steffanson went on deck and helped some women into lifeboat G. At 2:05, Collapsible D—the last boat to leave the Titanic—started down towards the sea. Woolner and Steffanson were standing alone by the rail. When they saw Boat D sliding down the side of the ship, Woolner cried: "Let's make a jump for it; there is plenty of room in her bow." Steffanson hurled himself out of the boat landing head over heel in the bow. The next second Woolner followed, falling half in, half out. A few seconds later they helped to haul Hoyt into the boat. Without the three men rowing, Collapsible D might not have made it to the *Carpathia.*

Steffanson became a Member of the Club on October 19, 1915, and remained one until his death in 1959. Some oldtimers still remember him reminiscing about those tense and dramatic hours.

Four days later the *Carpathia* approached New York with 651 survivors. Ten-thousand people watched her from the Battery as she steamed past the Statue of Liberty, and thirty-thousand more were waiting in the rain as she edged into Pier 54. Since no reporters were permitted on board at Quarantine, tugs filled with newsmen shouting questions through megaphones chugged beside her. Finally, at 9:35 on Thursday night, the gangplank was lowered and the first survivors came ashore. Mrs. Charles Hays and her daughter were met by a special train sent by the Grand Trunk Railroad. Madeleine Astor was met by two automobiles carrying two doctors, a trained nurse, a secretary and her twenty-year-old stepson Vincent. Three months later she gave birth to a son.

Madeleine named the baby John Jacob Astor. Historians later would call him the Sixth. He was brought up as a royal child, without, however, the royal means. When the will was read, the world learned that Madeleine had been treated rather miserly. She had relinquished her dower rights for a paltry $1,695,000 plus an interest in the Cottage in Newport and the house at 840 Fifth Avenue. Her son would receive $5 million when he came of age. Soon Madeleine was out of money, but her step-son Vincent disliked her and would not give her any. When a few years later she married the wealthy William Dick, Vincent not only retrieved the Cottage in Newport and the house at 840 Fifth but also the income on the $5 million trust. After a second disastrous marriage to the Italian prizefighter Enzo Fiermonte, Madeleine died of an overdose of sleeping pills in 1937, twenty-five years after the *Titanic* disaster.

John Jacob Astor VI received his five-million-dollar trust in 1933, and used it up with breathtaking panache. He bought a railway carriage and ten motor cars, one of which was a yellow Rolls Royce. Then he bought a house at 7 East 91st Street and staffed it with twenty-five servants. But most of the money was squandered on three disastrous marriages and all the lawsuits stemming from them. Finally in 1958 his affairs, marital and otherwise, had become so tangled that he applied to the New York State Supreme Court to find out to whom he was wed. No wonder his inheritance did not last long. Half-brother Vincent turned a deaf ear to all his requests for money.

In 1942, John Jacob Astor VI joined the Club. He was frequently seen in the Clubhouse and took an active interest in Club affairs. He served as a Governor for fourteen years, from 1945 to 1959. In 1970 he resigned to move to Florida. He has one son and one grandson, both named William Backhouse Astor.

There is an element of tragedy in the story of a middle-aged man who finally finds happiness with a girl much younger and considered unsuitable, who then dies prematurely leaving a mother and child to the tender mercies of a society with which they are not equipped to cope. Worse if they carry the name of Astor. Or the name Vanderbilt.

Reginald Claypool Vanderbilt, the son of Cornelius, Jr., became a Member on January 21, 1902. A few weeks before, on his twenty-first birthday, December 19, 1901, he had come into his inheritance, some $15.5 million with a yearly income of $775,000. He celebrated this event by heading straight to Richard Canfield's elegant, illegal gambling house on 44th Street and losing $70,000 that very night. He had grown up in the château at Fifth and 58th St. and in the Breakers. His first marriage ended in divorce and left him with one daughter, the exotically beautiful Cathleen, who had inherited the Vanderbilt oriental look. His brother was Alfred Gwynne Vanderbilt who went down on the *Lusitania.* One sister, Gladys (1886-1965), married to Count Laszlo Szechenyi, almost sold her house on 71st Street to the Metropolitan

Club during the financial crisis in 1945. His other sister, Gertrude Vanderbilt (1875-1942), married the immensely wealthy Harry Payne Whitney, and was a leader of the New York art world. She later played a fateful role in the life of her brother's daughter.

When the forty-four-year-old Reggie Vanderbilt met Gloria Morgan, who was his daughter's age, he had already wasted with reckless abandon his entire fortune and was living off the income of a $5 million trust fund which had been established for the benefit of his children. Gloria and her twin sister, Thelma, were beautiful and penurious and received a great deal of publicity from Maury Paul. Reggie and Gloria married and shortly after the birth of their daughter, Gloria, Reggie died leaving his widow penniless. The sad childhood and youth of the little girl, the sensational lawsuit between Reggie's widow and sister for custody, and the heartaches, ruined careers, and wasted efforts of the trial are fascinatingly told in Barbara Goldsmith's recent bestseller, *Little Gloria . . . Happy at Last.*

Not all men invited to become Members of the Club were industrialists or businessmen. Many were accomplished in fields more exalted than mere money-making.

One such eminent man was Charter Member Alexander Agassiz (1835-1910), son of the famous Swiss naturalist and geologist Louis Agassiz (1807-1873). Louis was an opponent of Darwinism and believed that a new species could arise only through the intervention of God. In 1846 he came to the United States to deliver the Lowell Institute lectures at Cambridge, Massachusetts. He gave a tremendous impetus in America to the study of science directly from nature and trained a generation of scientists. His son Alexander was born in 1835 in Neuchâtel, Switzerland and came here in 1849 to study at Harvard. In 1867, he went into mining in the West and became rich. He was one of the foremost zoologists in the country and remained connected in various ways with Harvard and the Museum of Comparative Zoology until his death in 1910.

Another Charter Member who left his im-

*Grief,* Saint Gaudens' sculpture for the grave of Clover, wife of Henry Adams.

print on America was Louis Comfort Tiffany (1848-1933), son of the founder of the famous New York jewelry firm Tiffany & Co. Today, he is best remembered for his lampshade designs; although, in 1980, Corning Glass had a Tiffany exhibition in which the center of attraction was the celebrated stained-glass windows from his lavish house in Oyster Bay, Long Island.

Of all the arts, architecture has best expressed what America has to say. Architecture, in an America grown to imperial might, expressed something new and vital. During the latter part of the nineteenth century, there was an abundance of first-rate architects in the United States. They not only beautified the formerly drab cities, but also invented the skyscraper in which walls and floors were supported by steel frames, a revolutionary new method. Henry Adams, in his *Education,* remarked that people would some day talk about Hunt and Richardson, LaFarge and Saint Gaudens, Burnham and McKim, and Stanford White when the politicians and millionaires were forgotten.

One famous architect of the period who was invited to become a Charter Member was George Browne Post (1837-1913). He became president of the American Institute of Architects. Among his best-known creations are the New York Stock Exchange Building and the Wisconsin State Capital.

Also among the Charter Members were three other artists who deserve special mention. Many of the Members made and left great fortunes, some assembled great art collections bequeathed ultimately to museums, others endowed hospitals, museums and colleges. But Stanford White, Charles Follen McKim and Augustus Saint Gaudens created works of beauty to delight their own and succeeding generations.

White and McKim and their importance to the Metropolitan Club have been mentioned earlier. Their good friend Augustus Saint Gaudens came from a different background from the two architects. Born in 1848 in Ireland of a French father and an Irish mother, he was brought to America six months after his birth. His father established a shoemaking business in New York. All their lives, Augustus spoke French with his father and English with his mother. When he was twelve-years old, he was given into apprenticeship to a Savoyard stone cameo-cutter. But he wanted to be a sculptor and in 1867 he entered the School of Fine Arts in Paris. Frequently traveling back and forth between France and New York, he met Stanford White in 1876 when he had taken a studio on 14th Street. Augustus loved to sing while he was working. One day White happened to be in the building, heard a loud voice singing the Andante from Beethoven's *Seventh Symphony*, walked in and a memorable friendship and artistic collaboration began.

Saint Gaudens' unusual genius for plastic expression, his thorough French schooling and his knowledge of the Italian Renaissance soon made him the foremost sculptor in the United States. His statue of Admiral Farragut in Madison Square set a new standard for public monuments as well as a new conception of the pedestal. On the base of this statue and on sev-

eral others, Stanford White collaborated. Saint Gaudens' exquisite nude figure of Diana, created at White's suggestion for the Tower of Madison Square Garden which White had designed, was a daring work of beauty. When the statue · was completed in 1891, one reporter wrote, "The Square is now thronged with clubmen armed with field glasses. No such figure has ever been publicly exhibited in the United States." Of special interest to Members is his statue of General William Tecumseh Sherman at the entrance to Central Park at 59th Street, visible from the Club's window.

One of the towering figures in American letters at the time was Henry Adams, of the fourth "royal" generation of Boston Adams. If he had written only *Mont-Saint-Michel and Chartres*, that "study of thirteenth-century unity," and *The Education of Henry Adams*, that "study of twentieth-century mobility," his place in American culture would be secure. Adams recognized similar spirits in White, McKim and Saint Gaudens—the three redheads—and they were good friends.

Henry Adams never joined the Metropolitan Club; he lived most of his life in Washington, where he was a member of the Metropolitan Club of Washington. His older brother, Charles Francis Adams, Jr., however, became a Charter Member. In 1873, Henry married Mar-

Augustus Saint Gaudens, in a portrait by Kenyon Cox.

ian (Clover) Hooper who was the "first heart" of a group which became the vanguard of the intellectual life of post-Civil-War America and which called itself "The Five of Hearts." The others were Clarence King and John and Clara Hay. Both King and Hay were Charter Members of the Club. Clarence King, born in Newport of Mayflower descent, shone among his contemporaries "like a kind of Apollo," says Otto Friederich in his book, *Clover*. Henry Adams wrote in his *Education*:

His wit and humor, his bubbling energy which swept everyone into the current of his interest, his personal charm of youth and manners . . . mark him almost alone among Americans. He had in him something of the Greek—a touch of Alcibiades or Alexander. One Clarence King only existed in the world.

John Hay was also a man of great charm and talent. He studied law in his native Indiana and joined his uncle's law firm in Springfield, Illinois, where one of the partners was Abraham Lincoln. When elected President, Lincoln took Hay to Washington as his personal secretary. There Hay and Adams met. After Lincoln's death, Hay spent five years at the U.S. Legation in Paris, then left to devote himself to writing. He edited Charter Member Whitelaw Reid's *Tribune* while the latter went on an extended honeymoon trip to Europe with his bride, the daughter of Founder D. Ogden Mills. Later Hay returned to politics, first in 1897 when McKinley appointed him Ambassador to the Court of St. James. He served as Secretary of State under McKinley and Theodore Roosevelt until his death in 1905. His daughter Helen married another Member, Payne Whitney (Oct. '01).

Others in this fascinating circle, all Charter Members, were Alex Agassiz, Henry Lee Higginson, Manton Marble, and Frederic Frelinghuysen, Secretary of State under President Chester Arthur from 1881 to 1885.

Henry Adams' world collapsed when in 1885 his beloved wife Clover committed suicide. Grief drove him to travel to far-away countries and he went with John La Farge on a lingering tour of the South Pacific. But before leaving he commissioned Saint Gaudens to sculpt a mon-

ument for his wife's grave. All he gave the artist as a guide was that he wished the figure to symbolize "the acceptance, intellectually, of the inevitable." Saint Gaudens created a masterpiece. Standing today in the Rock Creek Park Cemetery in Washington, D.C., the famous *Woman and Hood* is one of America's most extraordinary pieces of sculpture. "Infinite wisdom," said John Hay, "a past without a beginning and a future without end; a repose, after limitless experience; a peace, to which nothing matters."

Not to be overlooked was one Charter Member, who was neither an industrialist nor an artist but in a class of his own. Ward McAllister was the self-appointed arbiter of New York and Newport Society. When the Metropolitan Club invitations went out in February, 1891, he was at the height of his power and close to the end of his life. It was he who had established the famous list of the Four Hundred which he released to *The New York Times* on the occasion of Mrs. Astor's Ball on February 1, 1892. These were the people he deemed to be true members of New York Society.

Born in Savannah, Georgia in 1827, the son of a southern jurist who became rich in San Francisco, McAllister came East in 1853 where he married the heiress Sarah T. Gibbons. After a trip abroad to bone up on court procedure, knowledge of wines and other foreign refinements, he returned to New York, attaching himself pompously to a woman he called "his Mystic Rose": "The" Mrs. Astor. In 1872, he chose the "Patriarchs," a ball committee of the twenty-five socially most prominent men, half a dozen of whom later became Members of the Metropolitan Club. The balls became important, and he became a leader among his peers—who were almost exclusively engaged in money-making—and taught them to appreciate the pleasures of the dinner table. He soon had his own code of cookery, court etiquette and coat of arms. He divided Society into what he called "nobs," or old families, and "swells," or newcomers—and gave the latter advice on how to become the former.

His downfall came eventually as a result of the revealing book he published in 1891, *Society*

*As I Have Found It.* He was discharged from the Patriarchs by a Committee of Three—Hamilton Fish, Elbridge Gerry and Colonel William Jay, all Members of the Metropolitan Club. Mc-Allister died in 1895.

Among museums, as a rule, the most intimate, charming and interesting are those housed in the residence of the Maecenas who assembled the collection. Examples of such jewels can be found in all civilized countries. Paris has its Musée Jacquemart-André in the house of Eugène André built in 1869-75 and London has its Wallace Collection in Hertford House built by Sir Richard Wallace. America has a number of them. The Fenway in Boston is the home of the collection of Isabella Stewart Gardner (1840-1924), the McNay Art Institute is in the house of Marion Hoogler McNay in San Antonio, the Ima Hogg Museum is in Houston, Winterthur is outside of Wilmington, and there are others. But connoisseurs will agree that two museums tower above all others in the charm of the buildings and the choice of the collection within and both were at one time the residences of Members of the Metropolitan Club. One is the Frick Collection at Fifth Avenue and 70th Street and the other the Henry E. Huntington Library and Art Gallery in San Marino near Pasadena.

The story of Henry Clay Frick has been told elsewhere. He was interested in art from the time he was a young man. A story told in art circles has it that he once saw a portrait of a little girl which reminded him of his dead daughter. The purchase of that painting was the start of the Frick Collection. About the time he joined the Club, 1899, he gave up his business and devoted most of his time to this pursuit. His friendship and rivalry with Morgan and Mellon sharpened his taste and Duveen encouraged him to buy only the best. As his judgment ripened, he sold his earlier acquisitions; most of the masterpieces with which he filled his house at Fifth Avenue and Seventieth Street were bought after the turn of the century. His house was designed by Carrère and Hastings and furnished by the decorator Sir Charles Allom. He lived there with his wife and children and enjoyed sitting in one of the ducal Renaissance chairs, surrounded by his masterpieces, reading a popular magazine, while the huge ornate organ at the head of the marble staircase poured out sentimental songs. Today his legacy is one of the marvels among museums in the world.

Henry Edwards Huntington became a Member in 1900. Immediately upon joining, he asked to rent rooms at the Clubhouse, and on March 25, 1901, the Executive Committee gave him Rooms 5 and 6 at a rent of $2,000 a year. At just about this time he decided to retire and to spend his remaining years and his colossal fortune doing something that might justify for himself a place in the hall of eternal fame. This was the start of the Henry E. Huntington Library and Art Gallery, which found a home in the mansion he built some years later on the outskirts of Pasadena, California. The Huntington fortune had partly been earned by Henry E. himself, and partly inherited first from his uncle, railroad builder Collis P. Huntington, when he died in 1900, and then from his Uncle's once beautiful widow, Arabella, whom he married in 1913. Quite a personality herself, Arabella had been named in the 1905 trial of Colonel William D'Alton Mann as one of the select group who had made loans to the publisher of the scandal sheet *Town Topics*, along with many other prominent Members of the Club. It seems the worthy colonel had ferreted out the secret Arabella had desperately tried to hide all her life: that her son had been born out of wedlock. Alerted by her lawyer, she fled the State just before the process server arrived.

During the years when Henry E. Huntington lived in the Metropolitan Club, he stockpiled his rooms with whatever items he saw that struck his fancy. A good part of his collection he assembled with the help and guidance of Lord Duveen, the English antique dealer, decorator and purveyor *par excellence* of the world's greatest paintings to the American plutocracy.

S. N. Behrman, in his book on Duveen written a number of years ago, tells the following story of H. E. Huntington's acquisition of a masterpiece he liked—but which his wife thought immoral. To make matters worse, Duveen did not want him to have it either, because it was offered for sale by another dealer— and Lord Duveen took a dim view of such action:

H. E. Huntington strayed from the Duveen fold only once, and Duveen, in his customary fashion, made him aware that heavy penalties attached to such a lapse. One day in 1913, while H.E., then living at the Metropolitan Club in New York, was taking an innocent stroll down Fifth Avenue, he was pulled off the street by an English art dealer who had a Fifth Avenue branch. He wanted H. E. to look at a painting of two ladies in filmy garments sauntering against a background of clouds, which was, he asserted, a wonderful Romney of Mrs. Siddons and her sister, Miss Kemble. H. E. who, unlike his wife, had no prejudices against actresses, succumbed to the two sisters on the spot. As Arabella was in California and couldn't bring her scruples to bear, he had the heavenly girls sent to the Metropolitan Club and paid the dealer a hundred thousand dollars for affecting the assignation. Proud of the *coup* he had achieved on his own, he invited Duveen to lunch to show off his new acquisition. Duveen, whose opinion of paintings he hadn't sold himself was always candid, gave the two tall, lovely, cloud-framed girls a pentrating look. "I don't think this is a Romney, H.E.," he said. "It looks like a Romney, it is very like a Romney, it is Romneyesque, but it is not Romney." Duveen's reflection on the legitimacy of the painting ruined Huntington's lunch.

Behrman goes on to tell how Huntington sued to recover his money and Duveen eventually, after superb detective work, had his judgment justified.

Arabella Duval (Yarrington) Worsham Huntington Huntington was probably the most amazing personality of the Twilight of Splendor era so interestingly depicted by James T. Maher in his book. She was born either in Alabama or in Virginia sometime between 1847 and 1852 into a poor family. Her father Richard Milton Yarrington was a machinist and died early. Young "Belle" was a seductive beauty. Soft, dark, luminous eyes, dark hair, parted at the center, a small mouth, set with determination. After the collapse of the South, she fled Richmond in company of John Worsham, a gambler

who left his wife and children behind, and came to New York with his "friend." There in 1870 she gave birth to a son she named Archer Milton Worsham although she was not married to Worsham. A few years later she met the fabulously rich Collis P. Huntington and soon was known as his unofficial wife. She started to spend huge amounts of money for houses, travelling and art purchases.

When the first Mrs. Huntington died after a long illness in 1883, Collis married Arabella. He died in 1900 and left her with $150,000,000, which made her the richest woman in the world. Now she started on an incredible spending spree which made her one of the most important art collectors of her generation. But more was to come. Collis' favorite nephew, Henry E. Huntington ('00), had also inherited $150,000,000 from his uncle which, added to his own great fortune, made him one of the wealthiest men in the nation. Henry fell in love with Arabella and pursued her persistently. During those years, he started to build the fairy tale mansion San Marino as his main residence and the repository of his art and book collection. Architects Myron Hunt and Elmer Gray created a complex of beauty surrounded by an enormous park. Finally, Arabella yielded and they were married in 1913 in Paris where she owned the Hôtel de Hirsh at No. 2 rue de l'Elysée and spent a great deal of her time. Henry Huntington remained a Member of the Club until his death in 1927. The country was astonished by the magnitude of generosity his obituary revealed. He had left San Marino to the public with all its art treasures including the largest library ever gathered together by a single man in the United States. Arabella had died three years earlier. She took the secret of the illegitimate birth of Archer to her grave.

The National Gallery in Washington, D.C., is the third museum created by Members of the Club. Whereas the Frick and the Huntington museums each were the accomplishment of one man, the National Gallery was so huge in conception that its realization required the collaboration of many. The leader and most prominent of these was Andrew W. Mellon, a

Member since 1918. Andrew's brother Richard became a Member in 1915.

Andrew Mellon was an extraordinary man, whose enormous wealth was based on the heavy industries of Pittsburgh. He was often referred to as "the lord of aluminum and oil and steel." He served as Secretary of the Treasury under three Presidents—Harding, Coolidge and Hoover—from 1921 to 1932. He then became Ambassador to the Court of St. James. He became interested in art through his friend Henry Clay Frick with whom he used to travel to Europe to visit museums. Over the course of several decades he collected more than 150 paintings and sculptures. Doubtless Frick's decision to build a gallery in New York stimulated Mellon's thoughts about establishing a national gallery in Washington, D.C., which, unlike the capitals of every other important nation, had none. Finally, in 1936, Mellon wrote to President Franklin D. Roosevelt offering his collection of painting and sculpture to the American people together with a capital sum for the building of a gallery. He modestly requested that his name not be used for the Gallery, although for many years it was commonly referred to as the Mellon Gallery. The architect in charge of building the gallery was John Russell Pope. Unfortunately neither founder nor architect were to see their work completed for both died within twenty-four hours of each other in August, 1937.

In 1978, the Mellon family, at a cost of $100 million, added an impressive new section to the museum, known as the East Wing.

Since its opening in 1941, the National Gallery of Art has established itself not only as the primary home of Western art in the United States, but also as one of the greatest art collections in the world. In addition to the enormous gifts of Mellon, three other Members of the Metropolitan Club made major contributions. In 1937, Samuel H. Kress (Dec. '23), the rival of Woolworth and Kresge in supplying the popular market with inexpensive merchandise, donated over four-hundred paintings and thirty-five pieces of sculpture he had collected, all from the Italian Schools. In 1942, Joseph E. Widener (April '27) gave his collection of about one-hundred paintings ranging from Italian quatrocento to Renoir. Chester Dale (May '35), who earned a fortune as a financier in Wall Street, became an avid lover of modern French art. The collection of impressionism which he and his wife Maud assembled and which was the most extensive and representative in the United States was left to the National Gallery upon his death in 1962. Among the other donors were Members W. Averell Harriman (Oct. '13) and Walter P. Chrysler (Oct. '23).

Among "the many lawyers—barristers—as they style them in Pall Mall" who were Members of the Club were a number of men whose names still grace many of the most prestigious law firms in Wall Street, those firms which every Yale Law School graduate dreams of joining. John L. Cadwalader, founder of Cadwalader, Wickersham & Taft, has been mentioned before. There were also William H. Polk and Paul Cravath; Frank and William Chadbourne; and Lewis Cass Ledyard, who founded Carter Ledyard & Milburn. The present head of the firm is John H. Young, a Member since 1964. Other well-known lawyer Members were Frederick R. Coudert who founded the famous international law firm bearing his name; Ogden L. Mills and Carl de Gerstorff; William C. Breed and George A. Ellis, Jr. Many of these lawyers became industrialists as did Member Owen D. Young ('23), who became head of General Electric, and also gave his name to the famous Young Plan at the Reparation Conference of 1929. Or Alger B. Chapman, who became Chairman of the Squibb Corporation; and John P. McGrath ('58) who became head of East New York Savings Bank. There was Member Samuel Seabury who headed the investigation in 1930-31 of New York's political machine and forced the colorful Mayor James Walker to resign.

Among the Members who held the highest office in the country—all Republicans, of course—were Herbert C. Hoover, who joined the Club in 1917 when he was Chairman of the Commission for Relief in Belgium which secured food and clothing for that war-devastated country. He was later to become the thirtieth

President. General Dwight D. Eisenhower became an Honorary Life Member in 1948, when he had resigned as Chief of Staff and become President of Columbia University. He was the third Member of the Club to hold the latter office, the first having been Seth Low and the second Nicholas Murray Butler. Richard Milhous Nixon became a Member in 1963 while he was practicing law in Wall Street. All resigned when the prospect of the White House appeared on the horizon. Elsewhere it has been mentioned that Levi P. Morton, the second President of the Club, was Vice President of the United States during the administration of Benjamin Harrison.

Charter Member William L. Strong was elected Mayor of New York in 1894. He was a Republican and headed a reform administration, under which Theodore Roosevelt held the office of Police Commissioner. He was succeeded by Democrat Robert Van Wyck as Mayor in 1897. Two other Members were Mayors of New York. Seth Low ('93) was elected as a Fusion candidate against Tammany Hall in 1901. He reformed the police department, completed the electrification of the New York Central Railroad within city limits and attacked the unsanitary tenements. Joseph V. McKee ('32) was acting mayor in 1932.

Other Members active in politics, or the fringe of politics, were George E. Allen, lawyer and one-time head of R.F.C. and friend of Presidents; Clark M. Clifford, Secretary of Defense under Lyndon Johnson; John Jacob Raskob, James D. Shouse and W. Averell Harriman, ambassador to the Soviet Union, later to the Court of St. James, confidant of Presidents, and Governor of New York State.

One of the leading politicians in New York in the '30s and '40s who was very active in Club affairs was Grover A. Whalen, the original Mr. New York. In 1931 he joined the Metropolitan Club, and in the showdown over the sale of the Building, he sided with Lee Warren James and served as a Governor from 1945 to 1951. Whalen was connected with the city government most of his life and was Police Commissioner from 1928-1930. Faultless in dress and elegant in bearing, he gained wide notice as

the city's official host, and was president of the New York World's Fair 1939-40. He arranged for the Mayor's Committee to occupy offices in the Ladies' Annex for a time. His frequent guest at the Club was Mayor Fiorello LaGuardia, who loved good cigars, but hated to smoke expensive ones out of innate frugality. Gus at the front desk relates how Whalen instructed him to display a box of expensive cigars and mark it "2 for 5¢" whenever LaGuardia was his guest at the Club. Needless to say the "Little Flower" helped himself freely.

The Club had its full quota of that human species reputed to be "the richest man in the country." The first person who comes to mind is Thomas Fortune Ryan who became a Member in 1902. Born on a small farm in Virginia, he went to Baltimore to work, married the boss's daughter, moved to New York and soon owned a tangled, but vastly successful, web of railroads and street railroads, lighting systems and coal companies. Thomas Fortune Ryan's philanthropies, large as they were, were confined to the Catholic Church. His son, John Barry Ryan, joined the Club in 1915. He was a poet and a dreamer who published verse under the name of Barrie Vail and generally managed to spend as much money as he was able to get

Fiorello LaGuardia, mayor of New York, who loved a good cigar.

198

The Board of Governors of U.S. Steel dined at the Metropolitan Club on January 5, 1926, and sat for this group portrait. At the center in the front row is Judge Gary and on his right, George F. Baker. Behind the Judge is Mr. Farrell, President of U.S. Steel, and on Farrell's right is Myron C. Taylor.

his hands on. In 1919, son Clendenin J. Ryan also became a Member. His life was marked by stark tragedy. In 1939, he committed suicide in the family graystone mansion on Seventieth Street. Incredibly enough, eighteen years later, in the same house, his son, also named Clendenin, also committed suicide.

Daniel K. Ludwig became a Member in 1967. Born in 1897 in a small town in Michigan, he borrowed $5,000 to buy his first boat, which he renovated and sold at a profit. It was the beginning of his fascination with boats, and he became one of the great shipowners of the world. He developed the welding process to replace riveting in shipbuilding and made many improvements in tanker design. His main holding is concentrated in the National Bulk Carriers Inc. At present he is investing huge amounts in developing a pulp industry in Brazil.

The Club in its early days was like a magnet drawing to itself the leaders of American industry. The story has been told above how J. Pierpont Morgan used the Clubhouse for the initial talks with Elbert Henry Gary, the famous Judge Gary, which led to the formation of the giant U. S. Steel Corporation in 1901. Judge Gary became a Member on January 16, 1900. As chairman of the board, he was the dominant personality of U.S. Steel until his death. The steel town of Gary, Indiana, was named after

him. Gary believed in high wages, promoted the welfare of and safety measures for employees, but opposed the formation of unions. He organized the famous Gary dinners at which board members and key executives discussed management policies. These dinners were often held at the Metropolitan Clubhouse and a photograph of one of them is shown here. All the participants are lined up in the Foyer on the Third Floor. The dinner took place on January 5, 1926, and was one of the last the Judge attended for he died the next year. He sits in the center and to the right of him is Charter Member George F. Baker, Board Member and president of the First National Bank of New York. Behind the Judge is the then-president of U.S. Steel, James A. Farrell, (June 18, 1912) and on Farrell's right is Myron E. Taylor (Dec. 1920).

U. S. Steel showed great loyalty to the Club. When the first chairman of the Board, Gary, died in 1927, J. Pierpont Morgan, Jr., a Charter Member, took his place until 1932. His successor was Myron E. Taylor who served until 1938. Among those serving as presidents, Charles M. Schwab was the first, becoming president in 1901, the same year he became a Member. He had worked his way up from a laborer. He came to Andrew Carnegie's attention and Carnegie eventually made him president of Carnegie Steel in 1897. But he gave up the presidency of U. S. Steel after two years to become the head of Bethlehem Steel, which he made into the leading producer of war materials for the Allies in World War I.

Schwab was succeeded by William E. Corey who became a Member on May 17, 1904. he served as president of "Steel" until 1911 when he was succeeded by James A. Farrell who held this post until 1932.

The computer has changed our life and our society more than any invention during the last generation. Way out in front in this field is the International Business Machines Corporation of which Thomas J. Watson was the creator and its president from 1914 to 1949. He became a Member in 1933 and served as a Governor from 1935 to 1952.

Samuel H. Kress became a Member in 1923. Born in 1863 in Cherryville, Pennsylvania, he started in the retail business in 1887 and developed the S. H. Kress & Co. chain of 5, 10 and 25¢ stores. Over a period of years, he acquired many paintings and sculptures, particularly of the Italian School. His became one of the most important art collections in the country and most of it is now part of the National Gallery of Art in Washington, D.C., although he donated paintings to many other museums.

Alfred P. Sloan, Jr., of General Motors has been mentioned before.

The third largest unit in the motor car business was started by Walter P. Chrysler who joined the Club in 1923. His son Jack joined in 1941.

Arthur Vining Davis was born in 1867 in Massachusetts, graduated from Amherst in 1888 and became a Member in 1923. He was responsible for building the Aluminum Corporation of America to its present giant size. Later he assembled one of the largest holdings of real estate in Florida.

Frederick W. Ecker was born in Brooklyn in 1896. He joined the Club in 1919 and was a Governor from 1932 to 1947. He became President of the Metropolitan Life Insurance Company in 1953.

Samuel Insull, a Member since 1906, had an extraordinary career. Born in London in 1859,

he came to the States in 1881, was employed by Thomas A. Edison as a secretary, and subsequently built up one of America's largest utility empires—Middlewest Utilities Company. At the height of his career, Insull controlled over three-hundred steam plants and almost two-hundred hydroelectric generating plants throughout the United States. His empire collapsed 1932, and he left the country, but in a subsequent trial he was exonerated.

Conrad Hilton, whose name can be found all over the world on the chain of hotels he built up, became a Member in 1944.

Other well-known names on the roster are William Childs ('24) of the Childs Restaurant Chain; Floyd Odlum ('45) of the Atlas Corporation; Herbert E. Smith ('38), head of Uniroyal and a director of U. S. Steel, who lived in the Clubhouse during his last years and died there; Allen P. Kirby ('35), president of Allegheny Corporation; and Jeremiah D. Maguire ('34), chairman of Federation Bank & Trust Co.

Joseph A. Martino ('47) was head of the National Lead Corporation. He served as a Governor from 1949 to 1961. During those years he often invited the Board to hold its Meeting and have lunch on his beautiful yacht, *Captiva*, which he docked in the East River at the foot of 26th Street.

Many commercial bankers were attracted to the Metropolitan Club. The National City Bank was represented by Charles E. Mitchell ('17) who was president of the great institution from 1921 to 1929. Other names connected with the City Bank were James Stillman ('91), Frank Vanderlip ('01), Gordon Rentschler ('27), and John Rovensky ('19).

From the Chase, there were Albert H. Wiggin ('01), Winthrop W. Aldrich ('14), Nelson W. Aldrich ('99) and Carl J. Schmidlapp ('16).

George F. Baker of the First National Bank was a Charter Member and later a Governor. James G. Blaine, Jr. ('19), whose father almost became President of the United States but was defeated by the "Rum, Romanism and Rebellion" speech of one of his supporters, was president of the Marine Midland Bank. And Richard H. West ('50), the Club President from

1960 to 1966, was president of the Irving Trust Company. Benjamin Strong ('09) was president and then chairman of U.S. Trust from 1947 to 1962, and then held the powerful position of president of the Federal Reserve Bank.

Henry C. Von Elm ('30) was chairman of the Manufacturers Trust Company, Eugene W. Stetson ('18) was president of the Guaranty Trust, and James D. Callery ('17) of the Diamond National Bank of Pittsburgh.

As might be expected, the investment banking and brokerage community was heavily represented on the Club roster. There were so many that only a few can be mentioned. Among J. Pierpont Morgan's partners not mentioned before were Dwight W. Morrow ('15), Thomas W. Lamont ('03), and Russell C. Leffingell ('16). Charles E. Blythe ('21) was the founder of the investment banking house bearing his name. William A. Read ('97), Clarence Dillon ('18) and Frederick H. Brandi ('46) were each head at various times of Dillon, Read & Co. Brandi was a Governor of the Club from 1968 to 1973.

Clarence Dillon holds a special place in the hearts of oenologists: in 1927, he bought one of the greatest vineyards in the world, Château Haut-Brion of Bordeaux, and the family owns it to this day. Its wines have a remarkable history. After the Revolution, the Château was owned by Talleyrand, the great statesman and gourmet, once Napoleon's foreign minister, and the wine was his favorite. Napoleon's favorite wine was Burgundy's Chambertin and he always carried a supply of it on his campaigns. On the eve of Austerlitz, he served it to his officers in his tent. After Napoleon's fall, a defeated France sent Talleyrand to the Congress of Vienna. He accepted this appointment only on condition that the French Government would transport an ample supply of his wines to Vienna, among them the splendid wines of Haut-Brion. Talleyrand's soirées became so famous for their good food, choice wines and witty conversation and as a result so important in the diplomatic negotiations of the peace conference that he managed to walk away from it with more territory for a defeated France than she had when the war began.

Dominick & Dominick were represented by Bayard Dominick ('19), George F. Dominick ('97) and H. Blanchard Dominick ('92). Henry Harris Upham became a Member in 1924, Anthony J. Drexel in 1891, Charles Hayden in 1908, Edward H. Kidder in 1903, Grayson M.P. Murphy in 1914, W.K.K. Taylor in 1916 and Ed F. Hutton in 1926. There were three Delafields: Francis and Maturin L. Delafield, who were Charter Members, and A.W. Richard who joined in 1904. George Murnane of Lazard Frères joined in 1925, and the Honorable Charles Y. Bay of A.M. Kidder & Co. in 1945. Harry B. Lake of Ladenburg, Thalman & Co. became a Member in 1927.

A prominent family in the brokerage fraternity over the last hundred years have been the Fahnestocks. The original Fahnestocks came here from Germany in 1725. They became wealthy and Harris C. Fahnestock was invited to become a Charter Member. Not long afterwards, some of his sons joined; Gibson in 1893, William in 1894 and Harris in 1895. William founded the Stock Exchange firm of Fahnestock & Co. in 1881 which still exists at this writing. Father Harris C. Fahnestock bought the North Wing of the Villard House in 1882 and gave the adjoining house to the east to his son William as a gift. The story of the bachelor dinner given William Fahnestock in November,1898, is related elsewhere.

The Metropolitan Club was never very popular among the clergy. Perhaps the cold shoulder which the Founding Fathers gave to the Reverend Dr. Rainsford was not forgotten. The original Constitution provided for only one special class of Membership, i.e., Officers of the Army and Navy and according to the By-laws, Article XIX, they were required to pay only half the usual initiation fees and dues, but the clergy had to pay full fees.

The only clergyman who had been on the original list and who had accepted the invitation to become a Charter Member was the Rev. Dr. David H. Greer, rector of St. Bartholomew's. He was quite a clubman and belonged to five other clubs. The Century was the favorite of the men of the cloth and in 1894 had ten clergymen among its membership. They could be seen there frequently, especially on Saturday nights. Dr. Rainsford was a member of the Century and Bishop Potter was even an officer. The Union Club alone had no clergymen as members.

By 1929, the words "and Members of the Clergy" had been added to Article XIX of the Constitution, but the By-laws still granted the privilege of half dues only to Army and Navy Members. By 1940, however, the By-laws had been amended and granted Members of the Clergy half dues and fees. In the lists summarizing the professions of the Members, the Clergy was not listed separately until 1966, when there were two. Today there are seven, of which the best known is Reverend Dr. Norman Vincent Peale, who joined the Club in 1959. Born in Ohio in 1889, son of a clergyman, the Reverend Dr. Peale has been the pastor of the historic Marble Collegiate Church and has created a large following through his inspirational writings.

The outstanding educator on the Club's roster was Nicholas Murray Butler, who became a Member in 1903 and later became active in the Club's management, serving as a Governor from 1919 to 1936. He is the only non-President who has a Private Dining Room named after him. Born in Elizabeth, New Jersey, in 1862, he studied in Paris and Berlin through a Columbia University fellowship. He became professor of philosophy at Columbia in 1884 and, in 1901, succeeded Member Seth Low ('93) as president of Columbia University. He was an inspired leader, holder of the 1931 Nobel Peace Prize, active in Republican politics and the author of numerous books.

George Doubleday joined in 1910 and Frank Nelson Doubleday in 1923. They founded the publishing firm that bears their name in 1897.

Member Lincoln Ellsworth ('26) was a world-famous explorer. In 1926, on his second attempt, he flew from Spitzbergen over the North Pole to Teller, Alaska, in the dirigible *Norge*. He accompanied Admiral Richard Byrd, Roald Amundsen and Umberto Nobile on numerous expeditions in this area. His ship is on display at the Ford Museum in Michigan.

The Second World War established the military as a permanent and important branch of the Establishment. As a result, the Metropolitan Club also had many of the great military heroes and leaders either as Regular or Honorary Life Members. Some of them were:

General Douglas MacArthur (1951)
General Dwight D. Eisenhower (1948)
General George C. Marshall (1947)
General Albert C. Wedemeyer (1951)
General Robert L. Eichelberger (1946)
General Alfred M. Gruenther (1958)
General William Joseph Donovan (1957)
Admiral William F. Halsey (1945)
Admiral John W. Will (1959)
Admiral Arthur M. Radford (1959)
Colonel Maxwell Taylor (1950)
Colonel Earl H. Blaik (1959)

Famous foreigners who were Members include Frederick IX, King of Denmark, Olav V, King of Norway, the Rt. Honorable Winston Spencer Churchill, and Count Philip La Fayette, to name a few. Benjamin Seymour Guinness became a Member in 1902. His investments reached all over the world. He also was a partner of Ladenburg, Thalman & Co. An active Member was Count Charles Szechenyi ('46) and the Card Room shows his name as a frequent winner at gin rummy and backgammon. Dr. Tibor Eckhardt ('47), statesman and diplomat, was the founder of the Hungarian Small Holder's Party. Baron George Bessenyey ('50) was Hungary's pre-war Ambassador to Switzerland.

A man of national prominence who was very active in Club affairs was Elmer H. Bobst. He applied for Membership in 1945, became a Governor in 1966 and a Vice President in 1969. He died in 1978.

Mentioned above are only a fraction of the men who were Members over the years. Moreover, the story concentrates on the first fifty years of the Club's history. It is intended merely to convey an idea of the many important men who were attracted to Membership during its history.

# Chapter 18

# THE FIGHT TO SURVIVE: 1950 TO THE PRESENT

The last thirty years, from 1950 to the present, has seen a Renaissance of the Metropolitan Club. Many needed renovations and modernizations have been effected. Membership has risen again; activities have expanded; and, after almost ninety years of struggle, the Club appears to be financially secure.

On April 24, 1951, George W. Whitaker succeeded Lee Warren James as President. A native of Pennsylvania, Whitaker joined the Liggett and Myers Tobacco Co. and he was Vice President in charge of sales when he retired in 1944.

In December, 1951, an unusual and immense rug was acquired which for years was the much-admired showpiece of the Great Marble Hall. It was an Ardebil, measuring 47.9 feet by 31.6 feet, with a count of three-hundred Senna Persian knots per square inch, or fifty-four-million individual knots. Over 49,000 man-hours had gone into the weaving. Because the cost of repairs on the Ardebil became prohibitive, it was replaced in 1975 by the present rug which was bought for $2,500 plus the Ardebil. At this time, also, the private dining rooms, formerly known as Rooms A, B, C, D and E, were given the names of past Presidents or Governors. They became the Frank K. Sturgis Room, the J. Pierpont Morgan Room, the Levi P. Morton Room, and the Nicholas Murray Butler Room, after the head of Columbia University who served as Governor from 1919 to 1936. The fifth room had to be given up when the kitchen was moved to the third floor in 1966.

In May, 1955, the Warner-Lambert Pharmaceutical Company, of which Elmer Bobst was the head, asked to rent the ground floor of the Annex. They offered $21,000 a year for the first five years. Their proposal was accepted, and the rent has now been raised to $50,000 a year.

In December, 1955, Wilfred L. L'Esperance, Jr., who had been the front-office clerk for many years, retired. He was essentially a cigar salesman and in that capacity had worked for the Waldorf before joining the Metropolitan staff at a time when the selling of cigars was big business. The room now used as the Ladies Lounge behind the telephone booths was then the Smoking Room. A big cigar counter ran along the 60th-Street side of the room and in the east corner were a stock-exchange ticker, and a news tape. Chairs were placed in front of the ticker, where Members could sit, smoking, watching the tape and swapping tips. Gus, the present Front-Office Manager, remembers that one Member once placed an order for fifty

*Water leaf*

boxes of Larranaga Cigars. Attendance and business gradually fell off, however, and finally, in 1959, it was decided to get rid of the ticker, move the cigar counter to the office next door and convert the Smoking Room into the present Ladies' Lounge.

George Whitaker resigned because of illness and died two years later. His portrait by the English painter Gerald Leslie Brockhurst (1890-1978) now hangs in the Library. Brockhurst studied in London and exhibited in the Royal Academy before moving to New York in 1939. He is considered one of the best British portrait painters of the early twentieth century.

Upon Whitaker's resignation in April, 1956, Thomas A. O'Hara, who had been Vice-President of the Club since 1951, was elected President. O'Hara had been one of the old Calumet Club members. Born in Cincinnati, Ohio in 1888, he went to Dayton as an employee of Albert Emanuel, who was head of a vast utility holding system. When Albert Emanuel's son, Victor, took over the business and moved to New York, O'Hara followed and became Director of the Standard Power and Light Group and later of the Avco Group. O'Hara also became ill, occupying the Presidency for only about a

Cornelius J. Reid (1896-1980) President 1958-1960

year, and died on June 5, 1960. His portrait by Robert Tolman hangs in the third-floor Hall.

With O'Hara ill, Lee Warren James was again elected President on June 18, 1957, and accepted but only on a temporary basis. Dues were increased to $300 a year under his stewardship. In May, 1958, he underwent a serious operation, and at the Membership Meeting that month, Cornelius J. Reid was elected President.

Neil Reid was born in 1896 in Flushing, New York. In 1916, he succeeded his father in the insurance-brokerage business which had been established in 1895. In 1923, he married Muriel Jane Forester, they had six children, and in 1968 his twenty-fourth and last grandchild was born. He was one of the organizers of the Half Moon Hotel in Montego Bay, Jamaica. In 1972, he was elected Honorable Chairman of the Board of RBH/Reid & Carr, Inc., one of the large insurance brokers in New York.

The need for increasing the activities of the Club was obvious. Admiral John J. Bergen was the Chairman of the Special Events Committee in the late 1950s and, as a result of his naval background, was able to invite many naval officers to speak. On October 21, 1958, for instance, Commander William R. Anderson of the US Submarine *Nautilus*, addressed 340 Members at lunch. In June, 1960, Captain Edward L. Beach, commander of the submarine *Triton*, which had circumnavigated the globe completely submerged, addressed 344 Members at lunch. Many other notables spoke at the Club, including, in November, 1958, NASA's Wernher von Braun.

In May, 1960, Cornelius Reid told the Governors that his business activities had grown so demanding that he could not stand for re-election as President, and that after due consideration, he was taking the unusual liberty of nominating for his successor Richard H. West whom he felt would be in a better position to serve the Club adequately. The Board followed his suggestion.

Richard Haughton West was born in New York City in January, 1895. After serving in the Army during World War I, he joined the Irving Trust Company in New York in 1923 and became its President in 1949. He was a member of

Richard H. West (1895-1977) President 1960-1966

many boards of directors, and among his clubs were the Union League, Recess and Manhattan. In 1950, he married Lillian Nancy Fuller.

Under West's Presidency, the Womens' Committee came into existence and received much encouragement from him, and on January 12, 1966, he presided over the first Debutante Ball created by the Womens' Committee. He remained President until May 17, 1966, having held that office for six years: He too was made an Honorary Life Member and was a steady visitor to the Clubhouse. It was thanks to him that the Irving Trust Company extended a loan to the Club in 1969, although he was neither President of the Club nor of Irving Trust at that time. He died in June, 1977.

Richard H. West's portrait, painted by Paul Trebilcock, was displayed for many years in the third-floor foyer right next to the archway leading to the Main Dining Room. West's portrait is extremely lifelike and looked into the Room and toward the table to the left, where he and his wife dined so often, alone or with friends. Born in 1902, Trebilcock studied at the Art Institute of his native Chicago. He has painted a long line of famous men and women, among them President F. D. Roosevelt, Mrs. Reginald

Vanderbilt, Viscountess Furness, Benjamin Fairless, and Charles Hayden.

Under West's consulship, two major alterations were undertaken—the Clubhouse was air conditioned and the kitchen was moved to the third floor. The Clubhouse was built in the years 1892 and 1893 at a time when steel and concrete construction was a new method, gas was the accepted form of illumination, and electricity was just coming into use. All the original lighting fixtures in the Club were actually gas fixtures with electricity as an auxiliary. The elevators were hydraulic since the electric-powered lift had not yet been invented. The Building was heated with coal. Modern safety standards were unknown.

By the middle 1940s, the building was fifty years old. The roof was leaking and practically had to be replaced. A new State multiple-dwelling law imposed standards which were extremely costly to meet. First estimated at $150,000, they finally cost about half that, but still a sizeable amount. The old hydraulic elevators had to be replaced at a cost of $107,000. The electric alternating current had to be converted to direct current, and the cost of changing the wiring came to almost $50,000. New furniture, carpets and equipment were desperately needed. And then there was the problem of relocating the kitchen.

When the Building was constructed, the kitchen had been placed on the roof according to the fashion of the time. Food was conveyed to the Main Dining Room on the third floor, the Strangers' Dining Room on the mezzanine and the Ladies' Dining Room on the main floor by dumbwaiters to adjoining serving rooms where it was kept warm until served. Labor was then cheap and abundant and the large parties that have had to be accommodated in recent years were uncommon.

The move of the kitchen was discussed for at least twenty years, but the high cost and trouble of the changeover prevented its being done. In 1963, the cost was estimated at about $150,-000. Besides the obvious convenience of having the kitchen next to the Main Dining Room, it would save five men on the staff and would free space on the fifth floor for more guest rooms,

205

the rental of which would add to the Club's income. Finally, the renovation was begun in the summer of 1966, taking longer and costing more than estimated. The final cost came to $226,000.

The Building was not air conditioned and it was felt summer attendance would improve if it were. At the end of 1959, estimates for air conditioning the Building were requested and early next year the main social rooms had room air conditioners placed at the top of the windows. Comfort was provided but the real cost was not money. It was aesthetics. The unattractive boxes on top of the windows detract from the beauty of the rooms. Furthermore, the curtains now hang straight most of the time rather than in graceful curves as formerly.

In September, 1965, the entire outside of the Building, which had become grimy, was repaired, steam-cleaned and waterproofed. The gym was renovated the next year. A sauna was installed in 1968. In July, 1968, the marble in the Great Hall was cleaned. The beauty of the marble had been hidden by layers of dirt, soot and stains, as well as by marble stains from "bleeding" of the surface behind the marble. A poultice was applied to the surface, left for a day or two and then scraped off. The marble was thus restored to its original white beauty.

In March, 1969, the Main Bar was refurbished with new silk damask on the wall panels, the woodwork was refinished and the decorative designs regilded. New stained-glass windows were installed in the Library in 1970 to replace the original clear-glass ones. And in 1971, a contract was finally signed to build bedrooms on the third mezzanine, the space left vacant when the kitchen was moved to the third floor. The cost was to be $182,671, and would give the Club a total of forty-four bedrooms, of which thirty-seven were double rooms.

Accurate figures as to the amounts spent for rehabilitation, repairs and improvements are not available. A good estimate of costs since the Fiftieth Anniversary Dinner would be that about $2 million to $2.5 million has been spent, about one-quarter of this during the last six years. Such expenditures could never have

been met by the operating earnings. But in 1962, the Board had established a Voluntary Rehabilitation Fund asking each Resident Member for a contribution of $10 a month, to be added to the monthly bills. Non-Resident Members were asked for a contribution of $48 a year, and Widow and Foreign Members for $24 a year. The response has been very good, and the fund has yielded annual amounts of between $42,000 and $118,771. The total from 1962 to 1980 was just about $1.4 million. The purpose of the Voluntary Fund was redesignated in 1974 to be used for the reduction of debt, but whatever the name, it has been a most valuable source of revenues.

Special mention must be made of the many Members who again and again made liberal gifts, usually for a specific improvement or beautification of the Building. The cleaning of the marble in the Great Hall in 1968, which cost $12,500, and the redecoration of the Main Bar in 1969 mentioned above were paid for by anonymous donors. The valuable photograph collection of old New York now hanging in the Men's Grill was a gift of Frank A. Roe made in 1957. In 1967, a large sterling silver tray and cup inscribed with the names of ten old Members was donated. Another anonymous Member refurnished the entire Great Hall in 1968. Others gave amounts of $1,000 to $10,000, the most recent being Gert von Gontard, who in 1979 left $10,000 in his will to the Club.

Gert von Gontard was very much attached to the Club. He lived in the Clubhouse with his wife Hilde for many winters, spending the summers in Munich and later in Zurich. The writer Zuckmayer described him as a "highly cultivated and sensitive lover of the arts and humanities." The Gontards were Huguenots from Southern France who had emigrated to Germany during the second half of the seventeenth century. Son of Paul von Gontard and his St. Louis-born wife Clara Busch, Gert grew up in Germany. In 1929, he founded the literary and political magazine *Neue Revue* which was strongly anti-Nazi. When Hitler took power, he fled to America. He joined the Club in 1950; an uncle of his, Alex von Gontard, had been a Member since 1912. In 1980, Gert's widow gave his private library of 4,500 volumes, including a magnificent collection of Goetheana, to Washington University in Seattle.

An especially generous gesture was made in 1970, when a Member, who again preferred to remain anonymous, offered to give $50,000 a year for five years to reduce the debt of the Club provided other Members matched his offer. The offer met with limited success but the Club received a total of $100,000 from this Member.

More recently, in 1980, a generous group of Members contributed about $12,000 to clean and repair Armstrong's stained-glass windows in the Great Marble Hall.

Practically from the moment that the Clubhouse was completed, periodic rumors went the rounds that it was for sale and on the market. And just as often the Board passed a resolution that it was not for sale. So it was again, in October, 1962, that a resolution was passed stating it "was the consensus that the Club building should not be sold." Myriad plans were discussed regarding the Clubhouse. One of them was to build a large residential hotel where the Annex is. Another resolution was passed at that meeting stating that "it was undesirable for any Club Member to have any business contact such as supplying any goods or services for the Club."

As if the financial condition of clubs in general were not bad enough, a federal tax of 20% and a New York City tax of 5% was imposed on Club Dues in 1961. For the Metropolitan, that meant $75 a year on top of the Annual Dues which had risen to $300. In order to exert pressure for repeal of this impost, clubs banded together and some three hundred formed the National Club Association. The tax was removed in 1965. Today, a city tax of 8% remains on club dues.

In the late 1950s, the custom of conferring Honorary Life Guest privileges on prominent people was established. In 1959, Eugene Grace, who had been a member for forty-four years, was made an Honorary Life Guest. The same honor was conferred on George A. Bomann on his ninety-fifth birthday. In October, 1960, the King and Queen of Denmark visited the Club and were made Honorary Life Guests. By 1963, the following people had been designated Honorary Life Guests:

Sir Harold Alexander
Capt. William R. Anderson, USN
Mrs. William A. Barber
Capt. Edward L. Beach, USN
E. A. L. Bennett
Sir Winston Spencer Churchill
Lt. Gen. Garrison H. Davidson, USA
Frederick H. Ecker
Gen. Dwight D. Eisenhower
Frederick IX, King of Denmark
Gen. Alfred M. Gruenther
Hon. Herbert Hoover
Queen Ingrid of Denmark
Gen. Douglas MacArthur
Rear Adm. Redfield Mason, USN
Hon. Richard C. Patterson, Jr.
Adm. Arthur W. Radford, USN (Ret.)
Adm. William H. Stanley, USN (Ret.)
Gen. Albert C. Wedemeyer
Col. H.D. Woodruff, USAF

In addition, in November, 1963, the Board created a Senior Advisory Committee of those who had been Members for over fifty years. At the time, there were five men who qualified: Bedell H. Haned who had joined May 21, 1912; Dr. Owen H. Kenan, May 21, 1912; Lewis L. Clarke, May 17, 1910; Childs Frick (son of Member Henry Clay Frick), February 21, 1905; and Hall Park McCullough, October 16, 1894.

On May 17, 1966, the Honorable Spruille Braden, who had long been active in the Club's affairs and had been Vice President for seven years, was elected to the Presidency by the Board. Born in 1894 in Elkhorn, Montana, he was the son of William Braden, founder of the Braden Copper Company of Chile. He studied mining engineering at Yale, and later represented his father's and Anaconda Copper's interests in Chile. He became active in the Democratic Party in the early '30s, and in 1933 he was appointed advisor to the U.S. Delegation to the Pan American Financial Conference and began his diplomatic career. Subsequently, he became Ambassador to Colombia, Cuba and Argentina. His first wife, mother of his six children, having died, he married Verbina Williams Hebbard in 1964.

The first formal affair presided over by Ambassador Braden was the dinner given on November 2, 1966, to celebrate the seventy-fifth Anniversary of the Club's founding. Guests of honor were the two former Presidents, Cornelius J. Reid and Richard H. West, who were given Life Memberships and presented with gold Membership cards to commemorate the occasion. It was a family dinner and a glamorous affair, and also marked the opening of the new kitchen facilities on the third floor. The improvement was immediately evident, for the food served was hotter and more attractive.

A special feature of the dinner was a tasteful souvenir program, mailed to all Members, which reproduced the front page of *Harpers Weekly* of March 10, 1894, with a picture of the Marble Hall and Grand Stairway as well as views of the Ladies' Dining Room, the Main Dining Room, the Library and the Lounging Room.

Ambassador Braden was President of the Club for seven years from May, 1966, to May,

The Honourable Spruille Braden (b. 1894)
President 1966-1973

1973. During the first four years of his tenure, operations yielded small profits, averaging $35,000 after depreciation of $20,000. But then losses increased. They amounted to $147,000 in 1970, $56,000 in 1971 and $184,000 in 1972. Fortunately, in October, 1969, before losses became too heavy, the Board was able to negotiate a new loan for up to $1.5 million with the Irving Trust Company. The loan matured originally on May 1, 1972, but maturity was extended for two-year periods thereafter.

In an effort to put the Club on a sound financial basis, the Braden Administration increased the annual dues enormously to three times the level they had been several years before. Annual dues had been $300 until October, 1965, when they became $450. In November, 1968, they were increased to $500; in 1970 they jumped to $700 a year for Resident and $350 for Non-Resident Members. This led to massive resignations. When the Board met in January, 1971, there were eighty-eight resignations on the agenda. Regular Membership, the backbone of any club, fell from 591 to 486 between June 30, 1970 and 1972. While dues had been increased by sixty percent, total income from dues increased by only thirty percent. In addition smaller attendance in the Club's facilities reduced income from sales of food and beverages. In November, 1972, dues took another jump to $900 for Regular Members and proportionate increases in the other classifications. Effective January 1, 1973, another hundred Members handed in their resignations.

Regular Membership now had reached an all-time low of 434, lower than during the crisis of 1944-45. The Club has only recently recovered from this shock proving that dues cannot be steeply increased without causing severe consequences. With inflation solidly built into our economy, the level of annual dues must of necessity rise also. Such increases probably would be found less objectionable to the Membership if they were tied to the annual increase in the cost of living by an automatic escalation formula.

Over the last two decades, talks with various clubs regarding mergers or exchange privileges were held intermittently. Early talks with the Lotos Club came to nothing. In September, 1963, the Manhattan Club initiated talks regarding a merger, and in December of that year, talks were held with the Houston Club regarding exchange privileges. Nothing came of all of this.

Within the Membership, criticism of the management of the affairs of the Club began to grow and opposition became more outspoken. In March, 1973, Ambassador Braden announced that he would not stand for reelection. An opposition slate was nominated for the election of Governors, scheduled for April 25, 1973. This was done by petition under Article II, Part 7, of the Constitution.

At the meeting, the opposition slate carried the day. Elected were Howard J. Dirks, Harold B. Hamilton, Henry A. Otis, Gordon DeB. Joyce and John P. Gomulka, Jr. At the Governors' Meeting following the Annual Meeting, Peter Hilton was elected President. He had been a Member since 1959 and a Governor since May, 1972. At the same meeting Ambassador Braden was elected a Life Member and it was voted to give a special dinner in his honor.

The portraits of Cornelius J. Reid and of Ambassador Spruille Braden hang in the foyer leading to the Dining Room on the third floor; both were painted by Rudolph Anton Bernatschke, a Member of the Metropolitan Club since 1956. Braden is portrayed wearing the decorations of Bolivia and Paraguay in honor of his chairmanship of the U.S. delegation to the Chaco Peace Conference which settled the war between the two countries. Born in Salzburg, Austria, in 1913, Bernatschke was educated in Europe and America. He studied at l'Ecole des Beaux-Arts in Paris. He came to the United States in 1940 and served in the American army during World War II. Among the well-known men and women he has painted are Francis Cardinal Spellman, Desmond Guinness, General Albert C. Wedemeyer, CIA Director Admiral Raborn, Fritz Kreisler and the Prince Archbishop of Salzburg, among others. His works are on exhibit in a number of museums both here and abroad. His portrait of the late Senator Robert Taft hangs permanently in the Republican leader's office in the U.S. Senate.

Peter Hilton, who was in the corporate merger business, soon became ill. In September, 1973, he was unable to attend the Board Meeting. He died on May 9, 1974. Hilton was President for just one year. He tried valiantly to increase the Membership without much success. During this period, the possibility of getting together with the Canadian Club of New York was first discussed. They were not very happy with their quarters at the Waldorf-Astoria Tower since the terms of their lease had changed unfavorably. The overriding concern was to protect the identities of both clubs and three possibilities were discussed: an outright merger, which both clubs could not agree to; sale or lease of some club property, which was not feasible; or the creation of a new special class of membership by the Metropolitan Club, that of Associate Member. Negotiations dragged on over a protracted period. Finally, the last recommendation was agreed upon by Canadian Club President Phillips S. Trenbath and his committee, and on October 8, 1974, the necessary amendments to the Constitution of the Metropolitan Club were approved by a Special Membership Meeting. Two new classes were created, Resident and Non-Resident Associate Member. They have all rights except those reserved to Life and Regular Members.

The Canadian Club, founded in 1903, is twelve-years younger than the Metropolitan Club. In his book *The Kinship of Two Countries: A History of the Canadian Club of New York*, its twenty-fifth President, Hugh A. Anderson, presents the story of the club up to 1963 illustrated with some photographs. Many Canadians have come to live and work in the States over the years. Most of them are indistinguishable from Americans, except for those who have kept their "eh?", but few people who have not lived north of the St. Lawrence and the Great Lakes can recognize this speech habit.

Canadians have left their mark on many professions in the United States. To mention just one, the movies: Mary Pickford, Beatrice Lilie, Raymond Massey, Walter Pidgeon, Walter Huston and Norma Shearer were all Canadians by birth. Some Canadians felt the need of a congenial place in New York City where they could meet and entertain their friends. The first step toward that end, as Mr. Anderson relates, was a meeting in 1903 in a Y.M.C.A. (for where else would young Canadians foregather?) to discuss the organization of a club. The summonses were sent out by William T. Robson, formerly of Lindsay, Ontario, and from this meeting evolved the Canadian Club of New York. Starting at this point, Mr. Anderson relates how the new institution grew, how it graduated from the use of hired rooms for occasional meetings to permanent quarters, first in the Biltmore, then in the Belmont and finally in the commodious and attractive quarters they occupied in the Waldorf-Astoria. Along the way, he chronicles the many important world figures who visited the club as guest speakers.

New Year's Day, 1975, was the first day the new group was admitted to the Club Building, and those attending the Open House were given a printed Walking Tour to guide them through the Building. The Canadian Club was given separate quarters in the Annex, with its own entrance. The beautiful Ladies' Dining Room was remodeled and repainted, a new bar was installed and hand-painted coats-of-arms of the Canadian Provinces were hung, ringing the upper wall. A large handsome oil painting of Queen Elizabeth II of England hangs over the fireplace mantle. The painting was officially unveiled by the Queen Mother during a state visit to the Canadian Club in 1954. Hand-carved maple-leaf chairs and tables give the room a special charm. On May 28, the annual President's Reception was the first major function given in the new quarters.

Upon the death of Peter Hilton, the board elected Alger B. Chapman as President on May 21, 1974. Born in Hempstead, Long Island, in 1904, Chapman was graduated from Williams College and received a L.L.B. degree from Columbia University in 1932.

In 1934 Chapman became a partner in the Washington law firm of Alvord and Alvord. From 1945 through 1948 he was Commissioner

Alger B. Chapman (b. 1904)   President 1974-1977

of the New York State Department of Taxation and Finance and President of the New York State Tax Commission. Chapman became Chairman and Chief Executive Officer of Beech-Nut Life Savers, Inc., and in 1968 became Chairman of the Squibb Corporation upon the merger of Beech-Nut and Squibb. He was Treasurer of the New York Republican State Committee from 1950 to 1958 and was New York State Campaign Manager for Thomas E. Dewey in 1946, 1948 and 1950, and for Dwight D. Eisenhower in 1952 and 1956.

Chapman lives with his wife, the former Catherine Cox, in Amagansett, New York. His son Alger B. Chapman, Jr., is Co-Chairman of Shearson, Loeb Rhoades, and is a Member and Governor of the Metropolitan Club.

Alger B. Chapman was President of the Club for three years, from May 21, 1974 to May 23, 1977. It was under his stewardship that the arrangement with Canadian Club was finally consummated and he proudly presided over the Open House reception on New Year's Day, 1975, to welcome the new Members.

When Chapman did not want to stand for re-election, Harold B. Hamilton became the seventeenth President of the Club. He has been a Member since 1969 and a Board Member since 1973. Born in New York City, he attended Columbia Grammar School and Rice University.

After a short stint with the *Wall Street Journal*, he went into the air-conditioning business and started his own business under the name of H. B. Hamilton Company, of which he is now Chairman of the Board. He is said to have air-conditioned more hotel rooms than anybody else in the country. "Ham" Hamilton is married to Elizabeth (Betty) Wyhro, a gifted amateur painter. They have two children and three grandchildren.

The portraits of the two most recent Presidents of the Club, Alger B. Chapman and Harold B. Hamilton, were painted by the same artist, Dean Ellis. Born in Detroit in 1921, Ellis began his formal art education in 1941 at the Cleveland Institute of Art, but was interrupted for four years when he served as an infantryman in the Pacific theater of war. Paintings by Ellis hang in about twenty public collections. *Life Magazine* in 1950 selected him as one of nineteen promising American painters. His works have been shown at the Whitney and Metropolitan Museums and the National Academy. He resides in New York City and Amagansett, Long Island.

Hamilton has become very active in the management of the Club. It is a rare day when he is not in the Clubhouse, behind his desk in the office or for luncheon on Club business at his usual corner table in the Dining Room. His son has taken over the management of the air-conditioning business. As Chairman of the House Committee, Hamilton had already started to take over the management of the Club while his predecessor was still in office. Both men realized that their main objective should be to bring about better use of the splendid facilities of the Clubhouse. In other words, they wanted to fill the Main Dining Room and the private rooms for lunch and dinner and to stimulate the demand for large parties, receptions, balls and business meetings. In order to accomplish this, many of the Club facilities had to be modernized or enlarged, the food had to be made the tastiest, and the service, the best in town.

Many sorely-needed capital improvements have been made during the last few years. The Main Entrance in the Courtyard was carpeted and protected against wind, rain and cold by screens and heat lamps. A new heating plant was installed, practically the entire Building was newly-carpeted, and new furniture, such as the attractive and comfortable new Dining Room chairs, was purchased. The kitchen was enlarged and modernized. The program went into such seemingly minor details as having the lovely fireplaces in the Great Hall and Main Bar restored for use. During cold days, big logs are lit and their cozy fire creates an especially appealing atmosphere.

The result of all these efforts has been that the decline in the number of Members has halted. The number of Regular Members was 434 in 1974. At the beginning of 1981, there were 484 Life and Regular Members. Including all classes of Membership, there are 2,367 Members. Also, exchange privileges were negotiated with the old downtown luncheon club, the India House. This not only brought in more diners, especially in the evening, but gave the Metropolitan Club Members luncheon fa-

Harold B. Hamilton    President 1977

211

cilities in the Wall Street District.

The India House Club building on downtown Hanover Square is another of New York's landmarks. The elegant three-story brownstone began its history as the headquarters for the Hanover Bank in 1854 and later served the New York Cotton Exchange and the W.R. Grace banking house. Since 1914, it has been the home of the distinguished merchant's club. It contains a superb collection of Maritime objects. Other reciprocal agreements are in effect with the Union League Club in New York, the Union League of Philadelphia, the Carlton Club of London, Uebersee Club in Hamburg, the Manitoba Club of Winnipeg, the Australian Club of Sydney, and the Petroleum Club of Houston.

Indicative of the beneficial results of this expanded program is the increasing popularity of the Dining Room for lunch and of such established features as the Sunday Brunch given during the winter months in the Main Dining Room. The excellent seafood bar and the cold buffet attract an enthusiastic crowd, and recent attendance figures have averaged 250 and more. The Sunday Brunch enjoys a splendid reputation; Members and friends give glowing accounts of it. The elegant monthly Dinner-Dances usually attract two hundred of those Members who are fond of dancing. The Annual Ball in December, the main social function of the winter season, the Debutante Ball and the New Year's Eve party are usually oversubscribed.

The net effect is that the Club, under the leadership first of Alger Chapman and then of Harold Hamilton, is now financially secure for the first time in its history. During the five years 1976 to 1980 profits totaling $1,300,000 could be reported, over and above depreciation charges of $450,000. The voluntary fund for the retirement of the debt yielded another $450,-000. In 1981 for the first time in its history the long-term debt of the Club has been reduced to under one-million dollars.

*   *   *

The life of the Metropolitan Club began nine decades ago. There have been years of splendor and power, of crisis and struggle. The Members unabashedly enjoyed the period of splendor, but during the years of difficulties, it was the Building itself, that masterpiece of Stanford White's genius, that inspired the Members to great sacrifices. As a sodality of men, the Club is irrevocably linked to the Building, and the Building would lose its character and its meaning without the devotion of its Membership. Both represent the best: the Building, of the art and architecture of Western culture; and the Membership, of the dignity and high ideals of our nation.

# About the Author

Paul Porzelt was born on December 18, 1902, near Metz in Alsace-Lorraine, then part of Germany. His family came from Upper Franconia, where their name first appeared in town records in 1450. During the Thirty Years War, they fled before the hordes of Gustavus Adolphus into the fortified town of Kronach which resisted two sieges by the Swedish armies. Succeeding generations of the family migrated westward. The Rhenish branch of the family was founded by Melchior Porzelt (1811-1864) who went to Mainz and started a lumber business when he was a young man. In 1833, he floated down the Rhine on one of his logger's rafts and settled in Cologne. Not long afterwards, he married Sibilla, daughter of Ludwig Harperath (1777-1816) and niece of Johann Karl Harperath who participated in the Cannonade de Valmy as an officer in the army of the Duke of Brunswick and died on the retreat to Trier in November 1792. Before long Melchior Porzelt owned quarries and plants in western Germany, Switzerland, and Carrara, Italy, and became wealthy. He was a cultured man, who delighted in his large library of French and English classics.

One of Melchior's sons, Paul Porzelt (1844-1923) took over the business on his father's death. At the time, the firm furnished much of the marble and stone used in the completion of Cologne Cathedral. Paul married his cousin-once-removed, Helene Petronella, daughter of Bernard Heribert Joseph Harperath (1807-1865).

The son of Paul and Helene Porzelt, Dr. Paul Porzelt (1872-1949), studied medicine. He was highly educated and steeped in the humanities, his conduct guided by Kant's Categorical Imperative as well as by Sallust's *Esse quam videre*. His son, the Author, adored him and throughout his life has tried to emulate him.

The family fortune wiped out by the inflation following the Great War, the Author decided to terminate his study of law at the University of Bonn and to come to the country his mother's father had loved so much. Otto Müller (1847-1912) came to America shortly before the Civil War and, as soon as he was old enough, enlisted in the Union Army, Captain J. Lyster's Company B, 19th U.S. Infantry Regiment. After his honorable discharge in Shreveport in 1871, he made a trip to Germany, where he married and stayed to start a textile business. He prospered and his large house in Bad Godesberg was always full of American friends and relatives.

In January, 1925, the Author arrived in New York, with $63.04 in his pocket, his knowledge of English minimal, his ambitions to make a success boundless. In those first years, every hour and every cent he could spare was devoted to perfecting his command of English and to acquainting himself with the best of English literature. Within days of his arrival he was employed as a runner by the international investment bank Ladenburg, Thalmann & Co.; eventually he became head of their research department. In 1940, he joined the Stock Exchange firm Emanuel, Deetjen & Co. where he was a general partner from 1949 to 1968. During these years he served on many boards of directors. From 1958 to 1960, he was a governor of the American Stock Exchange. In 1968, he became Chairman of the Board of Can-Fer Mines Ltd., a company he had founded some years previously and which he later merged into Bralorne Resources Ltd. The latter became one of the fast growing units in the Canadian and American energy field. He resigned as Chairman of Bralorne in 1976 when fifty percent of its stock was sold to Canadian interests.

In 1952, the author married Klara von Csorba. Born in Budapest of an old Hungarian gentry family, she was a well-known artist before the second World War. Concert tours brought her to the Far East where she would watch from the window of her room at Shanghai's Cathay hotel as the Japanese planes sunk the English and American battleships. After her marriage, she devoted her time and efforts to charity work and, during the last eighteen years, particularly to her duties as Chairman of the Women's Committee in the Metropolitan Club. When the Committee was formed in 1963, she became its first Chairman. Social life in the Club was minimal at the time. She introduced the Monthly Dinner Dances and the Annual Debutante Ball, now among the most popular events of the season. She died suddenly on March 31, 1981.

The Author became a Member of the Metropolitan Club in 1955. He was a Governor from 1967 to 1971 and was elected to the Board again in 1979. When he was downtown, his luncheon club was the City Midday Club. He is Honorary Member of the Deutscher Verein, the second oldest men's club in New York, founded in 1842. He was its president from 1967 to 1971. After the defeat of Hitler, he devoted much of his time to improving American-German relations and in recognition received in 1971 the Commander's Cross of the German Order of Merit from the German Government.

The author lives at Westwood Farm in Sharon, Connecticut.

# Acknowledgements

The Management of the Metropolitan Club kindly put at my disposal the Minutes of all Board of Governors and Executive Committee Meetings. Unfortunately, the volume containing the minutes of meetings during the first five years is missing. Nevertheless, the material I had gave me an outline of the Club's history, the names of Governors, Officers and Members, the financial tribulations and major events; it shed but little light on the life of the Members within the four walls of the Clubhouse.

This life was carefully guarded from the eyes of outsiders for the first sixty years of the Club's existence. Fortunately, I found the interesting and detailed records of the Metropolitan Club Bridge Dinner Club which provided a partial answer to some of my questions. Whatever else I relate here about the life of the Club was obtained by indirect means.

Early in my labors I discovered that an immense amount of information is available in New York to those who know where to look for it. I spent a great deal of time in the New York Public Library and in the New-York Historical Society, both splendid organizations. I searched through the pages of the daily papers, especially those of *The New York Times,* and such weeklies as *Town Topics.* I found more information in the Museum of the City of New York, the Metropolitan Museum of Art, the Morgan Library and elsewhere.

Wendy Shadwell, Curator of the Print Collection at the New-York Historical Society, was most helpful, and several times patiently got out the extensive files and the architectural drawings of McKim Mead & White for me.

At the same time I assiduously studied the writings of the great historians of the social life of the period: Cleveland Amory, Dixon Wecter, Kate Simon, S. N. Behrman, Stephen Birmingham, James T. Maher, Walter Lord, and many others. They rarely mentioned the Metropolitan Club, but they provided a wealth of information and stories about many of the colorful early Members. At the beginning of my efforts, I had the pleasure of meeting the talented and erudite Brendan Gill who is working on a book about McKim Mead & White. When I told him about my plans, he was very helpful and encouraging.

When it came to writing about the Building, I was conscious of the fact that I lacked professional qualifications. I had had a humanistic education, was acquainted with the great writers, painters and sculptors of our civilization and the principles of classical architecture, but not with the history of architecture and the decorative arts. I started to read books on the history of architecture. I spent several weeks with my wife revisiting Venice, Florence, Rome and Athens and retracing the path Stanford White had taken over one-hundred years ago. I also established contact with the acknowledged experts in the field. The first was Dr. Richard Guy Wilson of the School of Architecture at the University of Virginia, author of *The American Renaissance: 1876-1917* and great authority on the subject. He read the first draft of my manuscript on the Building and gave me much advice and encouragement. He sent me the unpublished reminiscences of Egerton Swartwout which I quote in Chapter Five. Sometime later, Mrs. Justin Haynes, who is also an expert in the field, introduced me to Henry Hope Reed, author of several books on art history and president of Classical America. He read part of my manuscript, found it interesting and offered help freely. He put me in touch with his friend and collaborator, John Barrington Bayley, president emeritus of Classical America, who agreed to read and correct the chapters on the building where necessary. Architect, author, decorator and man of culture, Bayley spent many days with me going over each word of Chapters Four to Eight of the book. He gave it the authority it had been lacking.

Among old personal friends, Member John Hutchings Spencer, amateur architect himself, gave me many valuable pieces of information and put his large architectural library at my disposal. Member Marco Grassi also provided information on Italian art and architecture.

Member Dr. James B.T. Foster, a great Latin scholar, immediately recognized the Latin inscription above the Library fireplace as an excerpt from Cicero's oration In Defense of Archias (Pro Archia) and made the translation for me. A friend from Paris, Marie-Annick Flambard-Guy obtained for me the information on Gilbert Cuel.

I greatly appreciate the co-operation I received from everyone in the Metropolitan Club from President Harold B. Hamilton and General Manager Edward W. Soyer on down. Banquet Manager George Wm. Elkins called my attention to the story I told about Morgan's portrait in Chapter Nine. He also gave me information about many features of the Interior of the Building and checked the text for inaccuracies. Gus Schiffner at the Reception Desk, who joined the staff in 1941, regaled me with several anecdotes which I was happy to use, such as the one about Mayor LaGuardia in Chapter Eleven.

The color photographs of the interior were made by Joseph Farber who has a broad background of photographing the architectural works of the Italian Renaissance. The beautiful art work on the title page and the head of each Chapter is the creation of a Sharon neighbour, Mrs. Jan Fairservis. The editing and the assembling of the general photographs was done by Dr. Rosemary Eakins and her associates at Research Reports, New York.

My inspiration was my wife Klara who gave me the original idea, encouraged me throughout my labors and did not mind spending many hours alone when I was working on the book. It is a tragedy that she did not live to see this book completed.

Extracts from the following books have been included:

Pp. 110-111 from Edward Steichen: A Life in Photography, Doubleday & Co., Inc., New York, 1963.
Pp. 135-136 from James T. Maher: The Twilight of Splendor, Little, Brown & Co., Boston, 1975.
P. 180 from Kate Simon: Fifth Avenue: A Very Social History, Harcourt Brace Jovanovich, Inc., New York, 1978.
P. 183 from Dixon Wecter: The Saga of American Society, Copyright 1937 by Charles Scribner's Sons; copyright renewed (New York: Charles Scribner's Sons, 1937) Reprinted with permission of Charles Scribner's Sons.
P. 196 from S.N. Behrman: Duveen, Random House, Inc., New York, 1952

# List of Works Consulted

Amory, Cleveland. *The Last Resorts.* Harper & Row, Publishers, Inc.: New York, 1952.

Amory, Cleveland. *Who Killed Society.* Harper & Row, Publishers, Inc.: New York, 1960.

Amory, Cleveland. *The Trouble with Nowadays.* Arbor House Publishing Co., Inc.: New York, 1979.

Anderson, Hugh A. *The Kinship of Two Countries: A History of the Canadian Club of New York.* Quinn & Boden Co., Inc.: Rahway, N.J., 1964.

Baker, Paul R. *Michael Morris Hunt.* The MIT Press: Cambridge, MA, 1980.

Baldwin, Charles C. *Stanford White.* Dodd, Mead & Co.: New York, 1931.

Behrman, S. N. *Duveen.* Random House, Inc.: New York, 1952.

Bernier, Oliver. *Pleasure and Privilege.* Doubleday & Co., Inc.: New York, 1981.

Birmingham, Stephen. *Our Crowd.* Harper & Row, Publishers, Inc.: New York, 1967.

Charlick, Carl. *The Metropolitan Club of Washington.* Judd & Detweiler, Inc.: Washington, 1965.

*Club Men of New York 1903.* Mail and Express Company: New York, 1903.

Cowles, Virginia. *The Astors.* Alfred A. Knopf, Inc.: New York, 1979.

Downing, Antoinette F., and Vincent J. Scully, Jr. *The Architectural Heritage of Newport, R.I.* Bramhall House: New York, 1967.

Dunn, William J. *Knickerbocker Centennial.* Knickerbocker Club: New York, 1971.

Feller, Richard T. *For Thy Great Glory.* Community Press of Culpepper, Virginia, 1965.

Fleming, John, Hugh Honour and Nikolaus Pevsner. *The Penguin Dictionary of Architecture.* Harmondsworth, Middlesex, 1980.

Folsom, Merrill. *Great American Mansions.* Hastings House, Publishers, Inc.: New York, 1963.

Frégnac, Claude, and Wayne Andrews. *The Great Houses of Paris.* The Vendome Press: New York, 1977.

Friedrich, Otto. *Clover.* Simon & Schuster, Inc.: New York, 1979.

Girouard, Mark. *Historic Houses of Britain.* William Morrow & Co., Inc.: New York, 1979.

Goldsmith, Barbara. *Little Gloria — Happy at Last.* Alfred A. Knopf, Inc.: New York, 1980.

Hoyt, Edwin P. *The Whitneys.* Weybright & Tolley: New York, 1976.

Kimball, Fiske. *American Architecture.* The Bobbs-Merrill Co., Inc.: Indianapolis, 1928.

Konolige, Kit and Frederica. *The Power of their Glory: America's Ruling Class: The Episcopalians.* Wyden Books: New York, 1978.

Landmarks Preservation Commission of the City of New York. Research Report by Ruth Selden Sturgill, September 11, 1979.

Langford, Gerald. *The Murder of Stanford White.* The Bobbs-Merrill Co., Inc.: Indianapolis, 1962.

Le Jeune, Anthony, and Malcolm Lewis. *The Gentlemen's Clubs of London.* Mayflower Books, Inc.: New York, 1979.

Lord, Walter. *A Night to Remember.* Holt, Rinehart & Winston: New York, 1955.

Maher, James T. *The Twilight of Splendor.* Little, Brown & Co.: Boston, 1975.

Mathews, Charles Thompson. *The Story of Architecture.* D. Appleton and Company: New York, 1896.

Mayor, A. Hyatt, and Mark Davis. *American

*Art at the Century.* The Century Association: New York, 1977.

Meyer, Franz S. *Handbook of Ornament.* Dover Publications, Inc.: New York, 1957.

Miller, Nathan. *The Roosevelt Chronicles.* Doubleday & Co., Inc.: New York, 1979.

Morris, Lloyd R. *Incredible New York.* Random House: New York, 1951.

Palladio, Andrea. *The Four Books of Architecture.* Dover Publications, Inc.: New York, 1965.

Petrie, Sir Charles. *The Carlton Club.* White Lion Publishers: London, 1972.

Rense, Paige. *Historic Interiors.* The Knapp Press: Los Angeles, 1979.

Rives, Reginald, W. *The Coaching Club.* Privately published: New York, 1935.

Roth, Leland M. *A Monograph of the Works of McKim Mead & White, 1879-1915.* Arno Press, Inc.: New York, 1977.

Roth, Leland M. *The Architecture of McKim Mead & White, 1870-1920: A Building List.* Garland Publishing, Inc.: New York, 1978.

Sampson, Anthony. *Anatomy of Britain Today.* Hodder and Stoughton: London, 1965.

Shopsin, William C., et al. *The Villard Houses: Life Story of a Landmark.* The Viking Press: New York, 1980.

Simon, Kate. *Fifth Avenue: A Very Social History.* Harcourt Brace Jovanovich, Inc.: New York, 1978.

Steichen, Edward. *A Life in Photography.* Doubleday & Co., Inc.: New York, 1963.

Stillman, Damie. *The Decorative Work of Robert Adam.* Transatlantic Arts, Inc.: New York, 1966.

Strange, T. A. *French Interiors, Furniture, Decoration, Woodwork & Allied Arts.* Bonanza Books: New York, 1968.

Ware, William, R. *The American Vignola.* W. W. Norton & Co., Inc.: New York, 1977.

Watson, Ross. *National Gallery of Art, Washington.* Orbis Publishing Limited: London, 1979.

Wecter, Dixon. *The Saga of American Society.* Charles Scribner's Sons: New York, 1937.

Wharton, Edith, and Ogden Codman, Jr. *The Decoration of Houses.* W. W. Norton & Co., Inc.: New York, 1978.

Whicker, Sherrell. *Elements of Interior Design and Decoration.* J. B. Lippincott Co.: Philadelphia, 1960.

Williams, Henry Lionel. *Great Houses of America.* G. P. Putnam's Sons: New York, 1966.

Wilson, Richard Guy. *The American Renaissance, 1876-1917.* Pantheon Books, Inc.: New York, 1979.

Zinelli, Umberto, and Giovanni Vergerio. *Decorative Ironwork.* The Hamlyn Publishing Group Ltd.: London, 1969.

# Picture Credits